The Ocean of Grace

Tributes to Amma's All-Embracing Love

Volume 3

The Ocean of Grace

Tributes to Amma's All-Embracing Love

Volume 3

Edited by Ramana Erickson
Co-edited by Julius Heyne

Mata Amritanandamayi Center
San Ramon, California, USA

The Ocean of Grace – Volume 3

Tributes to Amma's All-Embracing Love

Edited by Ramana Erickson
Co-edited by Julius Heyne

Published by:

Mata Amritanandamayi Center
P.O. Box 613
San Ramon, CA 94583
United States

In India:

www.amritapuri.org
inform@amritapuri.org

In Europe:

www.amma-europe.org

In US:

www.amma.org

Contents

	Preface	**8**
	The Goal of Spiritual Practice *A Message from Amma*	**11**
1.	**Gratitude Brings Grace** *Aparna Mulberry - USA*	**13**
2.	**Living Amma's Life Lessons** *Hari Sankaran - USA*	**24**
3.	**Happiness is a Decision** *Sugama - France*	**35**
4.	**Amma's Infinite Grace in my Life** *Rajiv Nair - India*	**46**
5.	**Amma's All-Pervading Presence** *Sarala - USA*	**59**
6.	**Japa is the Seed** *Jyotirup - France*	**70**
7.	**See the Good** *Sribhavani - Germany*	**84**
8.	**My Tiny Teardrop** *Amritesh Ito - Japan*	**96**
9.	**Reaching Amma** *Sudha Borys - USA*	**108**
10.	**Insights on the Path to the Light** *Abhijit - Austria*	**119**
11.	**Divine Love Speaks in Silence** *Amritapushpa - USA*	**130**
12.	**Amma's Amazing Rescue** *Devadath - The Netherlands*	**143**

13. **Self-Confidence** 153
Dr. Vidya - USA

14. **Amma Is My Shade Tree** 165
Navaneet - Belgium

15. **It Is Amma Holding My Hands** 175
Purnima - Germany

16. **Sēvā — Amma's Transformative Path** 185
Amar Gressel - USA

17. **Seeds of Wisdom** 197
Madhurima - Austria

18. **You Prepared Us for This** 208
Priyan - Lebanon

19. **Devotion in Duality** 218
Yati - USA

20. **Child #9,800,012** 231
Nityanand - USA

21. **Embrace Your Own Nature** 242
Gati - Spain

22. **Hot Chai and Cold Lassi** 253
Benjamin - Germany

23. **Faith in Guru and God** 263
Guramrit - USA

24. **Gratitude** 274
Govinda Rohkitte - Germany

25. **Compassion is the Answer** 283
Amritasri - Spain

Glossary 295

Pronunciation Guide 310

Acknowledgements 311

“The love that you experience
is proportional to the love that you give.”

— *Amma*

Preface

'Vasantavat lōkahitaṁ charantaḥ' – this is a line from *Vivēkachūḍāmaṇi*, written by Śhrī Śhaṇkarāchārya[1]. When he talks about the nature of mahātmās[2], Śhaṇkarāchārya compares them to the spring season, constantly bringing goodness to the world.

Spring is the most beautiful of all the four seasons. Neither the unbearable heat of summer, the freezing cold of winter, nor the troubles of the rainy seasons are present in spring. The weather is pleasant. The canopies of green trees and the exuberant growth of plants and vines can be seen all around. Fruits and flowers of varying colors and sizes abound. Butterflies dance in intoxication as they sip nectar from the flowers. Birds and animals eat their fill of fruits and berries. Blissful Koels burst out in song. A gentle breeze wafts the fragrance of flowers to every nook and corner.

In this way, the golden spring has prepared a sumptuous feast for us to see, hear, taste, smell, and gently caress. Śhaṇkarāchārya has likened the mahātmās to such a glorious spring. Those who have experienced Amma's presence even once, will realize that his words are not an exaggeration. Wherever Amma goes, spring blossoms. Her children lose themselves in joy as they abide in her presence.

In nature, spring gives way to summer, and there is a yearlong wait for the following spring season to arrive. But this is not the case with mahātmās. Nothing external can negate the

---

[1] Saint revered as a Guru and chief proponent of the Advaita (non-dual) philosophy.

[2] 'Great soul,' a term used to describe one who has attained spiritual realization.

joy and contentment, the inner elation that ever arises in a mahātmās's presence. Because the mahātmā awakens spring within us, and provided we live our lives in accordance with her words, we will experience an inner peace and pleasure that nothing can deprive us of.

Like the spring season, Amma travels around the world, gifting the experience of the blissful inner self to all. Her children have enshrined this experience within their hearts. Even as they endure the burning embers of life, Amma's loving words of consolation soothe and cool their hearts.

Amma's children will never become weary as they live through the different seasons. Amma is our life-giving shade; she is our pillar of support, shielding us from the onslaught of the burning heat of this world. Amma is the warmth of love and hope when we suffer the freezing winter of life's disappointments. Amma is our refuge, our shelter from the pelting downpour of life's problems.

Each page of this book bears witness to her amazing grace. As we travel through these pages, we experience her presence akin to the spring season. And it will inspire and motivate us to seek the highest goal of human life.

Swāmī Jñānāmṛitānanda Puri

The Goal of Spiritual Practice

A Message from Amma

Children, many people seem to have wrong notions about what spiritual practices are and what their aims are. Remaining strong in difficulties, seeing God in everyone, and loving everyone equally – this is what we should gain through sādhanā (spiritual practice). The highest goal of all sādhanā is the ability to maintain an unshakeable inner peace amidst the ups and downs of life.

The purpose of meditation, japa (repeated chanting of a mantra), and other practices is not to gain some occult experience. Some people say that they see a green or red light during meditation. Once, a man told Amma, "I always see a green light when I meditate."

Amma said, "In that case, please don't drive any vehicle, son, because you will see the red traffic light as green and will not stop your car." It is not to gain such experiences that we ought to practice meditation and other forms of sādhanā. The real aim of sādhanā is to gain equanimity and peace of mind.

Some people inhale and exhale forcefully. When this is done continuously, the prāṇa (vital breath) in our head will decrease, and we will feel as if we are soaring into another world. This is not spiritual bliss. When their vision becomes dim, some spiritual seekers tell Amma that they see lights in their eyes. They don't realize that it is because there is a problem with their eyes. Instead, these people explain it as if they were seeing the effulgence of the Self. Amma advises them to see an ophthalmologist. Once the disease is treated, they will stop seeing the light.

Even if we get certain experiences as a result of our spiritual practice, we need not take them too seriously. They are also like dreams. If a beggar dreams that he has become a king, will that help him in real life? What we need is an inner poise in each and every situation while we are awake. That is real spiritual progress. Through spiritual practice, we must regain the natural peace and calm of the mind. We must develop the ability to remain patient under any circumstance. We must learn to see goodness in everything. This is true spiritual progress.

Self-realization is being able to see oneself in all beings, and thus love and serve them. This is the culmination of sādhanā.

1

Gratitude Brings Grace

Aparna Mulberry – USA

One year on the U.S. Tour, a friend ran over to me saying, "Amma said yes!" She had just come off the stage where Amma was giving darśhan.[1] While she was sitting beside Amma she asked a question in her head. She told Amma, "If the answer is yes, look to the right; if the answer is no, look to the left." She 'thought' her question, and Amma looked to the right!

She had a doubt, so she tried it again just to confirm. Again Amma looked to the right. Hearing this I thought, "I want to try this." I had never tested Amma before and my weak mind fell for this trick. I headed to the stage to test Amma myself. Before I could even formulate the question in my mind, Amma looked directly at me, pointed at me, and said, "You have a question, ask it." I was shocked. She not only allowed me to physically ask her, but she also answered it! Amma, please forgive me for ignorantly trying to test you. And thank you for not allowing my mind to doubt even for a moment that you hear every thought that passes through my head.

Amma hears our every desire and prayer. A journalist once asked Amma how she could hear all the prayers of millions of people all over the world. Amma said, "It is like the thousands of strands of hair on our head. We can feel when even a single hair is pulled." So if Amma can hear us, what are we telling her? What are we praying for?

---

[1] Darśhan is an audience with a holy person or a vision of the Divine. Amma's signature darśhan is a hug.

Years ago in Amma's āśhram[2] in San Ramon, California, Swāmī Amṛitātmānandajī during a satsang mentioned how we can transform the useless chatter in our heads into a conversation with Amma. Take random thoughts like, "Oh it's time for me to start work," or, "Oh I need to call my mother," or, "Oh no, I still have to finish that paper." See what happens if you simply add Amma in front: "Oh Amma, it's time for me to start work." "Amma, I have to finish that paper!"

This really helped me during my university days. I would invite Amma to come to class with me, sit in the car with me, and gradually I could feel Amma's presence so strongly when I was physically away from her. Telling Amma something transforms it into a life lesson. Each of us can choose what conversations to have with Amma. When we don't know what to say, we can just say, "Thank you!" Actually, let's say thank you even when we do know what to say!

Something I have learned from Amma over all these years is that every moment is a perfect opportunity to be grateful. So let me share how gratitude has helped me throughout my life and how I use it as a spiritual practice. In my opinion, gratitude is our key; it is synonymous with love. It lights up the same part of the brain as feelings of love do. This area of the brain is associated with understanding other people's perspectives, empathy, and feelings of deep relief. Research suggests that gratitude has many benefits, including better physical and psychological health, increased happiness and life satisfaction, decreased materialism, and more. Grace goes where there is gratitude.

---

[2] 'Place of striving.' A place where spiritual seekers and aspirants live or visit, in order to lead a spiritual life. It is usually the home of a spiritual master, saint or ascetic, who guides the aspirants.

We have all heard Amma say that happiness is a choice. Just like deciding which shirt to wear, we can choose to be happy... or not. Every day. This isn't so easy to grasp. Choosing gratitude comes more naturally to me. We can wake up in the morning and choose to be grateful for all that Amma has given us. We all have so much to be grateful for – a comfortable home, food when we are hungry, people who love us and whom we love. Most of all, we have the rarest of all blessings. We live alongside a mahātmā (a great soul) who instructs us down to the tiniest detail on how we can end our suffering and attain the state where we never feel separate from her again. We can keep drawing our attention to this fact and decide to choose gratitude again and again. By doing that we will absolutely be happy. Amma says, "The foundation of happiness is gratitude."

Some people are criers, and others are not. I am definitely a crier. When something touches my heart, I cry. When I see people's bhakti (devotion) or helpful nature, I cry. When I hear people's sweet Amma memories, I cry. One time in Amritapuri, I went for darśhan and started crying. Amma looked at me and asked, "Why are you always sad?" I was a little confused by this question because I didn't really feel sad. I was just crying for Amma. But for the rest of the day, I kept thinking about Amma's words. "Am I sad? Maybe I am sad. But why? Hmmmm... maybe I am not focusing on gratitude." Wow! There it was! I had not been counting my blessings for all the little miracles that happen every day right before my eyes.

Studies show how practicing gratitude may even be able to change and rewire our brain. When thinking shifts from negative to positive, 'feel-good' chemicals such as dopamine and serotonin surge. To shift the focus of my mind, I began to write down every single thing I was grateful for. The list got longer and longer till I wrote down 108 things that I was so lucky to have or experience in my life at that time.

I went to Amma from the side as she was giving darśhan. I offered my list to Amma while praying to always stay focused on the positives. Actually, I have had this breakthrough several times in my life, most recently when I began writing this satsang. I wasn't feeling very positive because I was physically away from Amma during the pandemic. The pain of that was taking a long time to dissolve. As I was writing about gratitude, I realized yet again that I was not practicing it. Gratitude makes us content with what we have. Amma says:

> "Gratitude is the ability to reminisce about all the support and help we have received, with an attitude of humility. It is a state of mind. When we lovingly recognize the goodness in another person, this helps to awaken the goodness in ourselves. In fact, gratitude benefits us more than anyone else. The positivity and goodness that awakens within as a result of being grateful in turn benefits society and the entire world."

***

Let me tell you how I first came to Amma in this birth. My parents were both on their own spiritual journeys in India when they met. They got married in Śhrī Satya Sāī Bābā's āśhram where they first heard about Amma. When my mother was pregnant with me, they went to see Amma for the first time in Switzerland in 1989.

With Amma's grace, there was never a 'before I met Amma' for me in this life. I received my first darśhan while in my mother's womb. In 1990 when I was seven months old, Amma came to Santa Fe where we were living. Apparently, Amma carried me all the way from the darśhan tent to her car and I was completely obsessed with her nose ring. Amma told me then that one day I would have a nose ring too, but that story will have to wait to be told in another satsang.

With Amma's blessings, in 1993 my parents moved to Amritapuri. I grew up here from the age of three to fifteen years old. I have so many precious memories of going to Amma's room; playing games with her; Amma feeding us children with her hand; letting us massage her; dancing with her; and swimming with her in random water tanks in the āśhram. We did all kinds of sēvā (selfless service) with her and helped build parts of the āśhram in whatever small ways we could.

One time, when I and some other children were playing hide and seek, a friend of mine stepped on some glass. We rushed her to her room and called the doctor who came to remove the glass from her foot. She was hugging her Amma doll very tightly, and as the doctor was removing the glass, she bit her Amma doll from the pain. After that, we took her to Amma who gave her a big hug and kiss, and jokingly said, "You didn't need to bite me!" Wow! Amma felt it when my friend bit her Amma doll!

Another time, when we children were rehearsing for a Christmas play in the Kālī temple,[3] Amma suddenly appeared and told us to take a break and come play with her. Play with Amma? Oh my goodness, yes please! We came to the area where the big darśhan hall is today, but back then it was still just sand and trees, and we played hop-tag. For those of you who are unfamiliar with this game, everyone hops on one leg and the leader, who is also hopping, tries to catch everyone. Of course Amma was the leader, and let me tell you, she was so fast! We played for quite some time until Amma hopped over

---

[3] Main temple in Amritapuri dedicated to Goddess Kālī.

to another friend, caught him, and then hopped all the way back to her room.

Once, when I was around ten years old, my mother took me to Amma's program in San Ramon. The night before leaving San Ramon to return to Amritapuri, I went for darśhan. Remembering all of her children in Amritapuri, Amma started filling my arms with packets upon packets of Hershey's chocolate kisses. She then gave me very detailed instructions on how to distribute them to everyone. She asked me to unwrap each one and feed the chocolate to her children one at a time. So, as Amma wished, all the other kids assisted me in unwrapping each chocolate as I fed them to Amma's Amritapuri āśhramites.[4] Whether Amma physically shows it or not, she always remembers each one of us.

I may not remember all the spiritual gems Amma shared with us during those times, however, the fruition of all these stories, experiences, and moments we have with Amma strengthens our bond with God. That relationship between mother and child, Guru and devotee, creator and creation, is the bridge that will ultimately take us across this ocean of birth and death. Throughout those precious years, Amma was molding me and preparing me for the life she had planned for me. Soon it would be time for me to go deep within and learn to practice all of her teachings in real-world scenarios.

***

After spending my childhood in this sacred place, I moved to the United States when I was fifteen years old to live with my father. The decision to move across the world happened just two weeks before I landed there and started high school. Straight from Amma's loving shelter to a superficial, materialistic

[4] Āśhram residents are also called āśhramites.

high school full of children with no experience of different cultures, diversity, or spirituality. I was completely clueless about American culture and how to be a teenager in the U.S. Luckily, Amma in the form of my father, his partner, and a few kids my age whom I had met five years earlier, helped me *a lot* during this difficult transition.

When I say I was clueless, I really mean it. I didn't know any of the games, music, or movies that the children there had grown up with, and they felt the same about me. There was no common ground between us, and it was very difficult for us to relate to each other. In the two years that followed I tried to become a 'regular' American teenager. I explored and experimented with all the things I was taught not to do, all in trying to fit in. I didn't always make healthy choices.

Though I always remembered Amma, my prayers became more infrequent and slowly I drifted further and further away from my roots. I thought by doing this I would be more accepted there, have more friends and finally fit in. What I did not realize is that by pushing away my roots, I was only hurting myself. These were the hardest years of my life. I got so lost because I forgot who I was and where I came from. Luckily, our most compassionate Amma didn't let me stray too far. The Divine Mother of the Universe had a great plan brewing; a series of small events that were a huge wake-up call for me.

After two years, I visited Amritapuri during my summer holidays. When I returned to the U.S., I was starting my senior year in high school (twelfth standard). I went to school on the first day with a great attitude. Unfortunately my mood completely changed as soon as I arrived. When I walked into the building, all the memories of the rough past two years came flooding back. It was horrible. I did not want to be there. That night I told my father that I wanted to change schools; I couldn't go back there. I didn't yet realize that the problem was in my own mind and that Amma had prepared me for this. I blamed the external circumstances. My father listened to everything, and what he said next changed how I lived my life for years to come. He said:

> "You have Amma inside of you. You have India inside of you. You cannot run away from who you are. If you don't face what is coming up within you, the same problems will chase you in your new school or wherever else you go. Instead of running, try to embrace who you are and share with everyone what Amma has filled you with."

Boom! That was it for me. There was no going back. The next day I arrived at school, beaming, so full of Amma's love. I started smiling at everyone, and it felt like I was watching the world in slow motion. When I smiled at someone, they would completely lighten up and turn to someone else and smile at them, who would also feel that joy. In that moment I truly understood what Amma says about the tremendous value of a smile.

I watched this butterfly effect as it spread throughout the school. It was so beautiful. Why hadn't I seen it before? I was so caught up in my own self-pity that I'd become blind to it. This is what we can see if our attitude is to ask, "What do I have to offer others?" This is exactly what Amma says: "If you have the attitude of taking, you become a beggar; but when you actually give, you become a king." As I started to allow Amma to shine through me, it was like night and day. An inner balance and acceptance between both worlds started forming. My inner confidence increased, people started noticing this confidence and I made some amazing friends that year. My desire to do sēvā, which Amma instilled so deeply within me, was reignited.

I started visiting an old-age home to spend time with people approaching the end of their life. The next year I spent ten months traveling around the U.S. doing service work with a non-profit organization. This was all Amma's doing through the sprouting of seeds she had planted in me.

Looking back, I see those hard years were some of the best years of my life because Amma gave me so much clarity on how I should live my life. She gave me such a firm conviction that wherever I am in the world, I will have something to offer, because Amma is in my heart. She taught me the powerful lesson of understanding the nature of the world; how unpredictable and unsatisfactory it becomes when we don't give the necessary importance to the unchanging Self within.

Amma has given us all the necessary tools to face any situation. And through tough times like the ones we are in now, she teaches us amazing lessons that we could only learn in these circumstances. It is through experience that these lessons get ingrained in our hearts. We can read about spiritual teachings and try to implement them, but our mind often forgets the teachings when hard times come. Teachings acquired through experience on the other hand, will remain firm within us. Amma says:

> "The circumstances of life will always keep changing. As long as we are unable to bring our minds under our control, sorrow will continue to hunt us down. However, once the mind comes under our control, then no problem or tragedy can devastate or paralyze us. In reality, the foundation of happiness is gratitude."

***

I'd like to share a story that happened during the pandemic which shows how Amma hears our every prayer no matter where we are in the world.

When I was a kid, maybe seven or nine years old, on the Indian tours Amma would take me with her in her car to visit devotees' houses for pūjās (worship rituals). Sometimes there would be other kids and we would take turns sitting on Amma's lap. Sometimes it was just Amma, me, and Swāminī Amma (Swāminī Kṛiṣhṇāmṛita Prāṇā). At each house visit, Amma would sit in front of the altar and sing this amazing prayer solo. I have never heard it chanted anywhere else; and when I remember it, Amma's voice still echoes in my mind. Over twenty years passed since I'd last heard it, and I held a strong desire to hear it again.

About three months ago, before leaving France to come here, my partner and I were sharing Amma stories and I told her about the days when I would ride in Amma's car and about this amazing prayer Amma would sing all alone during the pūjās, and how much I had I wanted to hear it again. I even mentioned if I ever gave a satsang, I would tell this story and ask Amma to sing that prayer again. This was on a Tuesday when Amma doesn't normally come for evening bhajans.[5] Literally thirty minutes later, Amma's voice echoed from the loudspeakers in Amritapuri, and from our computer speakers all around the world. Amma began chanting this same prayer from her room!

Amma's compassion knows no bounds. It is like a river whose nature is to flow. If your desire is pure, Amma just cannot help herself but make her children happy. She can only give, give, give.

Amma says:

---

[5] Devotional songs or hymns in praise of God.

> "Just call out. Let the call come from your heart. Like a child cries out for food or to be held and cuddled by its mother, call out to her with the same intensity and innocence. She cannot sit silent and unmoved when somebody calls to her like that."

We may call out to her, but do we really believe Amma will show up? Amma reveals herself to us in so many different ways every single day. May we have the innocence and faith to recognize her in whatever form she comes to us.

Amma, you have given me a human birth and also shelter at your beautiful feet. Please listen to my prayers, and fill me with the attitude of selflessness so I may serve you through every single action I do in the world, through my work on the internet, and with the people and animals around me every day. Please help me be more kind and helpful and take full advantage of the chances you give me to be your instrument. Help me make the right decisions and correct my wrong thinking and doing. Please help me accept all the results of my actions with an equanimous attitude as your divine prasad. And Amma, please help me always choose *Gratitude.*

2

Living Amma's Life Lessons

Hari Sankaran - USA

For two years of the pandemic, all those outside Amritapuri were pining to see Amma in person. That long period without our Amma, our everything, really made me treasure all my memories. Amma in her infinite compassion gave us the webcast and lovingly showed up every day so that we could see her. The physical separation caused by the pandemic, deepened my inner monologue with Amma, but the separation also had unanticipated side effects:

One is that the inner monologue unfortunately became an outer monologue. I thank Amma for masks as anyone seeing me walking alone and carrying a full-on conversation with 'no one' would wonder about my sanity. Also, as the live webcast starts at 6:30 a.m. my time and goes till 10:00 or 11:00 a.m., another unanticipated side effect is that I adjusted my schedule to allow only patient-care meetings before 11 a.m.

The last side effect is overwhelming jealousy towards my brother, Brahmachārī[6] Dr. Ravi Sankaran. Ravi chēṭṭan[7] will often tell us Amma called him for this pain or that pain. Or Amma would send some āśhramite to Ravi chēṭṭan for pain evaluation, etc. This has led me to seriously question my career choices. Why did I choose pediatric cancer, a specialty that for sure Amma would never call me about?

---

[6] Celibate male disciple. Brahmachāriṇī is the female equivalent.

[7] 'Older brother' in Malayāḷam.

Why does Ravi chēṭṭan have to tell me how tired he was because Amma called him to come from AIMS[8] late in the night? I get soooo jealous. However, that jealousy consumed my mind in a healthy way. I vowed that if Amma never called, at least I would make Amma hear me. I thank Amma that cars in the United States are somewhat soundproof. Had that not been the case, my loud shouting of Amma's name while driving to and from work every day for the past two years would surely qualify for a public noise disturbance.

To the bhakta (devotee), any remembrance of his beloved Lord whether happy, sad, remorseful, or even jealous brings sweet tears of longing. That longing brings us closer to our beloved. I know that everyone of you has made their own unique deep and lasting connection with their inner Amma during the Covid time.

I want to share some teachings I have received from Amma. Though few, I reflect on them daily (sometimes obsessively), and they have substantially shaped my life. Amma's teachings are like seeds. Some grow now, and some grow later. But they all grow.

Lesson 1: Don't waste money.

We met Amma in Chicago in 1989 when I was six years old. I cannot remember a moment in my life without Amma. Like most of the children in the āśhram today, I didn't know Amma was planting seeds in my mind and how they would help me navigate the choppy waters of life. All I knew was that there was something very wholesome in the love that Amma gave us, like a mother's milk, full of the necessary vitamins and calories needed during infancy.

---

[8] Amrita Institute of Medical Sciences, Amma's super-specialty hospital in Kochi, Kerala.

However, the mother must sometimes discipline her child, especially when he doesn't know what is wrong or what to correct. I received some lessons as a child that I remember to this day. My first experience of this happened in the early 1990's while I was kneeling in the darśhan queue. A lady handed me a bag of Hershey's chocolate kisses she had brought and asked if I would give it to Amma as she had forgotten to give it.

As we came up for darśhan, I innocently handed the bag of chocolates to Amma, and her mood went from a beautiful light smile to a stern look. I was perplexed. Amma asked: "Did you buy this?" Before I could say no, Amma said: "The money YOU spent to buy this could have fed a poor family for one month! Amma hates to see money wasted." Amma then quoted exactly how many rupees were needed to feed a poor family for a month in India, but I cannot remember exactly how much.

Needless to say, the rest of the darśhan was miserable due to the 'undeserved scolding,' especially as I had not bought the chocolate. I learned that I should be aware of each dollar I spent, even at that young age. Did I learn those lessons though? Around age twelve, I convinced my father to purchase a laptop for my entertainment and I went to get it blessed by Amma. Oh boy, was I in trouble! Amma said, "Didn't I tell you not to waste money? Why does a boy like you need such an expensive item? Are you going to become a computer specialist? Do you know how many starving people are waiting for a good meal and that this money could have been used for that?!"

This second dose was stronger, as if the first dose was not enough. I was taken aback that I had forgotten the scolding from six years before. This one teaching has shaped many of my decisions to this day. When I started my MBBS[9] in 2001 in India, this Amma teaching kept me from going out with the

[9] Bachelor of Medicine, Bachelor of Surgery.

other non-resident Indians to fancy restaurants, parties, etc. My brother who was already doing his MBBS at the same college also helped nurture the seed of frugality in my mind by setting an example. However, taking frugality to the extreme may not be to our benefit. Though I still spend a lot of money on coffee and other food indulgences, Amma's lessons prevent me from going overboard. This lets me help impoverished pediatric cancer patients who need financial assistance during their care.

During my pediatric residency in 2010, I asked Amma if I could share an apartment and rent cost with another male doctor. This doctor had a girlfriend, but he assured me that she would not visit as she lived far away. However, as soon as Amma heard these details, she said, "No way!" Thus, during my seven years of medical training I lived alone. I often joked with any women who wanted to stop by my apartment that they would be the first woman besides my mother to step inside! This joke kept me free from any unwanted company during my training.

***

On the U.S. Tour, our family works in the kitchen and snack shop, selling chai, samosas, and other items to people who come to the program. Amma has told us that the money generated from chai and samosa sales in the U.S. fund many of her charitable initiatives! These sweet words from Amma not only doubled our enthusiasm to do kitchen sēvā, but also highlight how Amma teaches us to value every penny.

My mother often told us growing up that whatever the Guru gives you is prasād[10] and you must accept it. During a Chicago program in the 1990s, I got in line to get Amma's darśhan. When my turn came, Amma looked at me mischievously and asked

[10] Blessed offering or gift from a holy person or temple, often in the form of food.

me to close my eyes and open my mouth. With excitement I opened my mouth, anticipating a sweet or some other treat from Amma. I heard a foil wrapper coming off a Hershey Kiss and my intuition was confirmed. My mouth started salivating and I prepared myself for the sweet taste of chocolate.

Imagine my surprise when I got a metallic taste instead! Amma had placed the aluminum foil in my mouth! I was now in a dilemma. According to our mother, you must take whatever Amma gives you. Though I was unsure of what would happen, my faith won over and I swallowed the foil. In the next moment Amma opened my mouth trying to fish out the foil and started laughing when she realized I had swallowed it! She then gave me a couple extra chocolates which I took to mean I had done something right. The play of the Divine Mother draws devotees close, and that feeling of Amma fishing around in my mouth and her laughter drew me to her like iron filings to a magnet.

Lesson 2: Studying is your sēvā.

As a child, no one wants to study. I am not sure what led Amma to say this to me ("Studying is your sēvā"), but before starting my MBBS, Amma said these words to me very seriously. In the U.S., I never had to study much to get decent grades and thought that would be so in the Indian system. However, coming from the U.S. educational system, the Indian system was very foreign to me. Memorize this WHOLE book? Write this sentence ten times? Studying for MBBS was like that.

Initially, those words of Amma didn't resonate in my mind. After a long day of classes, I would play outside till sunset and then sleep. I would ask my classmates how much they studied, and innocently believed them when they said, "Oh I don't study at all," or "I barely study." I was getting my first lesson in Indian education, as the best and the brightest struggled to get into this degree program. What you sow, you must reap, and for the

MBBS sessional exam at the end of our first year, I failed two out of three subjects.

This swift kick left me dejected but Amma's words rang in my ears. I took the loss as a lesson and started seriously applying myself. I ignored my classmates' invitations to come out and play until after reviewing the day's material. My grades improved, and by continuing to follow Amma's teaching regarding studying, I secured a first class in MBBS. Later I got admission to the third-highest ranked pediatric residency and pediatric oncology fellowship program in the United States. Now I work in the largest cancer research institution in the world, the National Cancer Institute, next to our Washington, DC āśhram. This is the fruit of following Amma's teaching, and all this material success belongs to our beloved Amma.

Amma says, "There is education for life and education for living." 'Studying is your sēvā' has a deeper meaning now, and I try to apply Amma's teachings to learn from every experience. I try to see Amma in every pediatric patient that comes to see me and care for them with compassion.

***

Here's a fond memory from my first long-term visit to Amritapuri:

Though I had been on tour with Amma many times, I first visited Amritapuri without my parents when I was seventeen. One of my sēvās was medicine sorting in the hospital. I naturally became close to our doctor-brahmachārīs. After sorting for long hours, sometimes I would fall asleep in the Amrita Kripa community hospital. The brahmachārī doctors adopted me and would lovingly bring me to their room to sleep. That small room with five brahmachārī doctors, though cramped, became my residence.

They taught me essential āśhram life-skills, like washing clothes on a laundry stone, etc. In the U.S., we had the luxury of washing machines, clothes dryers, and other amenities that made doing laundry easy. Learning how to beat the clothes against a stone, scrub them, and hang-dry them was a challenge. Unfortunately, I had a bad habit of leaving my clothes in a bucket with washing powder and forgetting to actually wash them. As I commuted between AIMS and the āśhram, I often left clothes in buckets at both locations.

One day, a brahmachārī-brother returned from AIMS and said to me, "Hey you rascal, I have brought you a gift." He handed me a plastic bag. Anticipating a gift, I opened it quickly and to my bewilderment, a foul smell greeted me and I saw what looked like my clothes. These clothes had spent many days unattended in a bucket and a fungus now graced them. The fellow doctor explained that the foul smell had attracted his attention. On further inspection he found my clothes with a complimentary lizard lying on top of them, as it had likely fainted due to the toxic fumes. He considered washing them for me, but decided I needed to learn a lesson.

Suffice to say, I learned a bit more about śhraddhā (attentiveness) that day. Amma's teachings came to me through these doctor-brahmachārīs who taught me self-sufficiency. For parents, teaching your children to do household chores at a young age is also an essential marriage skill. I have seen couples my age fight over who does the laundry! The doctor-brahmachārīs also taught me how to practice compassion-based medicine, as they often went to rural camps to serve the villagers. These inspiring examples awakened in me the desire to be a doctor and a brahmachārī also.

Lesson 3: Do you like research?

This was an innocent question Amma asked me in the Detroit airport in 2014. It was one of those lucky times when it was just Amma and a few others with her. I had just started doing research as part of my specialization in pediatric cancer. I had a special dislike towards research. How could Amma know that I felt that research was a waste of time, and that once I finished this training I planned to be done with research forever? "No Amma, not at all. I really don't like it. I just want to take care of patients and serve the world," I replied. Amma just said, "Hmmm..." and boarded her flight. I never thought much about that interaction afterwards. I completed my specialization in 2016 and joined AIMS as a cancer doctor. As I practiced at AIMS, I was thoroughly intrigued by the clinical questions that arose while treating patients, but did not have the expertise to study them comprehensively.

In 2018 our mother got sick and required ICU-level care. As both my brother and I were here in India, we were unable to take care of her. However, Amma took care of her through our Michigan satsang. I am forever grateful. Our mother's health crisis awakened in me a desire to return to the U.S. to make sure that one of us was always near her. Around this time, I got an unsolicited job offer to join the National Cancer Institute in the U.S. This would allow me to pursue cutting-edge cancer research, and also to treat and take care of patients.

This job offer came through a motherly figure that reminded me of Amma, and it felt as if Amma was giving me an opportunity to continue serving her while working abroad. The most important part was that my office was only twenty minutes from our Washington, DC āśhram! Amma took care of my job, my accommodation, and my spiritual company. Her grace has allowed me to develop skills and explore topics that are of benefit to the U.S., India, and the rest of the world.

Lesson 4: What are your thoughts about death?

Amma asked me this question once during a Dēvī Bhāva[11] program in Michigan, while discussing one of my cancer patients who was not doing well. I had just started my pediatric cancer training, and was having some emotional difficulty dealing with the poor prognoses and passing of some of my patients. I don't remember what I exactly replied, but it was superficial. I have reflected on this question throughout my career. Though science hasn't found an exact reason for all pediatric cancers, some are due to genetic causes. More importantly, pediatric cancers are very curable and treatable with some exceptions. However, the longer I practice medicine, the more death becomes a recurring companion.

One of the unique views that I can offer comes from what some of my pediatric patients have told me close to their time of passing. I remember one 16-year-old boy with an aggressive blood cancer who came from a religious background. A few days before his passing, he often said he saw angels, heard angelic voices and trumpets calling him, and he had no doubt he would go to heaven.

The room at his time of passing was filled with laughter and love, as he comforted his parents and everyone around. After his passing, his parents often told me that he was in heaven and they dreamt of him. Amma says:

> "Death is not the end of life. We end each sentence with a period. We do so, so that we can write the next sentence. Death is just like this period mark. Death

[11] 'The divine mood of Dēvī' when Amma reveals her oneness with the Divine Mother.

is simply a continuation of life. If we place our faith in God and are aware of the truth, we can definitely conquer death and the fear of death."

I have also seen the transformative power of death for parents who lose a child to cancer. I took care of a 15-year-old girl with an aggressive leukemia. After much discussion and different therapies, she was transitioned to palliative care. After she passed, her mother, who was a housewife, went back to school and became a nurse. She is now a cancer nurse on the very same floor where her daughter passed. She often takes patient assignments of terminally-ill cancer patients and gives them the love and care that they need.

Though this kind of response was not the case in all situations, I have many memories of children facing death with the full confidence that it was not the end. Death can be transformative, both for the people left behind and for the person experiencing it. I still have difficulty understanding unexpected sudden deaths and providing support to the families. In those cases, I find that chanting my mantra[12] and maintaining a respectful silence helps me to create a healing environment.

Lesson 5: Amma wants us to be a big family.

Some of the most powerful lessons are the ones that we don't rationalize with our intellect but rather absorb. We have all observed the sacrifice Amma makes for us, her children, and how painstakingly she takes care of us saplings from across the world to create a forest. While we grow under her care, we form root networks that connect all of us together. This forest

---

[12] Mantra is a sound, syllable, word or words of spiritual content. According to Vēdic commentators, mantras are revelations of ṛiṣhis (sages) arising from deep contemplation.

has helped me to grow strong roots. The constant support of the older, more majestic trees has given me confidence in many situations to move forward without fear. I have no doubt that no matter the distance, this network remains resilient and that Amma, our caretaker, will continue to fertilize us with her love and guidance. Though I cannot fathom the vastness of this forest Amma has cultivated, as a small sapling I will support the budding seeds as best I can with whispers of encouragement so they can sprout and thrive.

It's difficult to express what Amma means to me, and what the swāmīs mean to me. Amma has been there for us every moment of our lives, and she continues to plant seeds in us that I am excited to see grow and mature. Amma is a great farmer. I sincerely pray that Amma continues to help all of us to be open to her grace and live lives worthy of her teachings.

3

Happiness is a Decision

Sugama – France

Amma says that happiness is a decision.

Every single time I heard Amma say that happiness is a decision, I would feel so confused and frustrated. I would think to myself, "Of course I want to be happy but when I experience negative feelings or pain, I get stuck in it. I just don't understand! How can happiness possibly be my decision?!?"

In 2014 I had the rare opportunity to meet with Amma in her room to have her darśhan and receive guidance from her before she left Amritapuri on her world tour. The very last sentence Amma said to me before I left her room remained etched in my mind, "Daughter, remember, happiness is a decision." After leaving Amma's room, I was in bliss. But I didn't realize just how challenging it would be to take this critical advice.

My mother got pregnant at seventeen, and no one in the village knew who my father was. My mother was a brilliant student with so much potential, but she was forced to discontinue her studies as a result of the pregnancy. She went to work in a nearby city to provide for us, and I spent the first nine years of my life growing up on my grandmother's farm. It was a very simple and happy life.

Life on the farm taught me to have a deep love and reverence for nature. Amma says that if we approach nature with love, it will serve us as our best friend, a friend that won't let us down. Nature very much played this role for me.

From a young age life taught me that human love was very limited and conditional. Even those closest and dearest to us can suddenly withdraw their love, and express anger if their expectations are not met. I wanted so much to be loved and fully accepted for who I was, and to experience unconditional love! For many years I ardently searched for this unconditional love...without any success.

As a young person I went through a painful identity crisis, I longed to know who my father was. I thought that if I could find out who my father was, then I would know who I was, but only my mother knew and I resented her for refusing to tell me. I believed this world to be ruthless and cruel. As I grew older and was exposed to more suffering in the world — witnessing humankind inflicting so much pain on nature, animals, plants, and on fellow humans including innocent children, I was convinced that there was no such thing as a loving God. Only an insane God could allow so much suffering in his own creation.

My family wanted me to go to university, but at age eighteen, there was nothing I could think of that I wanted to study and do for the rest of my life, and so despite my mother's wishes, I left home and moved abroad.

Albert Einstein once said, "The woman who follows the crowd will usually go no further than the crowd. But the woman who walks alone is likely to find herself in places no one has ever been before."

I met people from all walks of life during those adventurous years, and I learned a lot from all of them. Looking back now I realize how arrogant I was. I thought I was getting by on my wits and luck. It never occurred to me that a higher power was looking over me and protecting me even when I made the stupidest decisions! Little did I know that God was lovingly protecting me from my own foolishness, and patiently waiting for me to come find her.

After four years of travel, I returned to France.

One night I noticed a very tall and large male figure standing outside across the street from my house. He was staring straight at my window. It was a very scary situation for an isolated young woman. This happened over many nights. He was terrifying!

I felt so desperate that without even thinking I ran to the nearest church, fell to my knees and started unburdening my heart to a statue of Mother Mary. I was surprised to feel a divine presence, and a deep sense of peace. It reminded me of what Rumi says, "When the world pushes you to your knees, you're in the perfect position to pray." That was all I could think of to do, and God responded.

The next day, the threatening shadow didn't show up, and to my relief, never returned. Soon after, I moved to Toulon, in the south of France. By then I was convinced that unconditional love didn't exist, but I knew that suffering existed and I wanted to find a way out. I was eagerly searching...and again, Rumi's words describe my journey:

"Yesterday I was clever, so I wanted to change the world. Today I am wise, so I am changing myself."

***

One day something happened that would change my life forever:

I looked within! I don't exactly remember why or what inspired it, but it was the first time I had ever done so before. I just noticed I was being judgmental towards someone when they were speaking, and realized that I was not able to love others unconditionally. I used to resent others for not being loving towards me, and I would judge them harshly. But this love I expected from others, I myself was unable to give to anyone, including myself.

That was such a revelation, as if the sky was opening over my head!

So I started observing myself very closely: every thought, emotion, and word, my actions and reactions. I intensely observed myself as much as possible, and there was a lot of very painful discovery, but at the same time I experienced a new hope. Even though I realized I couldn't change the world, I could start changing myself! "Our task," Rumi says, "Is not to seek for love, but merely to seek and find all the barriers within ourselves that we have built against it." I was definitely beginning to see the barriers.

I started looking for ways to work on myself and to heal. For years I tried various esoteric paths, attending workshops and reading lots of books about bringing light into the darkness. It helped, and I discovered that I could heal and change my inner world to some extent.

The Buddha says, "One moment can change a day, one day can change a life, and one life can change the world."

Then the true life-changing moment for me arrived. In 2002 during a workshop, a friend casually mentioned she was going to see Amma. When I heard that name 'Amma,' I felt an overwhelming feeling of love and expansion in my heart. I decided to go along.

Attending Amma's program was like being transported to a heavenly planet without any previous announcement! What an overwhelming experience it was to watch such a radiant divine being embracing each and every person with the same quality of love — and all this for hours and hours without ever showing any sign of aversion, exhaustion, or lack of enthusiasm!

For three days and nights, my whole being soaked in Amma's beautiful love and presence. Tears slowly and silently rolled down my cheeks. The unconditional love I had been searching for, for so long, did exist! and She was right there making herself so available to all...

After that I never again felt the need to know my father's identity, and because I finally understood that there was nothing to forgive, my relationship with my mother greatly improved. Many people die with the regret of not having known or met one of their parents. Due to Amma's grace, I was not destined to have this regret.

Rumi says, "Your heart knows the way. Run in that direction."

Most people fall in love with Amma first, then later on become interested in her teachings and start practicing. For me it was different. I understood right away that Amma's teachings were of great value and very practical, and so I put in efforts to understand and practice them. I wanted to discover if they would work for me.

After meeting Amma, my way of living radically shifted. I established a regular daily routine of spiritual practice. It was my food! I could not live a day without it. I started considering my job as sēvā, which allowed me the opportunity to pay attention to my shortcomings and work to correct them.

One day as I was busy in the shop where I worked, I noticed an old, short woman, with a beautiful smiling face looking at me. She said to me, "Ma fille chérie" — "My darling daughter." I froze — these were the same three words Amma had so lovingly whispered in my ear during my darśhan. I just stood there and looked at her, unable to speak. This is absolutely *not* something people say in France, and I couldn't remember meeting or having helped that particular lady before. When I turned to look again she had disappeared. I was stunned!

I started following Amma in Europe, each year doing a bit more of the tour. Then I visited Amritapuri...it was love at first sight! I felt so much dispassion towards my worldly life, and missed Amma and Amritapuri very intensely everyday when I returned to France. However, an astrologer told me that I would never live in Amritapuri, so I sadly assumed it was my dharma to remain in the world.

During Amma's tours, I would do sēvā at the jewelry table with Swāminī Kṛiṣhṇāmṛita Prāṇājī. Amma says that wherever we see individuals endowed with noble qualities and good dispositions, we will find a great mother who has inspired them to become what they are.

To me Swāminī embodies Amma's teaching in so many beautiful ways and by association with her I receive much support, inspiration, and many valuable lessons. Her inspiring presence is like a magnifying glass, and it has challenged me to grow out of old harmful patterns of thinking and behaving.

A few years ago, a dear friend of mine came to see Amma in Paris. Each year the local Amma satsang group holds a lottery as a fundraiser for Amma's charities. The lottery tickets are quite cheap, and the first prize is a round trip plane ticket to Amritapuri. Many people dream of winning this prize. My friend casually bought a lottery ticket at the program.

On the last night of the program, the lottery winners were announced over the loudspeakers in the hall, and I heard my friend's name read aloud as the first prize winner! I was so happy for her! To me Amritapuri is heaven on earth, and I knew that her coming to this sacred land would be of such benefit. She absolutely wanted her boyfriend to come with her to Amritapuri, but the travel agency had difficulties coordinating his schedule with hers. In the end, my friend never came to Amritapuri. A few months later, she became very ill, and then just when she needed him most, her boyfriend left her. Such is the nature of worldly love.

I have learned a lot from this story, and remember it often when I find myself starting to take my life with Amma for granted. We have all won the most divine lottery — the greatest prize is having Amma in our lives. Amma is very eager to give each and every one of her children the grand prize of Self-realization, unconditional love, everlasting happiness, and peace.

But it is not enough for us to hold the winning lottery ticket in our hand. We have to put forth the right effort to collect the prize. If we wander here and there following the dictates of our mind and ego, we may end up losing this most valuable treasure. Amma gives each one of us the necessary guidance to reach the destination, but only we can take the steps to walk the path.

This reminds me of something that happened to me a few years ago here in Amritapuri. I was visiting the dentist and she told me, "You really need to get in the habit of flossing your teeth!" To which I replied hastily, "What a waste of time! I'd rather do something else!" "Ok, you don't have to floss your teeth," she answered. I smiled. I like when people tell me I can do whatever I want! Then she added, "Only floss them if you want to keep them!"

***

I have found, time and time again, that doing the right thing rather than following my likes and dislikes, has had many benefits. Not only does it help me keep my teeth, it also teaches me to overcome aversion, and I find myself more willing and able to joyfully complete any sēvā that needs to be done at any given moment.

The Covid pandemic brought so many things to a grinding halt, and so many people suffered as a result. Only dear Mother Earth was rejuvenated, getting a much needed rest from humanity's heartless and indiscriminate exploitation. But the pandemic also gave us a great gift — time to contemplate what really matters in life.

I was deeply shocked and pained to read that nowadays even six-year-old children sometimes struggle with depression. We have no control over what life will bring our young ones, but we can try to give them a spiritual education and teach them good values; just like Amma does for all of us, big and small. Spiritual education empowers both children and adults so that they depend less on the outer world for peace, happiness, and sense of fulfillment, facing life's challenges with more courage and equanimity of mind.

Amma is reaching out to all her children all over the world, telling them not to despair, and to never lose hope or self-confidence. She knows it is possible to stay peaceful and happy in all circumstances.

The *Tao Te Ching* says, "She who is centered in the Dao, (which I understand to be the Self), perceives universal harmony even amidst great pain, because she has found peace in her heart."[13]

Amma lovingly reminds us that God is always with us, guiding and protecting us, and that she will give us the energy and enthusiasm we need to transcend any obstacle in life.

All spiritual masters teach us that this human birth is meant to attain Self-realization. That is why it is of major importance for spiritual seekers to watch ourselves, and have the courage and patience to compassionately face our shortcomings and kindle the faith and endurance to keep on trying.

That reminds me of a story. A couple watched television together every night for twenty-five years. One evening, the husband looked at his wife, and with a twinkle in his eye asked, "How about doing something different tonight?" The wife became so happy, immediately thinking about what dress and jewelry she would wear to the restaurant or dance club they'd be going to. "What do you have in mind?" she enthusiastically

[13] *Tao Te Ching* by Lao Tzu, Chapter 35. Translated by Stephen Mitchell.

asked. "Let's swap seats," he replied. "Tonight you sit on the right side of the sofa and I'll sit on the left."

Let's not be like that. Sometimes it may seem hard to change, but Amma's grace rewards every small effort we make. No effort is ever wasted on the spiritual path. If we try to sincerely practice spiritual truths, we cannot remain the same, and it will not only benefit us but society as a whole.

Robert Adams said that you have to want liberation more than anything else in this world. So think of the things you're attached to that come before liberation. That is a question we all can ask ourselves, "What is it I am attached to that comes before Amma?"

I thought I was doing pretty good spiritually until some weeks ago when Amma gave us all a pop quiz! Amma asked us if we had been present or thinking of God while brushing our teeth or showering that morning? Such a simple question led me to realize that I was living my daily life mostly lost in my mind and hardly ever present; engrossed in useless thoughts of the past or future. I felt a little sad realizing that after all these years of spiritual practice, I still allowed my mind to wander as it pleased almost all day long.

Amma recently mentioned that many of her children are not afraid to die. After all, why should we fear death when Amma is with us? But what about life? Shouldn't we be at least a little afraid of not making the best use of it, and missing out on our own life? Life only happens in the present moment. If we miss this very instant, we miss life. Wise men say that neither fire nor wind, birth nor death, can erase our good deeds. So let's make sure that we foster thoughts and actions that support our spiritual evolution and the welfare of all.

In the book *Silence of the Heart*, Robert Adams says, "The sage is not confined to a body whatsoever. A sage is pure awareness.

To be in contact with the sage, all you have to do is think of the sage."

By making proper use of our imagination, Amma can always be by our side, and we can spend as much time with her as we want, and create meaningful memories of her. Amma herself has said that if we think of God without wasting even a moment and move forward with total detachment, we can reach the goal in a short time.

Once during a Europe tour I was seated in the very last row of the plane, about to take off for Ireland. Looking out the window, I noticed a white car pull up to the plane. I watched as Amma emerged from it! At first I was happy about traveling in the same plane as Amma. But as I was at the very back of the plane, and Amma was seated in the front, I was disappointed that I couldn't see her at all, not even a hair of Amma's head!

I was tired from the previous program, and my mind took over and started complaining, "You don't have a close relationship with your Guru! See, you are always so far from Amma. She never keeps you close."...on and on my mind went. By the end of the short flight, I was completely exhausted and heartbroken!

As they opened the back door for us to disembark, I realized with amazement that Amma would be exiting the plane at the same time using the front exit! Because I was at the very back, I was the first to exit, and could easily join Amma at the gate. We walked side by side to the luggage area. Amma lovingly smiled at me, and my broken heart was healed in an instant.

Sometimes we may feel sad that we are not as close to Amma as we wish, but that might be one of the many ways Amma uses to pull us closer to her. It is Amma's nature to love all of her children equally, and she has many creative ways to reach out to us when we long for her presence.

Let us practice trusting in her rather than believing our crazy, wandering minds. When the time is right, life will pull us into Amma's arms, and one day with her grace, we will become one with her. We are all the children of the goddess, and as Amma says, "If we so decide, we can create an empire of happiness. Because happiness is our true nature."

4

Amma's Infinite Grace in my Life

Rajiv Nair – India

Compared to many present here, I have very basic and limited knowledge about spirituality. From childhood, my devotion was limited to temple worship. Satya Sāī Bābā bhajans were held regularly in our house, but I must confess, at that age I was more interested in the potluck prasād that followed the bhajans, and playing with my friends. I often visited temples and performed special pujas (vazhipadu) for divine assistance to overcome particular situations. In fact, I often did five śhayana pradakṣhiṇams (circumambulating a temple by rolling on the ground as a form of austerity) in one go at Guruvayur. But once I met Amma, somehow the urge to do all that simply fell away. People began to comment on my changed behavior though I couldn't explain it to them. Every time I felt lost, insecure, or in need of support, my thoughts automatically turned to Amma. I continued to visit temples but even in those places, my mind would try to visualize only Amma's form. I didn't try to analyze all this. It happened and I was content to let it be that way.

Looking back, I realize that my relationship with the divine was very transactional: I will do this pūjā and you fulfill my desire. Along with this, I gave a lot of importance to horoscopes and astrology. Nothing bad was ever my fault. It was all because Jupiter, Mercury, Saturn etc. couldn't get along with each other or me. After I met Amma, listening to Amma's satsangs, hearing her bhajans, and reading her books made me think that although astrology is indeed a science, I have to do my part too.

As Amma often tells us, our karma[14] has a vital influence on the situations that we confront in our lives. I realized through experience that as long as I had faith in my Guru and put forth my best effort, I would be alright and though a 'difficult event' may still occur, with Amma's grace its severity would be greatly reduced. Now I just try to do each task to the best of my ability. If I succeed it is Amma's grace. If I don't, then it's still Amma's grace that I didn't fail even more spectacularly. As my perspective changed, I thought why rely on interpreters — astrologers — when I am with the scriptwriter herself? All I have to do is constantly try to be her instrument while she etches out my role.

After meeting Amma, when faced with seemingly insurmountable situations, I have prayed to her and turned to the *Awaken Children*[15] book series. Invariably, I find an answer there. Amma teaches us how to bring the scriptures into our lives. Not a moment goes by without her showing us the role of spirituality in our everyday lives. Spirituality for me is Amma, her words, and her teachings. My knowledge of spirituality is what I have learned from my journey with Amma, and from her infinite grace in my life.

While composing the bhajan *Ṭhumaka Chalata Rāmachandra*, Gōswāmī Tulsīdāsjī sought to compare baby Rāma's face with something of beauty. After various attempts he found that no comparison was adequate. Eventually, he wrote:

> *tulasīdās ati ānand dēkh ke mukhāravinda*
> *raghuvar chhabi ke samān raghuvar chabi baniyān*

---

[14] Action; mental, verbal and physical activity; chain of effects produced by our actions.

[15] One of the first compilations of Amma's teachings written by Swami Amṛitaswarūpānanda.

> 'Tulsīdās is thrilled by the face of Rām which has the glory of the sun,
> Rām's face can only be compared to Rām's face.'

I feel this is true for any attempt to describe Amma. Words by their very nature are limited and bound by their meanings and contexts; how can I use them to describe the limitless, unbounded, unfathomable, all-pervasive Amma? Is it any wonder that Amma's ardent devotee Śhrī Ottoor Namboodiripad wrote:

> *ōm vāṇī buddhi vimṛigyāyai namaḥ*
> 'Salutations to Amma whom speech and intellect cannot apprehend.'
>
> *108 Names of Amma, 11*

Amma tells us that sweetness cannot be known by writing 'honey' on a piece of paper and licking it. Similarly, Amma cannot be described in words.

***

During the dire times when the world was still reeling from the Covid-19 virus, Amma kept us safe in an environment where the travails and troubles of the outside seemed like anecdotes. If anything, Amma made life even more comfortable for us. Who would have imagined room service in the āśhram![16] And best of all, she ensured that none of us missed meditation or bhajans by arranging the live streaming of the evening programs. She assured us that whatever we may need, she would do her best to provide it. I can't help thinking that I missed a golden opportunity to tell Amma that all I want is *her*!

---

[16] At the height of the pandemic when the āśhram was in lockdown, all meals and groceries were served to the āśhramites in their rooms.

Amma's compassion is incomparable. In Hindu temples, it is a custom to ring the bell that hangs at the entrance of the sanctum sanctorum. By doing so, we announce our presence to God, and draw his attention to us. But here in Amritapuri, Jagadīswarī — the universal mother — comes to us and rings a bell to remind us that she is here. All we have to do is wake up. Amma has come to wake us up from our deep sleep of ignorance which we have been immersed in since time immemorial. Every day during Amma's 'White Flowers of Peace' meditation, at certain moments Amma would ring a bell, and I would obediently wake up for a few seconds before dozing off again. So, the gentle, melodious, tinkling bell was replaced by a gong. WAKE UP! I am here. There is a saying that you can lead a horse to water, but you can't make it drink. However, Amma's compassion is such that she brings her river of love to us and won't rest until we've all had at least a sip.

On a summer day in 1980, I set out from Ottapalam town in Kerala to meet Amma. However, there was resistance from the elders in my family, so we never completed the trip. That journey concluded nineteen years later in 1999, when I finally met Amma. Although I only met Amma in 1999, when I look back, I'm certain she had been with me long before that. From the fluid in my lungs miraculously clearing up after my open-heart surgery at the age of five, or escaping unscathed after my car was crushed under a sixteen-wheel trailer-truck in Dubai — only Amma was able to save me.

My parents-in-law were the first in our family to meet Amma in 1997. My father-in-law gave us the Dubai Satsang contact details, and we went for bhajans for the first time on the auspicious occasion of Guru Pūrṇima. The mesmerizing bhajans, especially *Sunlē Pukār*, did the magic, and we became regulars at the weekly satsangs.

In 1998, my parents got their first darśhan in London. They showed Amma a photo of our son, Pranav and she blessed the photo. The next year, during Amma's North India Tour, my in-laws went for darśhan in Ahmedabad, and took another photo of Pranav to Amma. The minute she saw the photo Amma said, "I know this son. His other grandparents also showed me his photo in London." The two photos were different and in the months between the London and Ahmedabad programs, Amma must have met thousands of people, and yet the recognition was instantaneous; Amma joined the dots and knew the relationship between all of us, who were in three different parts of the world — London, Ahmedabad and Dubai! But here's the twist in the tale: though our parents had met Amma, we hadn't yet!

> *sṛiṣhṭiyum nīyē sṛiṣhṭāvum nīyē*
> 'You are the Creation and the Creator.'
>
> Amma's bhajan *Sṛiṣhṭiyum Nīyē*

Amma needs no introduction to her creations.

After that, our longing to meet Amma became stronger by the day. I had recently changed jobs and moved to Bahrain, so the earliest I could get leave was in October, coinciding with Amma's London program. When we went for darśhan, Amma gave us a huge smile and said, "*Makkaḷ ettiyo? Evide āyirunnu?*" (Have you Children arrived? Where have you been?) Then she drew me into her hug. Nothing was ever this welcoming and secure. Never before had I felt that this is indeed where I belong. I remember lying on Amma's shoulder and feeling tears roll down my face. It didn't feel odd to cry on the shoulder of someone I was meeting for the first time; even crying had become effortless! Thereafter, I split my annual leave into two parts — one to be with Amma here in Amritapuri or on part of her tours, and the other part during Swāmī Amṛitaswarūpānandajī's annual visit to the Middle East.

Amma says that sincere prayer from the heart will always be answered. In the Middle East there are many people who are forced to stay away from their families, unable to come home for years together. Through Swāmījī's words, these people long to rest on Amma's shoulder for a while, hear a word of compassion and love, and unburden their sorrows at her feet. In 2000, Amma answered their prayers by making her first ever visit to Dubai. Among those multitude of prayers, our prayers were answered too.

We had an intense desire that Amma should perform Pranav's vidyārambham.[17] Our only desire was that Amma should conduct it whenever she felt the time was right. But coming to Amritapuri for Vijayādaśhamī was looking highly unlikely as I couldn't get the time off from work. As our frustration grew, so did the intensity of our prayers. Compounding the problem, Pranav's pediatrician advised us to get Pranav's adenoids surgically removed. My wife Jayshree was very upset and scared by this prospect.

Then we heard that Amma was coming to Dubai at the start of Navarātri. We immediately made our travel plans to Dubai. The first day of Amma's first ever Middle East program was super-mega-crowded and we decided not to go for darśhan that day. However, Amma had her own plans. A volunteer came and took Jayshree and Pranav for darshan saying Amma had called mothers with infants.

When they reached Amma, Amma sat Pranav on her lap and started playing with him. When Jayshree mentioned his

---

[17] Ritual done for the commencement of a child's studies, usually performed on the Hindu festival of Vijayādaśhamī which comes right after Navarātri — the nine nights devoted to worshiping the Divine Mother.

adenoid problem, Amma smiled and asked, "*Ivano?*" (for him?) and lovingly stroked his throat. That was it. When we went back to Bahrain the puzzled doctor said there was no need for the surgery after all. Amma took care of that prārabdham.[18]

During the Dubai program, Amma visited a devotee's house. Before we left for their house, out of the blue, Jayshree decided to buy the items required for a vidyārambham – a plate, a packet of raw rice, and some fruits. When we received darśhan Amma put Pranav on her lap and asked us, "*Enta vēnde makkale?*" (Children, what do you want?) We asked Amma if Pranav's vidyārambham could be done and Amma said yes, but that we would need a plate with some raw rice in it! We hurriedly produced the needed items, and Amma conducted Pranav's vidyārambham ceremony.

When her children, who long to be in her divine presence, are unable to come to her and cry out to her from their heart, Amma traverses millions of miles to be with them to fulfill their desire of being held in her embrace. Amma is the only guru in the history of mankind who does this.

> *ōm vāñchhitārtha pradāyinyai namaḥ*
> 'Salutations to the one who gives what is desired.'
> *Lalitā Sahasranāma, 989*

This is our Amma.

***

In the aftermath of 9/11, I was made redundant and following Amma's advice, returned to Dubai looking for a job. I had two Masters degrees, was a Chartered Management Accountant

---

[18] Malayāḷam for 'prārabdha karma,' the fruits of actions from the past that need to be experienced in this life.

and had worked in senior management of some of the best companies in the world for more than fifteen years.

These were my strengths, or so I thought... till then. I attended many interviews and one after the other they rejected me for the same reason: I was overqualified, and my experience far exceeded their requirement. What I thought were my greatest positives had now become my biggest negatives. One morning, after archana,[19] I thought to myself, "I give up. Let Amma do whatever she thinks is best."

Within a few minutes, I got a call from a company I had interviewed with many months previously. They asked if I could go over right then to sign a contract and start work the next day. The point here is, I see in retrospect that I was attached to my achievements and that was nurturing my ego. It was only when I gave up and left it to her that Amma could respond to my call for help. I am convinced that the grace was always right there, which is why I kept getting called for interviews — maybe Amma was giving me multiple chances to develop an understanding of surrender...but the story doesn't end there.

During this time, our biggest concern was Pranav's schooling. He needed a resident visa to continue in school but until I got a job and a resident visa, he couldn't get his. By Amma's grace now that the job situation was sorted, I got my visa stamped a day before the deadline given by the school. The next day, I was in the immigration office. I had until 1:00 p.m. to get the papers to the school. By 12:00, I was at the final stage of the process but was about twentieth in the queue.

An old colleague who was well connected with government officials suddenly called me. We had not spoken for many months. When I told him my situation, he spoke to the official at

---

[19] Chanting the 108 or 1000 names of a particular deity, in this case, the 'Śhrī *Lalitā Sahasranāma*' (The Thousand Names of the Divine Mother).

the counter who then took my documents straight to the director's office. I stood there waiting and chanting my mantra. The director issued my visa at around 12:40. Calling out to Amma, I prepared myself for a desperate hunt for a taxi. There was a taxi waiting right outside the immigration office. By Amma's grace there was hardly any traffic and I handed over Pranav's visa to the school just in time! After all, Amma had performed his vidyārambham; she took care that there would be no break in his education. Yet again, she protected her children like a 'mother hen' keeping us under her 'divine wings.'

At work, I was held responsible for things I had no part in, and my boss recommended that I be dismissed. After cursory investigations, the recommendation was accepted but needed the Group CFO's (chief financial officer's) approval too; which usually was just a formality. Unexpectedly, I got a call from the Group CFO's office telling me that he wanted to meet me. As I walked to his office, I prayed to Amma, "Amma you know I haven't done anything wrong, but I am unable to prove it." As I finished that thought, I felt something grip my left palm. I looked down and saw a dark hand holding my palm. As I looked on, the hand faded but I could still feel the strong grip in my palm as I walked into the CFO's office.

At the start of the meeting, I recall him saying, "Tell me your side." The meeting lasted ninety minutes but to date, I don't remember what transpired during that time. When I became aware of my surroundings, I was back in my office. I was mentally preparing to start hunting for another job, but again Amma had her plans. Apparently, the CFO was convinced that I was being framed and instead of terminating me, he promoted me to deputy CFO. Effectively, I was now my boss's boss!

Actually, it's not strictly true that I don't know what happened in those ninety minutes. I do know. Amma happened — as simple as that. She came there and spoke for me.

In 2007, I asked Amma for the first time if we could move to Amritapuri and Amma said, "*Amma parayam*" (Amma would tell me). Over the years I repeatedly asked her, and she repeatedly gave the same answer. In 2011, I had to undergo an emergency angiogram[20]and took medical leave. When I resumed work, I discovered that because my four-day medical leave had coincided with the annual budgeting exercise, the CEO was displeased and had decided to lay me off.

We came to Amritapuri and when we went for darśhan, Amma asked Jayshree and Pranav to stay. Amma gazed at me with a faraway look and said, "You go back and continue there." I was like, "Are you sure Amma? You know I don't really have anything to go back to. Plus, I was the one pestering you for permission to stay here, remember?" But Amma was firm — go back. So I did. However, the following days were full of desolation and despondency. I would often ponder on a poem I had written earlier:

You ask me not to think of the past
And I constantly
Live in the moments I spent in your presence.

You ask me not to think of the future
And I constantly
Dream of the moments when I'll be with You again.

---

[20] X-ray test that shows how blood flows through the blood vessels or heart.

You ask me to live in the present
And I constantly
Fill each moment with my memories and dreams of You.

You ask me to always be happy
And I constantly
Grieve that I'm so far away from You.

You ask me to understand that You are with me, anytime, anywhere
And I constantly
Need to see Your picture before I can pour my heart out to You.

You ask me to act without expectations
And I constantly
Pray to you, expecting You to call me to You.

You ask me to make my mind free of desires
And I constantly
Tell my mind to desire Your grace.

You ask me to act selflessly
And I constantly
Perform acts in order to try and come closer to You.

You ask me to be without ego
And I constantly
Find ways to see if anyone loves You more than I do.

I ask you when my obedience will bear fruit
And You constantly
Gather this disobedient child in Your embrace.

I would visit Amritapuri every opportunity I got, and Amma did not miss any opportunity that *she* got to pull my leg and announce to everyone around her, "Now he will start again like a child trying to avoid going to school, 'Do I have to go back, Amma? Can't I stay? Don't send me back Amma!'"

One day when I was visiting in 2013, I was sitting next to Amma's pīṭham [21] during darśhan. She was talking to one of the administrators of Amrita Vishwa Vidyapeetham [22] and suddenly said to him, "This son's prayers have borne fruit, let him come here and join the MBA college." Amma had never asked me about my academic background or discussed my job profile; but of course our omniscient Amma knows where each of us fit in her jigsaw puzzle.

Amma had told me, "*Nī padikkukayum vēṇam padipikkukayum vēṇam*" (You should study and also teach). I took it to mean that I should study so as to teach. And then she dropped the bomb — do a PhD. After getting my MBA in Scotland, I was offered a PhD position. I joked that I would do it when I grew old. Amma even fulfilled that wish — I was almost fifty when she asked me to do it!

My PhD had to be completed by November 2018. Deakin University rules were non-negotiable, complete on time or don't graduate with no credit for any work done up till then. By October 2017, I was skeptical whether I would be able to finish on time and decided to tell Amma. It was a Dēvī Bhāva night in London and when we went for darśhan I had barely uttered, "Ammē..." when she said, "*Thīrthe pattu*" (you have to complete it), and asked me to sit by her side. As I sat there my mind was in a turmoil because I really couldn't see how I could achieve what Amma had entrusted me with.

I was thinking, "Amma, I don't mind not getting the PhD but I don't want to bring a bad name to you or our university

---

[21] Seat for the Guru.

[22] A private, deemed, multi-campus, multidisciplinary university created by Amma, currently ranked among the best in India.

by failing in this." As I thought this, Amma turned to me and gave me the most beautiful smile I have ever seen. That smile and look calmed me down completely. I felt that rather than giving up, I had to continue to put in more effort. Amma often reminds us that instead of trying to change the paristhiti (circumstances), we should change our manasthiti (perspective). I knew in my heart Amma would take care of things.

Ultimately, Amma completed my PhD ahead of schedule.

Let us all pray to Amma that our faith in her grows stronger every moment and with her grace, we follow her guidance unquestioningly until we become one with her. Ammē, please hold on to me tightly and make me worthy of being known as your child.

5

Amma's All-Pervading Presence

Sarala - USA

O Amma, 'kōṭi kōṭi praṇāms' (millions and millions of prostrations) to you for coming out of hiding and revealing yourself to me. How long have you been hiding? Even if I don't get it right before this self trapped in māyā passes away, please let me know you are there with me. Please do not stay hidden. But how can Amma ever be hidden? Amma is everything and everyone; everything and everyone is Amma. If I just sit in silence for a moment I can feel her all around me. I can feel Amma here with me in this physical realm of time and space. If I focus, I can feel that Amma is the universe and everything therein.

Never Lost

I would like to share a verse with you from the *Bhagavad Gītā*.[23] I continually strive to grasp and realize its meaning. It also comforts me as it reminds me that since Amma is always with me, I have nothing to fear. Lord Kṛiṣhṇa says in Chapter 6, verse 30:

> *yō māṁ paśhyati sarvatra sarvaṁ cha mayi paśhyati*
> *tasyāhaṁ na praṇaśhyāmi sa cha mē na praṇaśhyati*
> 'One who sees Me everywhere, and sees all things in Me,
> I am never lost to him, nor is he ever lost to Me.'

[23] 'Song of the Lord,' one of the most sacred texts of India. It is a practical guide to overcoming crises in one's personal or social life and is the essence of Vēdic wisdom.

As I understand it, Lord Kṛiṣhṇa repeats this point in different ways — that he is everywhere and everything — throughout the *Gītā*. This is what I am striving to remember. I remember, then I forget, then I remember... We hear it, we know it... Then we forget and fall deep into the clutches of māyā again. It is one thing to *believe* that Amma is in everything, and everyone is in Amma. It is an entirely different thing to practice it and to experience it.

When I reflect on some of the lessons I have learned since reuniting with Amma in this lifetime, sometimes the lesson is just knowing Amma is always with me, and she knows my heart. That alone gives me the faith and reassurance to continue along the path. That alone quells my fear. Sometimes by some cosmic mysterious grace, Amma makes her all-pervading presence known.

***

I met Amma in the summer of 2008. I went to only two programs on that U.S. Tour — Los Angeles and Toronto. At the time I did not have many photos of Amma, so at the Toronto program I bought a small photo of her and kept it in my archana book.

Behind my house in the high desert are two paths in the hills where I liked to hike, chant archana and meditate. When I returned from the Toronto program, I immediately went hiking and did archana at the top of a hill.

After that hike I discovered my new photo of Amma was missing. A few days later, I hiked on the other side of this hiking area to chant archana. Over on that side was a giant rock where I like to meditate sometimes. After I finished archana, I glanced down and saw something white on the ground. It looked like a bit of laminated paper. In this area you never see any garbage. I thought, "This looks like the size of the Amma picture I lost.", I picked it up and looked at it. Lo and behold! It was the same photo of Amma that I had lost, but now it had little teeth marks around the edge where rodents must have nibbled on it. Somehow it had traveled all that way on its own to the foot of my meditation rock, about 350 meters away.

***

Six months later, we were at a chai stop on the South India Tour with Amma. Before Amma arrived, they put her chair in one place, and the tour people rushed over and crowded around it. I wanted to avoid the crowd, so I walked far away from everyone. A couple of minutes later, they moved Amma's chair and set it down right in front of me. When Amma came, she immediately sat down, and I was able to sit down right in front of her. I even talked to her a little bit. At that time, I was trying to learn Malayāḷam. (Actually, I am still trying, but progress is very slow!)

I told Amma that we had seen some wild elephants on the drive. We were all so excited that many of us got off the bus and started walking towards them. Then we realized maybe that was not such a good idea, and we all ran back to the bus. In Malayāḷam, I said to Amma, "*Amma, ñān āna kaṇḍu.*" — 'Amma, I saw an elephant.' Amma laughed a lot and lovingly mimicked my Malayāḷam, repeating what I said and how I said it so that everyone else could laugh. I was ecstatically happy.

After everyone settled in around her, Amma asked if anybody wanted to tell a story. I thought, "There is absolutely no way I am going to tell a story." Amma asked three times for someone to tell a story. Each time, a brahmachāriṇī sitting behind me leaned forward and said, "You tell a story!" After the third time, I hesitantly took the mic from Amma. Amma looked at me and said, "You?" I nodded 'yes.'

I told the same story that I just shared with all of you about finding Amma's photo at my meditation rock. After I told the story I asked Amma, "Did you do that?" She nodded 'Yes!' and smiled a smile that lit up the entire sky.

Amma was giving me a peek at her omnipotence and omnipresence. She was showing me that she was definitely with me, in her supreme form. I would hike up those same hills and cry that I wanted to be with Amma right now! And the hills would respond, "You are with me, you are standing on me." I would answer, "Not that Amma — the one in the form of the cute little Indian lady."

Going All In

As I mentioned before, I met Amma in this particular life in LA in the summer of 2008. Right away I got that strong message of, "Come running, darling children." So, I dropped everything and moved to Amritapuri within six months. Between the time of meeting Amma and moving to Amritapuri, I hopped on part of Amma's Europe and the Fall U.S. Tours. When I was not on tour with Amma, I just imagined that I was.

While making plans to move to India, someone told me that I could not simply move here on my own. I needed to ask Amma's permission first. That was like a kick in the teeth — the thought that Amma, my own mother, could possibly reject me and not let me come home. So, when I was at the Paris program, I asked Amma specifically if I could come to Amritapuri. I didn't say 'India' because if she had said, "No," I was going to move to the village right next to the āśhram and then ask her every day if I could move here. Amma did say yes, and I was greatly relieved.

After arriving here in the āśhram, within a few months I went on the tours to Singapore, Mauritius, Reunion, and Kenya doing darśhan token[24] sēvā. I really love a challenge and that was definitely a challenge because I had no background knowledge in it whatsoever. Actually, it was thrilling. I slept very little as I was always being called for something urgent. This is how Amma teaches us to overcome our bodily limitations.

Serving the Ever-Expanding Universe

In the summer of 2009, I started doing various sēvās in the āśhram — I am so grateful for these opportunities. I was fortunate to be a part of the formation of AMMACHI Labs,[25] as well as being present for many other milestones. One of the first things I did was to put together a computer vocational course (CVET) on plumbing for village women. There I was, designing a plumbing course, and learning a lot more about plumbing in the process.

For example, I now know the correct slope to position a sewer pipe for sewage waste so that the waste will flow down on its own. It depends on the diameter of the pipe. If the slope is too steep then all the liquid goes down, but the solids don't and the pipe will clog. If the slope is not great enough, then no flow happens and once again, the pipe will clog. While I was working on this day and night, my fellow āśhramites were meditating, doing yōga, learning scriptures and Sanskrit, getting their minds centered on the divine. However, the metaphorical context was not lost on me. I knew that Amma

---

[24] Darśhan tokens are numbered tickets given to devotees wishing to receive Amma's darśhan.

[25] AMMACHI Labs is an academic and research center at Amrita Vishwa Vidyapeetham that brings an interdisciplinary approach to addressing societal challenges. AMMACHI Labs creates innovative educational tools and skill development solutions to help uplift entire communities, especially women and girls in rural villages in India.

was plumbing out waste products from my mind — at a proper slope tailor-made for me.

From this experience I learned that Amma has many ways of teaching us and that āśhram life isn't only about sitting in the lotus position and chanting. Of course, for some people, that is strictly their path. I just try to accept what comes my way as Amma's prasād. This is an ongoing process by the way.

That very first batch of plumbing students are the same women that you used to see around the āśhram and the university before the pandemic lockdowns started. What grace it was to be able to work with the first known all-women group of plumbers in India. I would always tell them how proud I was of them in Malayāḷam: "*ñān niṅgalekurichu vaḷare abhimānikkunnu.*"

Over the years, AMMACHI Labs has expanded and become its own department at Amrita University, with many PhD students. What an unbelievable honor it has been to watch how this department has evolved, and even to be of help a tiny bit here and there. Even the sky is not the limit in Amma's ever-expanding universe.

A Wonderful World

We often take our lives and the existence of the universe for granted. We see things only from our tiny perspective. But look at flowers; flowers are beautiful in so many ways. Actually extraordinary, really exceptionally extraordinary, but we take them for granted. How can they be *that* beautiful — in color and design, fragrance and abundance? I know about biology. I studied biology and ecology in college. I do not deny the process of evolution. But it's not just the flowers' beauty. It's also about our ability to appreciate their beauty. Where does that come from? Where does our ability to see the splendor of sunsets come from?

One of my favorite phenomena to contemplate is how the moon is the perfect size and perfect distance to get perfectly between the sun and the earth to make a perfect solar eclipse. What are the chances of that? If the moon were larger or smaller or closer or farther, the perfect solar eclipse showing only the annulus of the sun would never happen. Think about it. It is truly amazing how much we take for granted. We never seem to be able to step back and observe what a wonder this world really is.

Bhakti – the Blessed Soul

I am always amazed at the extraordinary respect that Amma gives to all of nature, seeing all as different aspects of herself. Amma can be seen bowing to, and serving plants, animals, and all living beings. I had the great blessing of witnessing first hand Amma's relationship with her beloved daughter Bhakti. Bhakti was a very special dog... no ordinary dog. I'd like to share the story of when Bhakti first met Amma.

One of Amma's brahmachārīs rescued her when she was a tiny puppy, and she lived at Amma's engineering college across the backwaters from the āśhram. She would sleep on the brahmachārī's chest at night. During the day she would take rest on whatever new mat the college administrator got for her office, and Bhakti would claim it as her own. After some time Bhakti figured out that the administrator's guest chair was much more comfortable, and that also came to belong to her exclusively. If you sat on 'her' chair, then she would come and sit on you.

But Bhakti also liked to sleep in a somewhat dangerous place – near the tires of parked cars. One day someone in a car backed out without seeing her there, and they ran over one of her front legs and broke it. The brahmachārī set it with a splint; I was so worried about her. I said we should bring her to Amma, but the brahmachārī was reluctant to do so. So I took Bhakti myself.

When Amma saw her, she lavished her with love and affection. She kissed the paw of her broken leg, fed her prasād and put sandal paste on her forehead. I was so in awe of the love Amma gave her that I blurted out, "Name!" meaning please give her a name. Amma told me to come back in a week with a list of three or four names. We were all so excited and happy for this yet unnamed dog. The next week, the brahmachārī carried her back to Amma. Amma looked at the list thoughtfully, and then said, "Bhakti!" I held her up for everyone to see, calling out, "Bhakti, Amma named her Bhakti!"

We all have miraculous stories to tell about Bhakti, but the best part about her was watching her interact with Amma. Bhakti was so devoted to her, and Amma would often tell stories about Bhakti's devotion and intelligence to teach us lessons about the spiritual path. She brought so much joy to all of our lives; in fact, she was a veritable boon.

Bhakti, Amma's darling daughter passed away early morning on November 21st, 2021. Bhakti was given a full funeral ceremony after the evening bhajans and was buried by a tree on the beach. Blessed soul.

Laying Our Burdens Down

I want to talk about something personal, and private, because I think it is important to bring general awareness to this issue. Amma discusses it quite often, but individuals rarely share about it. I have depression. I am shy to mention it because there is often such a stigma that goes along with it. But even though I have this reservation to be public about it, I know it's common and Amma has given me 100% support over the years. Without this loving support, I might not be here right now.

It's kind of scary to be so open about this because, as I said, I'm a really private person. But with such support from Amma over the years, the least I can do is try to give something back. And if talking about it now can help someone in some small way, then it is definitely my good fortune.

What to say about my depression? Often just getting through the day can be a challenge for me. Amma told me it is due to my prārabdha karma.[26] On one hand, I secretly pray to Amma to just let me burn all the prārabdha karma that I can without any intervention from her. On the other hand, I get very lost in it and pray for any kind of help whatsoever, as if I were a complete failure. But I know that I am strong. I must be strong because I am Amma's daughter.

Trying to bring yourself out of a depression is not unlike trying to still the mind. Even if you have some methods and tools to help you, it takes a lot of effort and grace to steer the mind into a positive space, to even remember to remember to try.

However, with Amma's help, I have an excellent support structure, and I have been making progress. I can honestly say that I am getting better, that I have a little bit more control over my mind. As Amma has said that my depression is due to my prārabdha karma, I can only say that burning karma in the lap of the divine is pure grace. I also have to put forth my own effort and reach for help when I need it.

Anyway, we are in Kali Yuga.[27] It's not supposed to be perfect. Everyone has their own worries and sorrows. This reminds me of one time when I went to Amma when I was feeling depressed

---

[26] The results of past actions that are the cause of one's birth and whose effects one is destined to experience in this lifetime.

[27] The dark age of materialism and ignorance where unrighteousness predominates.

and frustrated with my mind. I asked Amma how to get rid of this problem. Amma said, "You just have to keep trying, you just have to persevere."

Now for a humorous story of an experience I had with Amma long back. Once on a retreat during a North American tour, Amma was giving a question-and-answer session. One person asked Amma what happens to us after death. Amma said there are three possible outcomes. One is that you have accumulated so much bad karma that you become like a balloon tied to a rock and you can't move. The second possibility is that you become like a balloon that rises on a long string, but still its ascension is also limited because of attachments and whatnot. The third is that your balloon rises up into the air with no string attached and you merge with the divine.

I found this all very fascinating, and I decided to talk to Amma about it. I posed a question to her that Swāmījī translated: "Amma, what percentage of living beings at the present moment will be stuck to a rock, or rise up like a balloon on a string, and what percentage will merge into you?"

Amma replied, "You can't even count the hairs in your own nose! Why do you want to know where everyone else is at? You should just worry about yourself."

We all started laughing, and I told Swāmījī that I thought, if I had the proper scope, it would be possible to count the hairs in my nose. The laughter went on and I thought to myself, "Wait, I should worry about myself? Is there something I need to worry about?" I walked away shrouded in this concern. Then someone came running up to tell me that Amma was calling me. I rushed back, and Amma told me that I don't need to worry because I have Amma's helium in my balloon.

I can see two lessons in this. One is that the spiritual growth of others is none of my business. I'm doing my best to imbibe that. I do try to correct myself when I find my mind taking a detour to judge the spiritual progress of others. The other is that Amma is with me, and I do not need to worry. We can all put our burdens down. No need to carry the luggage. We are on Amma's ship crossing the sea of transmigration. Amma is with me — Amma is with all of us.

6

Japa is the Seed

Jyotirup - France

> 'Fix your mind on me [...] taking me as the supreme goal, you will come to me.'
>
> *Bhagavad Gītā 9.34*

Amma says, "The mind cannot be fixed on a single point in the beginning. It should be tuned by doing mantra japa (repetition) continuously." Mantra is the tool to connect our inner Self to Amma. Amma tells us that a small key is enough to open a big box. Our mantra is one such small key. When we open a box, the space inside and outside the box merge, like the jīvātman (individual soul) merging into the paramātman (supreme Soul). Amma says we just have to turn the key in the right direction — in the direction of love, bhakti (devotion), and śhraddhā (faith).

As we chant our mantra, we begin to hear a whisper echoing in the depths of our heart. This is the inner mantra revealing itself. It's always a moment of wonder. As this inner mantra becomes more powerful, more audible, it gradually replaces the outer mantra. Then we only listen to the chanting of the inner mantra, which has always been present. It was just hidden, buried under our vāsanās[28] and thoughts. The outer mantra clears the way to reveal the inner mantra that never stops vibrating within us.

[28] Latent tendency or subtle desire that manifests as thought, motive and action.

The bhajan *Ōmkāra Svarūpiṇi* says:

> *ōmkāra svarūpiṇi uṇarū*
> *nīyenṭe hṛdayāntarālaṅgaḷil*
> *mṛdu tantriyil oru mantramāyi*
> *ātmāvin varavīṇayil uṇarū*
> *ōmkāra svarūpiṇi*
> 'O embodiment of Ōm, awaken. You who are the mantra that emanates from the soft strings of the veena of the Self in the depths of my heart, awaken.'

By continually chanting the mantra, we become silent and listen with joy to the pulse of the inner mantra. The mantra is God revealing himself in silence. The mantra invites us to silence; silence of the vāsanās, the mind, the world. It is vibration — the original source.

I am amazed at the power of the few syllables comprising the mantra. They seem so fragile in the face of the hubbub of the world. But the mantra has the power to take us deep within. Kṛiṣhṇa says to Arjuna in the *Bhagavad Gītā*: "I am the Self residing in the heart of all beings." (10.20) The mantra can carry us into that sanctum sanctorum, the inner Self.

In Awaken Children 2, Amma says:

> "The mantra will take you to the destination, the threshold of God-realization. From there, the beloved himself will lead you to the supreme state, realization."

Chanting, singing, and repeating our mantra invite God to reveal himself. Seemingly ordinary syllables are filled with Amma's divine śhakti (power). Recently someone asked Amma for her blessing to chant the Gāyatrī Mantra. With love and compassion Amma said it's fine to chant it, but then reminded her that there is no greater, more powerful mantra than the one given by the Guru.

In *Awaken Children 9*, Amma explains:

> "When Amma gives you a mantra, she sows a seed of spirituality within you. She transmits a part of herself into your heart. But you have to nurture that seed by meditating, praying, and chanting your mantra regularly, without fail. You have to be totally committed."

Amma transfers 'a part' of her divine energy. But isn't a part of the indivisible infinite already the infinite whole? Maybe that's why the scriptures say there is no difference between the Guru and the mantra. The mantra *is* the Guru. At the same time, the Guru (God) is beyond the mantra. The 846th name of the *Lalitā Sahasranāma*[29] describes the Divine Mother as:

> *ōm mantra sārāyai namaḥ*
> 'She who is the essence of mantras.'

Thousands of people may have been initiated into the same mantra, yet each one is a priceless treasure because Amma infuses it with her energy in a way that is unique for each person, according to their saṁskāras (mental impressions), their vāsanās, their spiritual path. Only Amma knows.

***

About ten years ago, I used to meditate daily at the aśhram beach. Every evening, the same brahmachārī would come and do his mantra practice with his mālā (rosary) for about an hour. For the first few days, I would sit in 'meditation' just a few

[29] Thousand Names of Śhrī Lalitā Dēvī, a form of the Divine Mother.

meters behind him. From time to time, I would quickly peek to see if he was really practicing or if he was faking it. The one who was faking it was me, not him. Crazy mind. By his abhyāsa, or constant practice, he unknowingly inspired me to practice my mantra even more.

Amma tells us to see the good in others. By practicing this, I have discovered many role models. One inspired me with his commitment to meditation; another with his sincerity performing sēvā; another with her warm smile; another with his courage and strength; another with her intense bhakti; another with his scriptural knowledge. Let us be inspired by the best in each other, and use this inspiration as a ladder for our spiritual upliftment. I am grateful to all of you who are a precious, invaluable support on my path.

I also wish to express my gratitude to my wife Mitra. For twenty-five years she has been an unshakeable support and source of inspiration and encouragement. She always tries to pull me up. I feel Amma uses her as an instrument to make the flower in my heart bloom. It's not always easy, but we are like spiritual siblings on our way to the vānaprastha[30] stage of life where the couple leaves the world and moves to the 'forest' to dedicate their lives to spiritual practice.

Time is most precious. Amma always tells us not to waste our time. It is possible to recover a million dollars lost, but we can never recover a single wasted second. I used to record the number of mantras I chanted per day in my diary. One day, I reached the bhajan hall early and realized I was nowhere near my usual quota of daily mantra repetitions. I decided to chant

---

[30] One of the four stages of life in traditional India; they include brahmacharya (celibate student life), gārhasthya (householder life), vānaprastha (retired life dedicated to spiritual practices) and sannyāsa (life of complete renunciation).

my mantra while waiting for the bhajans to start and between each bhajan. By the time bhajans ended, I had chanted almost 250 mantras! We are not even aware of the precious time we waste. Wasting time is not just sitting idle or gossiping. Every time we think, say, or do something without love and śhraddhā (attentiveness), we are wasting time.

In her satsang for the seventeenth anniversary of the AmritaSREE women's empowerment program, Amma said:

> "Everything in the world — every region, every place, every grain of sand, every individual, every house, every forest, every ocean has its own vibration. That vibration is its mantra. Similarly, there is a mantra for this entire universe."

Amma also says, "This mantra is yajña, which means 'giving' [...] real enjoyment comes only when we all share wealth, prosperity, and natural resources equally with respect and love."

The mantra allows us to harmonize with the universe, to vibrate at the same rhythm of love and giving. The inner mantra, the one not sung but heard, opens the door. In the fourth century, Saint John Chrysostom, one of the Fathers of the Christian Church, spent decades in the desert searching for God. He had the same idea:

> "To rise [...] to the prayer of the heart, which opens up the Kingdom of God within us."[31]

Mantra is vibration. We all know about Einstein's theory of relativity and most of us have also heard of quantum physics. They are currently the two most serious theories explaining how the universe functions. But these theories contradict each other on certain points, and for a few decades alternative theories

---

[31] From the book *The Pilgrim Continues His Way.*

have tried to reconcile them. One is string theory which says that the universe is composed of very subtle elements that look like strings. These strings propagate throughout the universe, interact, and are animated by an ultimate energizing element called vibration.

Amma also talks about the vibration of the universe from a spiritual perspective. Science and spirituality intersect. God is vibration. Mantra is vibration. The mantra connects us to God and to the universe. Amma says that sometimes the telephone network might not work, but the divine network is always available everywhere.

Twelve years ago, I was walking in a forest in France chanting my mantra. My mantra and I were like two friends out for a walk. Suddenly my phone rang. The call was from abroad. When I answered, no one said, "Hello." Instead, I heard Amma's divine voice singing a bhajan. It turns out that one of my brothers thought to call me during bhajans so that I could hear Amma's voice.

This is Amma's magic, the magic of the mantra, irrefutable proof of its power to connect us to the divine, even thousands of kilometers away in a forest in France. God is everywhere, but it's up to us to dial the mantra number on our "parāśhakti-smartphone."

One of the most difficult things to do is to surrender our old habits to God. Our oldest habit is to constantly fill the mind with thoughts. Some say the most effective way to change is to change our habits by creating new saṁskāras. To change our habits, we have to replace them with new ones. They say our thoughts become our actions; our actions become our habits; our habits form our personality; and our personality determines our destiny.

In *Eternal Wisdom 2*, Amma says, "To constantly remember God is not your natural habit, so you have to cultivate it. Japa is the prescription." And Amma also says, "Japa should first become a habit."

***

The more I progress on the spiritual path, the less I seem to know. I am more of a beginner today than I was a year ago. Sometimes, I feel like I am going backwards. How many times have I forgotten my mantra? Amma had to remind me one year during a room darśhan[32] to remember to chant it. Another time, Amma gently touched her wrist mālā while chanting a mantra and counting the beads...a subtler reminder. Only her grace can save us. Let us be patient and continue our efforts.

When I was teaching the IAM[33] meditation technique, many people shared that they did not have time or energy for their daily spiritual practices. I had to face the same issue when after eight years of living in Amritapuri, I had to return to France to work for a whole year. I was so busy with my job that I had no strength or time for sādhanā (spiritual practice) in the morning, let alone at night after a full day's work. How to stay connected to Amma in such circumstances? I had to be realistic. I decided to focus on four points that I felt I could sustain for a whole year.

First of all, I resolved never to complain about my situation. I decided to accept it one hundred percent. Secondly, on

---

32 A 'room darśhan' is when Amma meets individually with āśhram residents in her room.

33 IAM, or Integrated Amrita Meditation Technique, is a meditation practice formulated by Amma that integrates gentle relaxation stretches with an effective and easy-to-practice breathing and concentration technique. It is based on traditional methods and designed for the time constraints of modern life.

weekends I would do archana and the IAM meditation to stay connected with those practices; and I would walk in nature. Amma says that nature is the 'visible form of God.' Very often I could feel nature absorbing all the tensions and negativities I accumulated during the work week. I would experience peace and joy reconnecting with the natural rhythm of nature and of life.

When Swāmī Rāmakṛiṣhṇānandajī joined the āśhram Amma told him he still had to work at a bank. I remembered how Amma told him to be welcoming, to smile and be helpful to each person, imagining that he or she was Amma. Inspired by this, my third resolve was that when I was at work, I tried my best to imagine that Amma was there watching me and was happily smiling.

As a fourth resolve, I decided to chant my mantra on my twenty-five minute bus ride to work in the morning. The first few days it took some effort to remember. But after a few weeks, I joyfully realized that as soon as I stepped on the bus, the mantra would start automatically. I didn't even have to think about it. A new habit was created — getting on the bus meant chanting my mantra.

The power of the mantra is immense and hard to fathom. Discovering it day after day is like lifting a tiny corner of a huge veil. Amma says, "The fullness of a mantra can only be experienced when your mind attains perfect purity." In the Rāma bhajan *Mukhi Asudē* Amma sings:

prabhuchē jithē smaraṇa nāhī
dukhtyā manāchē jhāvē nāhī
rām nām japē vinārē
śhānti kōṇi pāvē nāhī

> 'Sorrows will remain if we fail to chant the name of God. Without repeating the name of Lord Rām, no one will attain peace of mind.'

The power of the mantra redirects our scattered worldly thoughts to the thought of God. It has the strength to overcome our habitual thinking, thinking, thinking. Let our mantra become the habitual functioning of our mind, then we can deal with the ebb and flow of our negative emotions and thoughts. In verse 15 of the *Guru Gītā*, Śhiva instructs Pārvatī:

> *gurumantram sadā japēt*
> 'Always repeat the Guru's mantra.'

In the Bible, Saint Paul exhorts people to "Pray without ceasing." Amma tells us, "Chant your mantra while brushing your teeth, even while going to the bathroom or taking bath."

In his book *Meditation and Spiritual Life*, Swāmī Yatīśhwarānanda, a senior monk of the Rāmakṛiṣhṇa Mission says we worship our ego and our worldly thoughts much more than God. He says: "If we watch our thoughts during the day, we find hundreds of worldly 'iṣhṭas'[34] there instead of our iṣhṭa dēvatā — our chosen deity. We must cling to our real iṣhṭa and dissolve all the false iṣhṭas into the true iṣhṭa dēvatā. There is no other solution."

Because our mantra is divine it can help us move from the apparent plurality of the world to its underlying unity. The mantra is itself the substratum, the primordial vibration. In Amma's terms, it is seeing the unity in the diversity.

In *Awaken Children 2*, someone asks Amma, "Can one attain God by merely chanting the divine name?" Amma replied, "Certainly, why doubt? But concentration is a must."

---

[34] Iṣhṭa means 'that which one likes.'

So we must chant the mantra with love, faith, and concentration.

***

The *Muṇḍaka Upaniṣhad* tells the story of Śhaunaka. He was a mahāśhāla, a great householder. He lived in the world with possessions, family, and reputation, but he realized that all this did not make his life complete, so he decided to approach a Guru named Aṅgiras. That's exactly how it was for me. Before I met Amma, I had 'everything' — a rewarding job interacting with business leaders and politicians, and living in one of the most beautiful regions of France with my wonderful wife Mitra. Yet I experienced the truth of this story from the *Muṇḍaka Upaniṣhad* when I was twenty-nine years old. One day I was in my office, and I received a booklet about the 'Who's Who' of my profession in France; a whole page was dedicated to me.

I realized in a flash that name and fame are not the ultimate goal of life. They come and go. I felt my career in the world was over. It had not made me happy and could never make me happy. I had to find out who I really was and what real happiness is. This was before Mitra and I met Amma. At that time, I was reading a lot of spiritual books from different traditions. Two of them touched me deeply.

One was the nineteenth century Orthodox Christian book *The Pilgrim Continues His Way*, one of the best books in the world on mantra. It tells the story of a Russian man who is sincerely seeking God. He meets a *starets* (Russian for Guru) who teaches him the Christian mantra '*kyrie eleison,*' meaning 'Lord, have mercy on me.' He begins by chanting a thousand mantras per day, increasing until finally achieving 10,000 repetitions. He tells how his inner life and the world became divine, and he experienced profound peace.

The second book was *'Les Chemins de la Sagesse'* (The Paths of Wisdom) by Arnaud Desjardins, a French spiritual master who hosted Amma in France in the early years of her travels. In the beginning of the book he warns the reader:

"If you have neither a Guru nor a mantra, then it is impossible to follow a serious spiritual path. So don't waste your time reading this book. Close it now!"

It was a profound shock. I started praying every night for a real Guru and a mantra. In my childlike faith, I started chanting the Christian mantra saying to God, "If you are not happy with me chanting this mantra, then give me another one!" This proved to be very effective because in less than three months Mitra and I met Amma in Toulon, France.

I remember very well that first meeting with Amma and also the first Dēvī Bhāva. Mitra and I asked for a mantra during our darśhan, and we were directed to the mantra line. I innocently thought it would take five minutes. It actually took four hours! A long line of people sat in chairs snaking around behind the stage. To advance, the person in front had to move forward. However, that person was exhausted and fell asleep as soon as he sat down. I would wake him up and he would open his eyes, grunt, and slide to the next chair without even standing up and go straight back to sleep. I felt bad for waking him up again and again, but I had no choice if I wanted a mantra! This was my first sēvā for Amma! I must have woken him up at least forty times that night! It makes me smile. Isn't Amma also trying to wake us up all the time? And don't we just fall back to sleep?

Thousands of us have been on this path for a long time. I am reminded of the story of Nārada in the *Chhāndōgya Upaniṣhad.* He approached the sage Sanat Kumāra with a long list of all the subjects he knew, but he had to admit that the supreme knowledge was still unknown to him. I also had my list — different from Nārada's but a list nonetheless!

The spiritual path begins by renouncing aparā vidyā — knowledge that takes us away from the Self, concentrating on parāvidyā or ultimate knowledge, and on starting a sādhanā under the protection of our beloved Amma.

After all these years, I feel more and more that I do my sādhanā not for myself, but for the world, to be in harmony with this universe, to stop polluting the world with my thoughts, and one day to be able to share this wisdom. Following a sādhanā is probably the most perfect act of compassion, the most beautiful gift to the world.

At the end of the Dvāpara Yuga,[35] Nārada asks Brahmā, the creator, the best method to attain mōkṣha (liberation) in the dark age of the Kali Yuga. Brahmā answers that the best method is chanting the mantra. Amma sings in *Bōlō Śhyām Rādhē*:

> *sūr mīrā sabnē pāyī ānanda kā dhām lēnā*
> *kabhī na bhūlē vō giridhāri kā nām*
> 'The great saints Soordas and Meera attained the state of bliss by never forgetting to chant the name of Giridhāri[36].'

The qualities I strive to develop are mumukṣhutva, the intense desire for liberation, and lakṣhya bōdha, one-pointed focus on reaching the goal. Intensity is that inner fire that burns away all desires and thoughts so that our focus is on God alone. The truth is we are alone with God, and only God is truly with us.

---

[35] One of four 'yugas' or world eras or ages. The first era is called 'Satya Yuga,' the age where righteousness predominates. The subsequent three other yugas Trēta, Dvāpara, and Kali see a continual decline in righteousness in the world, ending with Kali Yuga where unrighteousness predominates.

[36] Another name for Kṛiṣhṇa.

In the *Rāmcharitmānas,*[37] Rāma tells Śhabarī:

> *mantra jāpa mama dṛiḍha bisvāsā*
> "Chant my name with steadfast faith."

It doesn't matter how many mantras we chant. The most important thing is how we chant — the intensity of our devotion, and the degree to which we are tuned to the divine.
In Chapter 1, verse 28 of the *Patañjali Yōga Sūtras*[38] it states:

> *tajjapastadartha-bhāvanam*
> 'To repeat and contemplate the meaning of the mantra.'

Settling into the meaning of the mantra becomes clearer as sādhanā continues. Just repeating the mantra is not enough; descent into the heart is essential. Saint John of the Cross, a great European mystic from the sixteenth century, wrote a very famous spiritual poem called *The Dark Night of the Soul.* He says, "With no other light or guide than the one that burned in my heart." I pray that this inner fire will ignite in the hearts of us all and that we will burn with love for the divine.
Kṛiṣhṇa asks us to fix our mind on him. The mantra is not separate from our beloved deity — our Guru and God. Thus, it becomes a great tool to reach God in this Kali Yuga. Let us not waste time; life is short. Let us chant our mantra with faith, love, and enthusiasm, as our offering to the world.

After the curtain closes at the end of every Dēvī Bhāva, a voice says over the loudspeakers: "Amma says there are no words to express her gratitude for the tireless work of her children in making this program a great success." I cry every

---

[37] A devotional retelling of Rāmāyaṇa (the story of the life and times of Lord Rāma) composed in the Awadhī language by Gōswāmī Tulsīdās.
[38] Aphorisms composed by Sage Patañjali on the path to purification and transcendence of the mind.

time I hear it. O Amma, we your children have no words to express our gratitude for your tireless efforts to guide us to true happiness. From the bottom of our hearts, we thank you Amma.

7

See the Good

Sribhavani - Germany

> "Try to see the goodness in everyone. That is the best way to become good in word and deed." — Amma

What does it really mean to 'see the good?' We 'see' with our eyes, but our eyes see everything equally. They do not judge. They are totally impartial. Therefore, this advice cannot be meant for the sense organs.

The mind illumines our eyes. The mind is the one that divides the seen into good and bad. So 'seeing the good' has nothing to do with 'good' vision. Seeing the good is a mental attitude. But is this an invitation for us to turn a blind eye to all the so-called 'bad?' Amma often tells us to see the good in everyone, but she also tells us to see the world as it is, to have the right understanding about the ever-changing world.

How to behave in situations where adharma (unrighteousness) takes place, and still see the good? To see the good requires dispassion and discrimination. We have to point out adharma and protect ourselves and others when it is needed. In every interaction we should remember that everyone has goodness in them even if their actions fail to express it. Amma's advice to see the good in everyone invites us to look beyond actions and words. By doing so we will find the good. This is not an easy sādhanā, but it is worth trying to do, and is part of the vision of prasāda buddhi, seeing everything as God's gift.

We have all experienced the power and importance of someone seeing the good in us. How fortunate that we have all met Amma, the master who sees good in everything, with all her light and the universal power of her saṅkalpa (divine resolve). This leads to a lot of changes in everyone.

During the Covid years, people shared so many experiences of how deep their first meeting with Amma was, and what profound transformations happened from her first glance and touch. Amma's glance and her saṅkalpa are beyond comparison and have a strong effect on everyone. Her every action and her every breath is only for the good of the world. Amma is the embodiment of goodness, and she awakens the seed of goodness in us.

Amma never gets tired of encouraging us, uplifting us, day in and day out, for years, without rest, and with utmost patience. And this is our rescue; our treasure. There was a huge change in my life after I met Amma for the first time in Mannheim in 2005. Even now after so many years, I still have no words to express the experience of my first darśhan.

At first I was not aware of the many changes that occurred afterwards. But a year later when I was preparing to go to Amma's program, my fifteen-year-old daughter decided to come with me. A teenager willingly going somewhere with her mother at that age, in the West, is a miracle. I thought my enthusiasm about Indian music, culture and food had convinced her. But when somebody asked her what brought her to Amma, she replied, "I saw a big change in my mother after she met Amma. At that time I had a lot of problems, so I thought it might help me too." This says everything.

***

When I visited Amritapuri the first time in 2010, somebody told me to get my chart read by an āśhram astrologer. When he spoke of my relatives as "good, virtuous people," I got a little confused. Does he have *my* chart? When he continued to speak about a bright future for me, I was convinced he had the wrong chart. However, somehow I was still open to reflecting on which person's vision about my life was correct. Today I realize the astrologer was right, and that my perception was clouded.

When I saw the *Mahābhārata* movie, I was very disturbed by the scene where Draupadī was insulted. How could Draupadī live happily and in peace with her five husbands after they silently stood by and failed to rescue her, making them complicit in the crime? How could she manage it? I knew I wouldn't have been able to. I thought that if I found the answer to this question, maybe I could find a way to make peace with my relatives. It is always easier to enquire about somebody else because you have the needed emotional distance and are not so identified with the situation.

I analyzed Draupadī and her virtues. Certainly, there is her deep bond, unshaken faith, and love for Śhrī Kṛiṣhṇa. Concerning my question, the following three points also seemed relevant:

- Draupadī still saw the goodness in her husbands, even after the insult.
- She knew that all this was part of her karma.
- She saw the good in herself too.

What could I learn from this? I was born in Romania while the country was governed by a very harsh and rigid communist dictatorship. I was born into a German minority which was at the top of the communist agenda to be eliminated...and they succeeded. That minority culture does not exist in Romania anymore. So my birth circumstances were not favorable even for life. It was a world pervaded by political oppression, corruption, continuous fear, violence and alcoholism.

From a very young age, almost every day I experienced that 'today's friend might be tomorrow's enemy and vice versa.' This was not limited to just 'friends.' It was true even with those closest to me — my parents and my family.

The darkest time of my life was when I was five years old. I desperately needed protection but no one was there to help me. Seeking help, God (Amma) came into my life, not physically but within me. She helped me protect myself and turned my life into a life of tapas (austerity). She guided me and carried me throughout. This was my rescue and my good fortune. Therefore, how to see the good in my family when they didn't protect me when I was so small and needed it most?

When you really search for answers, Amma never leaves you to figure it out alone. I started to notice that when Amma spoke about her own childhood and the values she was taught, I felt very disturbed and uneasy within myself. Finally I had to admit that I saw many of these same values in my family too. Some of those values were: not to sit idle; to honor the guest; to have gratitude and reverence towards nature; to be modest. They were (sometimes) living these values and telling me to do the same, but I couldn't accept what they were saying because they lived by those values only on 'good' days. On other days it was another story. The 'not-good days' totally dominated my point of view.

This reminds me of a story. A grandfather was teaching his grandson about life. He said, "A fight between two wolves is going on inside of me. The dark wolf is evil. He is anger, selfishness, sorrow, greed and fear. The light wolf is good. He is joy, peace, love, compassion, humility and faith. The same fight is going on inside you and inside everyone on this earth." The grandson thought for a moment and then asked, "Grandfather, which wolf will win?" The grandfather simply said, "The one you feed."

This story showed me that it was up to me which memories I feed: the experiences from the good days or the experiences from the other days. When I pondered on it, I realized that I expected my whole family to have acted like saints, but they were not saints. They were ordinary, simple people who were struggling in that very challenging environment, and still did not let go of the good completely.

Amma says, "The mind is like water; it naturally flows down." This means to feed the dark wolf naturally happens by itself. No special effort is needed. We feed our dark side through gossip, complaints, carelessness, guilt, and laziness.

To feed the light wolf we must put in effort. We must bring in fire (the light) to heat the water so it can rise upwards. Likewise, we must bring the qualities of awareness and discrimination into our daily lives. This requires deliberate effort.

With effort, slowly I was able to acknowledge and understand that it was my karma to go through all that had happened. Looking at everything in this way allowed me to find peace in regard to my parents and family. I was able to connect with this inner peace only because all of them have already passed away. Having learned from Amma that my spiritual practice will benefit up to three previous generations of family members is a strong motivation for me to do my sādhanā. I wish and pray for peace for all of them wherever they might be.

The wolf story helped me find outer peace with my family, even though the grandfather spoke about it as an inner fight. However, the story is even more relevant for the inner fight which goes on in most of us.

This brings me to the next point about Draupadī: she saw the good in herself too. This part I have to admit was not easy for me at all. First, I had to feed the light wolf and change my perception of myself. There was good in me, but I couldn't see it. I'll share one of many incidents of how Amma greatly helped me with this.

During my first visit to Amritapuri, I was blessed to be able to participate in a small North Kerala tour. The first stop was in Calicut. I didn't know anything, and everything was new for me. On the first day, I got a 'face wiping' shift at the beginning of the program. Face wiping is when a person assisting the darshan line wipes devotees' faces with a tissue before they reach Amma for their embrace. I received instructions and started doing this sēvā. Soon I realized I did not feel comfortable doing this at all.

It was very crowded. Within just ten minutes I had been touched by more people than I had been in my entire life. Plus, the fan broke, and it got extremely hot. No air flowed and it started to smell. When all this came together, my mind quickly concluded, "This sēvā is not for me." Soon I was convinced that India was not for me either, though I knew nothing about India at that time.

I started looking for the sēvā supervisor to get a replacement. I just wanted to get out of there so no one would touch me... Amma had other plans. Just when I started to look for the supervisor, an old woman came up. She was very skinny and clean, but you could see from the many repairs on her sāri that she was very poor. I wiped her face. Then she bowed down and touched my feet. I was shocked and luckily speechless.

I felt so uneasy. I didn't know what it meant when someone touches your feet, but I knew no one should do that to me. If at all it should be the other way round. Then she took my hands in hers and started to speak to me, but I didn't understand. She looked straight into my eyes. Only questions arose in me,

"What went wrong in my life? How does this poor woman have so much light in her? Where did I lose this light?"

Another woman came over and translated. The old woman said that she wanted to thank me from the bottom of her heart, as I had made it possible for her lifelong wish to meet Amma come true. Our devotion and dedication to Amma makes so much possible.

When I heard this, I really felt bad. I knew I had just been complaining and that there was not much devotion or dedication in me then. This interaction stopped the whole darśhan line, but no one interrupted us. When she reached Amma I looked directly into Amma's eyes. She had been watching us. Amma's glance revealed that this is what I should contemplate on. Amma's gaze went completely through me.

After this, face-wiping sēvā didn't bother me anymore. When my shift ended, I immediately fell sick and had to stay in my room for the rest of the program. This gave me plenty of time to contemplate on the question: "What went wrong? How did I lose the light in me?"

At the end of the program Amma sang bhajans. First, I felt sad not to be there, but I couldn't dwell on it because an Indian man entered the women's dorm with a plate of sweets. He said, "Amma sent this for you to thank you for the good work you did." I replied, "Sorry but you are in the wrong room. I was sick the whole program. I didn't do any work."

He asked, "Is this room 304?" and I said "Yes." Then he set the plate of sweets in front of me and left. Honestly, I was thinking he just wanted to get rid of the plate and return to Amma. It took a while before I could see Amma behind this and get the messages she was sending:

- Introspection is good.
- Introspection is also work.

- Introspection is precious for spiritual growth.

Questioning everything — life, its purpose, and the way of living — from a very young age and not being satisfied with shallow answers, was not at all in tune with the communist regime. I got into a lot of trouble for it. Finally, I stopped seeing anything good in this introspecting tendency and tried my best to get rid of it. Luckily Amma stopped me.

After two days of self-reflection in Calicut, even though without spiritual knowledge but in Amma's presence, and thanks to her grace, I got deep insights. My bond with Amma and the spiritual quest strengthened very much. Seeing good qualities in myself was the first lesson I had to learn, and it was practice for feeding the light wolf.

This version of the two wolves is a modern short version. The original story doesn't end there. After the grandfather said, "The one you feed, that one will win," he continued, "If you feed them both correctly, they both win." You see, if I only feed the light wolf, the dark wolf will be hiding around every corner, waiting until I become distracted or weak. At that moment, he will jump out to get the attention he craves. He will always fight the light wolf.

The dark wolf has many important qualities that we need as well, like perseverance, courage, fearlessness, and straightforwardness. Actually, the two wolves need each other. Feeding only one and starving the other will eventually make both uncontrollable. Caring for both allows them to serve you so that you can do something good with your time on earth.

Peace is our goal. How we choose to treat the opposing forces within ultimately determines how we live. What did the grandfather mean by 'feeding both?' Did he advise his grandson to express the negative qualities of the dark wolf? Not at all. Let me share an experience to explain:

Soon after moving into the āśhram, there was a sister I did sēvā with, who I found very difficult to work with. Every day she tried to provoke a reaction from me. I saw this as Amma training me in patience, forgiveness, being a good daughter of Amma, and developing good qualities. I gave my best and I felt happy about my progress. Then one day, this sister crossed all my boundaries. I exploded and shouted, "Stop! That's enough!" This came out with such force that I scared myself, and I left the office before doing something I might regret. All my 'progress' was gone at once.

After I calmed down and introspected, I approached our Swāmī in charge to tell him what had happened and to ask for permission to look for another sēvā. As I was telling Swāmījī what had happened, he started laughing. I got irritated and said, "Swāmījī, I tell you that I acted completely inappropriately, and here you are laughing. How should I understand this?" His answer was, "I've expected this to happen for a long time. I've observed you for months. You were only suppressing your feelings when you never spoke out. This had to happen! Tomorrow, sit on the other side of the office." Saying this, he left.

No scolding, no punishment, but what a teaching! Swāmījī showed me that I didn't have the necessary skills for handling such situations without reacting. I thought I had made spiritual progress, and was developing good qualities, but actually I was just suppressing my discomfort and anger towards that sister. When I analyzed what had happened, I saw that I had a big habit of suppressing emotions. I was suppressing nearly every vital force in me, so I started to be more watchful.

Growing up in an unfavorable environment had left its impressions on me. I hadn't acknowledged that. Even after I had studied psychology and had done a lot of self-study, I didn't have the courage to be honest with myself. I still wanted to be somebody else. I didn't want to look at the imprints and stains in me, so I tried to deny them — but that didn't work. Denial didn't work because the dark wolf was starving and was messing up my efforts. I never accepted him, so he was very canny and knew how to get me where he wanted me.

In this way I learned: acceptance is the first step in feeding the dark wolf, and acceptance itself can bring change. Amma says in *Awaken Children*, "Each reaction that arises within us causes a delay in our attaining the goal. Whereas acceptance will cause grace to flow without any break."

From then on, I tried to be honest with myself and to accept what is. By doing this, a lot could change, but sometimes I still wasn't sure what I was doing. Was I still suppressing? Finally I asked Amma, "What is the difference between suppressing and controlling."

I got a long, elaborate, wonderful answer. At first I thought Amma hadn't answered my question. She only spoke of the importance of knowledge and the importance of the deep conviction that I am not the body-mind-intellect. She also highlighted the importance of living this knowledge. She didn't mention anything about suppressing and controlling. Only later did I understand her teaching: only by imbibing spiritual knowledge can we overcome a deep habit of suppression. Assimilation of spiritual teachings is the only way to transcend these deep tendencies.

I understood that the proper food for the dark wolf is acceptance and spiritual knowledge. Then he can show his good qualities of perseverance, courage, fearlessness, straightforwardness, and determination. And aren't these some of the daivī sampat (divine qualities) that Śhrī Kṛiṣhṇa teaches us in the 16th Chapter of the *Bhagavad Gītā* that we should develop?

***

The biggest miracle for me is that Amma has slowly begun to open my heart. Amma, the creator, knows everyone's heart and she didn't give up on me. Again and again she has created situations where my heart spontaneously opened. She used each and every person possible for that, even when I felt blocked towards her. For this I am endlessly grateful.

I want to thank everyone wholeheartedly who have made themselves worthy of being only instruments — nimittamātram — in Amma's hands, providing me with countless opportunities to train the subtle heart to open, and to feel secure and comfortable in that state. Only this training has made it possible to open up to Amma and has brought me to this point where I can open up to all of you and give this satsang.

Now I can say sincerely for the first time:

- I love life.
- I am at peace with myself.
- I feel deep gratitude for all I had to undergo.
- All is Amma's prasād.

The more I dive into spiritual knowledge, the more my heart opens and the more I see the good in all of my life's hard lessons and experiences. They reveal their hidden treasure through which my love for Amma deepens and grows.

To properly feed both wolves — the opposing forces inside and outside — is to feed them the food of awareness, discrimination, acceptance, and spiritual knowledge. This is how to turn our inner battlefield, our Kurukṣhētra[39] into our dharma-kṣhētra, the field where the seeds of good actions are sown. This attracts the grace we need to walk the path and reach our goal of Self-realization. Seeing the good everywhere can be a sādhanā. It is also a service to the world which creates

---

[39] Name of the battlefield where the *Bhagavad Gītā* was revealed.

ripples that can spread. I feel this is the most needed service we can offer to the world in this dark age of Kali Yuga.

I want to conclude with a prayer for all the children in this world who haven't had God introduced into their lives. Divine Mother, please reach out to these poor lost children of yours. Find a way into their lives and hearts so that they can have you to hold on to no matter what their karma might be. Let their lives turn towards good and their hearts open to you. And make all of us who are so fortunate to be with you, your nimittamātrams or mere instruments, in this mission.

8

My Tiny Teardrop

Amritesh Ito – Japan

I know that I do not have any qualifications to sit here and talk about spirituality. I would just like to talk about what Amma has given to me. Before I met Amma in 1995, I was a young investment banker working in New York and in Tokyo. I thought that success in life meant increasing your income, living in a bigger house and occasionally enjoying a vacation at some resort area. The people around me were actually living like that. I didn't even know that the soul exists. I thought that when you die, that's it.

In February 1995, a group in Tokyo asked me if I wanted to help them prepare for Amma's visit to Japan in May. I had never met Amma but I said yes. I translated Amma's English pamphlets into Japanese. The pamphlet said that when people meet Amma, they would often cry and burst into tears. While doing the translation, I wondered if that was true and if I would also cry. We all went to Tokyo International Airport to greet Amma. Amma came out of immigration and while walking toward the exit, hugged each of us gently in her arms. I was delighted to receive Amma's hug but I remember noticing that I didn't shed any tears.

During the morning program on the second day, I watched Amma hugging people one after the other continuously. While watching I thought, "She is incredible. Every single day, she continues to hug people, hugging, hugging, hugging...for nothing, with love." Something touched me and tears overflowed from my eyes.

At that very moment, Amma turned her head towards me. She was smiling at me. I wondered who she was looking at, but it was me. Nobody else was nearby. I don't remember how long it was, but it seemed quite a long time that Amma was smiling at me to make sure I understood. "Oh, did she really understand my thoughts? The pamphlet's words are true. Very mysterious," I thought. Later I realized that Amma had not only read my mind, but also answered my question, "Will I also cry?"

Seeing Amma hugging people, I also pondered Amma's greatness but in a strange way. In the company where I worked, people took pride in their multi-million dollar project revenues. As a finance man I wondered, wouldn't people gladly offer millions of dollars to support Amma's charitable activities and enable her to give her tireless hugs and consolation? I felt that she is truly extraordinary, and that the work going on at my company suddenly seemed very insignificant in comparison, like child's play.

At the end of my first Amma program, somebody asked me to drive Amma from her accommodation to the airport. Initially, I declined due to lack of sleep after Dēvī Bhāva, but the coordinators kept asking so I agreed. This led to a big change in my life. There were four of us in the car: Amma, Swāmī Amṛitaswarupānandajī, Swāminī Amma and me. After our departure, everyone became silent. A question came to my mind, so I asked Swāmījī if I could ask it. First let me explain the context in which I asked the question:

While I was doing sēvā during Amma's program, I happened to visit the resting room we had prepared for Amma at the program hall. It had only a futon (bed mat) and a cover on the bare floor. I thought it would be nicer if I brought a carpet for the room. I happened to have a brand new, beautiful Persian rug in my home. Next morning I rolled up the carpet and took it on the train to the program venue.

In Amma's room I noticed some dirt on the floor so I thoroughly cleaned it. Honestly I'm not fond of cleaning, but I remembered a pamphlet I translated for Amma called 'Selfless Service' which introduced me to Amma's humanitarian activities. I thought, "Is selfless service really possible for me, since I don't like cleaning very much?" Nonetheless, I was happy that Amma's room had now become much nicer after cleaning it and adding the carpet.

In the car I asked Amma, "I know Amma talks about selfless service. But is selfless service really possible?" Then I explained about the thoughts I had after cleaning Amma's room. Amma smiled at me and said, "Selfless service is certainly possible. It may be difficult at first, but if you continue doing it, anyone will gradually be able to do it." I felt relieved.

Then another question came up for me: "Amma, I really enjoyed these three days with you, and I feel as if I've become a better person than before. I feel like I want to do something good. But in the coming weeks and months, I'm fully confident that I will revert to being the same old person. If I get to see Amma again next year, I'm afraid I will remain the same unchanged person. What can I do?"

Amma lovingly replied, "It would be nice if everybody could get together every week or so to sing bhajans and talk about God. That would be good, because then you can maintain and remember God." When I returned from the airport, I discussed this conversation with my friends. We decided to get together like Amma said. Thus the first satsang (spiritual discourse, gathering) was set for July 7th, 1995 on the evening of 'Tanabata,' Japan's traditional Star Festival Day. Once a month we rented a public space to meditate, talk, sing devotional songs called bhajans, then finish with the ārati[40] while singing along to a cassette.

Our satsang was very simple because our only tools were Amma's bhajan cassettes, a cassette player and a bhajan book. A year passed like that when I suddenly thought, "Maybe we should put Amma's photo in the front during satsang." Until then none of us had ever considered that; everyone agreed. Just think...We finally brought in Amma's photo after holding satsangs without it for a whole year. Looking back I realize how naive we were.

***

Amma returned to Japan the next year, and before I knew it I was playing the role of main coordinator. It was a long program – the first time that Amma blessed us with a six-day program. It felt like a never-ending paradise with Amma. After Amma left Japan I started reading *Awaken Children* every day during my bus commute to work, discovering how amazing Amma is. I said to myself, "Amma must be someone like Christ or the Buddha. If such a person lives in India, I have to go see her there to find out more."

From *Awaken Children,* I also learned that in India, Amma personally serves everyone chai and rice balls. I thought, "Oh my god! I'm so envious, I want to be there too!" After holding the first Amma birthday celebration in Japan in September of that year, I seriously considered going to be with Amma in India. However, I realized there was no way I could possibly take time off from work as I had many duties to attend to at that time. Then I received a beautiful letter from Amma and became extremely happy that Amma had remembered me.

[40] A traditional ritual involving the waving of a lighted lamp to the Guru or deity usually done towards the end of pūjā or worship.

Amma helped me by gradually arranging things so that I could remove myself from the company, and after a few months I was able to join Amma.

Immediately upon arrival in India, I joined Amma's North India Tour. Sure enough during the tour, Amma served chai to everyone during the chai stop. Finally, it was my long-awaited moment to get chai from Amma. I was overjoyed to receive that prasād! As I was drinking my chai, Amma asked me, "Japan, seconds?" Surprised but with great pleasure I responded, "Yes!" At each chai stop afterwards, Amma called me "Japan" and asked me, "Seconds?" Every time I received the prasād gratefully. Thinking that Amma loves me, I was immersed in bliss.

In May I decided to return to Japan temporarily to help prepare for the Japan program a few weeks before Amma's arrival. So in the middle of Amma's Madurai program, I returned to Amritapuri alone. With Amma on tour, only a small number of people remained in the āśhram. I was looking forward to tasting one last āśhram chai before returning to Japan, but I arrived a few minutes after the chai is usually served and missed it. I felt very disappointed as I walked towards my room. Suddenly a woman wearing a colorful sāri appeared and offered me a hot chai, extending a trayful of cups filled with chai in front of me. She was someone I had never seen before.

I thanked Amma from the bottom of my heart, "Amma, you're in Madurai 300 kilometers away giving darśhan to thousands of people, yet you've kindly sent chai all the way here to me knowing my trivial wish. How grateful I am!" The all-knowing, all-powerful divine loves me, knows my heart and protects me. I realized that there is nothing to fear. This realization came from Amma, and gave me tremendous confidence in my life, freeing me from anxieties and worries.

I also prayed to Amma, “Amma, I really thank you, but I feel sorry for bothering you about this. From now on, please forget about my chai. I can live without it. You are very busy, and I now know that you are taking care of me. I don’t want to trouble you about this anymore, Amma.” However, Amma still continues to give me ‘chai’ in many different ways.

After spending one dream year with Amma in Amritapuri, I returned to Japan. Amma blessed the Japanese people by sending Swāmī Shāntāmṛitānandajī to live in our Tokyo āśhram for many years until he moved to the Chicago āśhram. Amma also sent Swāmī Pūrṇāmṛitānandajī every year to tour all over Japan. I have been very fortunate to be part of these activities, including translating Swāmī Pūrṇāmṛitānandajī’s satsangs at many of the programs and retreats for the past twenty years. In this way, Amma has continued to bless us.

On March 11, 2011, there was a great earthquake in northeastern Japan. A huge tsunami killed 22,000 people, and a nearby nuclear power plant was damaged and exploded. That year, Amma came to Japan in July, four months after the earthquake. Upon arrival, Amma asked about the damage and the present situation. She announced the donation of one million dollars for the education of children orphaned by the earthquake and tsunami, and expressed her wish to go to the disaster area. However, the disaster area was 400 kilometers (250 miles) northeast of Tokyo. We told Amma there was no spare time scheduled during her stay. On the final day in Tokyo, Amma calculated the time needed to visit the affected area, and she called us to discuss. We looked into all the options and came up with a plan:

Right after Dēvī Bhāva we would leave the hall for the disaster area by car. We would visit, then take two bullet trains (via Tokyo) to Osaka where the next program was scheduled to take place, arriving before 9:00 p.m. the same day. Amma indicated that when she visited the refugee shelter, she wanted to take some helpful household items like clothes and towels to the people who had lost their houses. Amma's compassion never stops. However, there would be between 300 – 400 people in the shelter. Where could we find so many supplies? It was late Sunday night, and there were no stores open where one could purchase a lot of clothes.

While Dēvī Bhāva was still going on, I decided to drive around and see what I could find. The Tokyo bhajan group was scheduled to start singing at 12:00 midnight. I was supposed to play keyboards, and had been told, "Please come without fail." But I had no choice since I had to go buy clothes for the tsunami victims.

I explained this to the bhajan group leader, apologized to her, and went shopping. By Amma's grace, after visiting just three shops, we had miraculously purchased everything we needed. I looked at my watch which showed that it was past midnight, and my thoughts went out to the Tokyo group bhajans happening in the hall.

***

The Dēvī Bhāva ended at around 5:00 a.m.. Amma's camper immediately set out for the disaster area. Amma comforted and spoke with 400 refugees in the shelter. After that we went to the beach and prayed together with Amma.

On the train back to Tokyo, Amma suddenly said to me, "During Dēvī Bhāva last night, Amma could hear you singing bhajans beautifully in your heart." Even though I hadn't told Amma anything about the bhajan situation, she knew what had happened. I was amazed. My heart was filled with tears of gratitude for Amma's words, and my sadness about not being able to join the bhajan group disappeared.

There is another unforgettable story about this bullet train ride. Our group had a lovely forty-minute wait at Tokyo Station with Amma. Finally, we got on the train to Osaka, and I was supposed to sit near Amma to translate if any Japanese people wanted to speak to her. However as the departure time approached, I didn't see Swāminī Kṛiṣhṇāmṛitā Prāṇā sitting near Amma, so I was worried and stepped off the train to look for her.

Soon the departure time came and I panicked, not knowing what to do. As the final bell rang, I thought, "I can't leave Swāminī behind." The doors closed and the train departed. As it turned out, Swāminī was on the train! She is a very experienced traveler, and would never have made such a mistake. Not only did my own misunderstanding cost me the golden opportunity to sit beside Amma for three hours, but I also couldn't fulfill my dharma (righteous or sacred duty) translating for her. This left me feeling deeply traumatized. It was the biggest mistake of my life. I remembered it for many years, kicking myself for my mistake. I kept trying to find the lesson for me from the incident.

After more than a decade, I finally understood that my arrogance and lack of surrender to Amma were my mistakes. I thought 'I' had to save the situation, and ended up missing the train. Amma and the swāmīs were there leading the whole tour group, but I decided on my own without calling or consulting with anyone to see if Swaminī had already boarded the train, and thereby neglected my most important dharma. I realized this while listening to the satsangs during Amma's daily programs, comparing my experiences with other people's experiences. Amma has given me many years to reflect on this incident many times which has helped me learn more about myself.

By 2015, twenty years after I first met Amma, Amma's Tokyo program had grown as did the number of devotees and activities. The project to make M.A. Center Japan a religious corporation was initiated that same year under Amma's guidance. This was actually the second time I tried to do this, as the first attempt hadn't gone well. The Japanese government has always been very cautious about approving new religious organizations. I was in charge of the application process. I submitted the application, and then three years went by without much progress. We had reached an impasse.

However, in 2018 Amma probably thought we needed more of her divine grace because things started picking up after her visit! The administrator who had originally been assigned to our case had been transferred somewhere else, but now returned and was in charge again. She asked, "So you haven't been allowed to submit your application yet?" "I will help you from now on," She continued and then asked, "The religion of the Japan M.A. Center is Hinduism, isn't it?" I gave a long and convoluted answer about Sanātana Dharma,[41] which ended up complicating things more.

At Amma's next program, I explained the situation and asked Amma how to explain Sanātana Dharma. Amma smilingly said, "Sanātana Dharma is to see God in everybody. Serving everybody and all beings is equal to serving God. To serve God is to help the poor and underprivileged, and to take good care of nature." I understood this to be the root of all Amma's charitable activities and spirituality. The woman in charge seemed very happy with this, and we overcame a big obstacle.

---

[41] 'The Eternal Way of Life.' The traditional and original name of Hinduism.

They conducted several rigorous on-site inspections. I especially wanted the registration to happen for future generations of Amma's children. By Amma's grace we received permission to submit the final application, and did so in December 2019. From then on it was a waiting game.

When 2020 arrived, we still hadn't received approval of our application. I planned to visit Amritapuri for a week in early February, however the night before my flight, the Indian government suddenly shut its doors to Japan due to Covid. With the tremendous agony of severe disappointment, I had to cancel my trip to Amritapuri. By March, while the whole world was full of fear about the pandemic, my main concern was about the āśhram-registration approval process.

Around noon on March 23rd, I received a call from the administrator, saying, "Congratulations! The committee has approved your application! You need to come to our office and receive the official letter of approval. Can you come right now? It seems likely that the Governor of Tokyo will declare a total lockdown of Tokyo (14 million people!) this afternoon. After that, nobody will be able to enter our office."

I was two hours away, so I dashed out the door. I had to change trains several times to reach their office, but managed to arrive just before the inevitable lockdown began. It was clearly a miracle of Amma's grace that we were able to receive the approval before the lockdown. In addition, we were the first-ever Hindu religious organization given authorization by the government in Tokyo. Without Amma's grace, it would never have happened.

I was overjoyed! Amma had fulfilled my desire. Before getting approval I thought, "I can't die before completing the aśhram registration." Amma blessed us all with this tremendous boon. I don't know how we can express our deep gratitude. Soon after the registration of M.A. Center Japan went through, we received Amma's blessing yet again by procuring a new āśhram. This is our third āśhram, following the previous two that were located in Inagi and Oita. Amma's grace is truly immeasurable.

***

I have dreamt the same dream many times. In the dream Amma is giving darśhan, but I am in the next room unaware that the program is about to end. When I finally realize it's ending, I rush in only to find darśhan has just finished. I feel so shocked that I wake up.

I also remember a story Amma tells about a conversation between a grandfather and his grandson: One day the grandson woke up very early to study. Seeing his grandfather sitting with eyes closed in the next room, he waited for his grandfather to open his eyes then asked, "What are you doing so early in the morning with your eyes closed?" His grandfather asked a question in return, "Why did you wake up so early this morning?" The boy replied, "Nowadays in school they give us pop quizzes; we always have to be prepared for them." The grandfather replied, "I am also preparing for a pop quiz."

Amma also uses the analogy of pop quiz when explaining unexpected situations where the Guru tests the maturity of the disciple.

I felt like *my* pop quiz came when the Indian government closed the door on my flight to India. Between the Indian government shutting down my flight, and my recurring dream of missing Amma's darśhan, I wasn't prepared for either situation and therefore they both caused me a lot of pain. However, when Amma spoke to her children all over the world via the internet, she said, "Children, be courageous. Happiness is a decision. Smile, fear nothing!" These words have since echoed in our hearts giving us hope, and have helped me to move forward. I deeply thank Amma for such life-saving words.

I translate many of Amma's bhajans into Japanese. My first translated bhajan was *Anantamāmī Lōkattil*. I love this Malayāḷam bhajan and it expresses my own prayers. Here it is in Japanese:

> *Hiroi Sora no shita*
> *Kono chippoke na watashi*
> *Kamisama kite kudasai*
> *Nagusamete kudasai*
> *Mainichi anata o utai masu*
> *Mainichi anata o mitsume masu*
> *Hitori kiride omou anata wa*
> *Muneno okuni sumau*
> 'O Lord, come. Come, to console me
> who am a mere atom in this infinite world.
> I sing Thy praises forever. To see Thee before me always,
> I meditate in solitude upon Thee, who reside deep in my heart.'

It is said, "If the entire earth were turned to paper; all seven seas turned to ink; and the forests turned into pens to write with, they would still not suffice to praise the Guru's glory." Nevertheless, I wish to offer my story, as a tiny teardrop, into the seven seas of ink in praise of the glory of Amma. I offer my humble prostrations to Amma, the mother of the universe.

9

Reaching Amma

Sudha Borys - USA

Throughout history, stories and epics have been written about the great masters. Who can read about the divine lives of Kṛishṇa, Rāma, Buddha, or Christ and not wish to have lived when they lived? Saint Teresa of Avila burned in her longing for Christ for her entire life though she never met him in his physical form. Mirābāi was consumed with thoughts of her beloved Kṛishṇa to the extent that poison could not harm her because her Lord did not give permission for the poison to do its job. Yet she did not live at the same time as her Lord. Souls all over this earth long to live with a real master.

We have all also longed to experience God's pure love, and therefore have reached Amma's doorstep. Each one of us was born during this auspicious time because Amma wanted us to take part in her līlā (divine play). I am not speaking only of those living in Amma's āśhram. Every single one of Amma's children, wherever they are in the world, has been placed there by Amma to share certain gifts in their lives. Amma's bond with each of us is so powerful we cannot conceive of it.

Going deeper into this line of thought I recall an incident from Paramahaṁsa Yōgānanda's book, *Autobiography of a Yogi*. This is the story of when Lāhiri Mahāśhaya meets his Guru Bābājī for the first time. Lāhiri Mahāśhaya had been mysteriously reassigned from where he worked and was posted to a branch in an isolated area high in the Himālayas. He spent his free time wandering in the majestic mountains. One day on one such walk, he met a forest ascetic — a mahātmā — who lovingly invited him to rest in his cave. This saint knew Lāhiri Mahāśhaya's name, and also mentioned that it was he himself who had made sure Lāhiri Mahāśhaya was posted in this place.

Of course, Lāhiri Mahāśhaya was astounded that the mahātmā knew so much about him. With the love of a mother who had been separated from her child, the mahātmā asked Lāhiri if he remembered the time they had spent together in a previous life, as he had cherished the memory of that time for many years, longing to once again be with his beloved disciple. Surprised, Lāhiri Mahāśhaya admitted that he had no such memories. The mahātmā then tapped him lightly on his head and the memories of his past life with his beloved Guru Bābājī came rushing back to him.

Bābājī then described how he had been watching over Lāhiri through the afterlife, his birth, his childhood and every moment of his life. He had been longing for the moment he would meet his beloved disciple once again. For years he had kept Lāhiri's meditation mat and brass cup ready and clean for him.

In this way the love that the Guru has for the disciple is unimaginable. It spans lifetimes and is not confined by time and space.

This is the same as our Amma. She has carefully watched over each of us through lifetime upon lifetime until this very present moment. Amma's only thought is, "My children... my children... my children... how to uplift my children? how to make them happy? how to lead them to the unending bliss of the ātman (true Self)?"

Amma once said that, as a mother waits eagerly for her child to crawl, sit up, and take its first steps, so too Amma eagerly waits to see us take our first steps in spirituality, to see compassion, patience, and love blossom in our hearts.

***

What can we possibly do to show our gratitude to our mother? We all want to serve Amma physically. What a joy it is to stroke her back, bring her a glass of water, and say loving words to her. Loving Amma is so effortless. It is important to nourish the bhakti in our hearts. But Amma is pūrṇam (complete) in herself and is not in need of our love. Those in need of our love and compassion are all the people we encounter throughout every day.

Amma is happy whether we praise or blame her, but the people we interact with will be sad if we blame them or say nasty things to them. Amma's happiness is her children's happiness. If we show anger or are unkind, aren't we being unkind to Amma? Even though I smile at everyone and intend to be kind, if I get 'pinched' in the wrong way I can have a nasty sting! To anyone I may have hurt, please forgive me. Amma is overjoyed when we blossom and spread the fragrance of love to the world. This is the only way to show our gratitude to her.

A pāda pūjā[42] to Amma may last only ten minutes, but when we do the 'pāda pūjā' of selfless service along with our daily practices and introspection, it not only shows our gratitude to Amma, but can last for generations and its positive effects can impact many lives. This is the supreme pāda pūjā, the ultimate flower to offer at Amma's feet.

In the Mahābhārata,[43] King Yudhiṣhṭhira was conducting the Rājasūya Yajña, a coronation ceremony declaring a king's sovereignty. During this fire ritual massive amounts of gold, grain, precious gems, and other riches were to be given as gifts to everyone. At one point during the yajña, a strange

---

[42] Ceremonial washing of the Guru's feet as a form of worship.

[43] Ancient Indian epic composed by Sage Vyāsa, depicting the war between the righteous Pāṇḍavas and the unrighteous Kauravas.

looking mongoose was seen rolling around in the dirt near the sacrificial fire. Half of its body was gold, and the other half was a normal brown color.

Finally a spectator asked the mongoose what he was doing. The mongoose replied: "Many years ago a severe drought caused a horrible famine in a nearby land. Food was almost impossible to find. One family living in that place had not eaten for days; perhaps even for weeks. Somehow they found some grain and made a small loaf of bread with it. As they were about to eat it, there was a knock at the door and a hungry visitor arrived. The family unhesitatingly gave him a good portion of the bread. They were about to eat what was left of their bread when another famished beggar arrived at their door. The family gave the last of their bread to him. Their tremendous sacrifice invoked the unending flow of God's grace, and at that moment they merged into pure consciousness."

The mongoose continued, "I ate a few crumbs of that bread which had fallen on the floor. In my joy at finding food, I rolled in the dirt there, and the side of my body that touched the sacred earth blessed by their sacrifice turned golden. Ever since, I have visited many sacrificial ceremonies and rolled in the dirt trying to turn the other side of my body gold, but I have never found a sacrifice like that one, not even this Rājasūya." It is a great thing to be generous when you have plenty to give. It is divine to give when you feel you have nothing to give. May all of us practice such self-sacrifice.

***

I was fortunate to be born into a family who valued spirituality. My parents are practical in worldly matters, but monetary success was not their main goal in life. They wanted me to use this life to be spiritually uplifted. Both of my parents had a thirst for God. They met while they were training to teach Transcendental Meditation.

In 1988, a few months after I was born, my mother met Amma for the first time holding me, a small babe in arms. This happened in our home city of Seattle. In those early years Amma would give darśhan in someone's living room, and only twenty to fifty people would attend. Amma would rock back and forth blissfully singing to the heavens as she held each person in her lap for a long time, sometimes for the duration of a whole bhajan.

As I was an infant, I have no memory of meeting Amma for the first time. But as I grew up, Amma was always a part of my life. My mom worked from home as a massage therapist in the early nineties. Sometimes her clients would call and four-year-old me would pick up the phone. They would ask if my mother was home, and I would tell them my mother is in my heart, leaving the poor clients truly confused! I thought everyone knew Amma is in our hearts!

When I was four or five years old, I used to think that even if someone just heard a bhajan it could change their life and lead them to God. I would yell out the car window as we drove through the neighborhood, "*Chāmuṇḍāyē Kāḷī Maaaaaaa! Kāḷī Maaaa Kāḷī Maa Kāḷī Mā!*" This was to my older sister's dismay, as she was trying to fit into the harsh world of middle school, and I was not giving our family a very normal reputation! I thought everyone knew that God-realization was obviously the goal of life!

Amma has said many times that even children who grow up around Amma may stray during their teenage years. But because of the strong values instilled in early life, they will come back to their spiritual roots and will never permanently leave Amma. I too strayed during my teenage years. I would see

Amma once or twice a year on her North American tours. A year after last seeing Amma, I fell in with the 'party-hardy' crowd and I jumped right in to see what that was all about.

I had heard people say they were a little afraid of Amma as she could see right into the depths of their hearts and minds. I could never understand how anyone could be afraid of Amma until the beginning of my questionable teenage behavior. Suddenly, I very much understood this fear. I was now in the darśhan queue about to come face to face with my maker — the all-knowing mother. I was pretty sure she would look at me, shake her head in disappointment and say, "I wasted so much time on you. Look what you have become!" I shyly moved up in the line.

When it was my turn, Amma gave me an extraordinary, brilliant smile, as if she had been waiting the whole day just to see me! Then she took me in her arms and said very loudly in my ear, "My darling darling darling darling DARLING DARLING DARLING DAAAARRRRRLLLLLING DAUGHTER!" With each 'darling' she leaned into me while holding me strongly in her embrace; each darling got louder and longer. I knew that Amma was saying, "No matter what you do, have done, or will do, I will love you absolutely and unconditionally."

In my life with Amma I have had doubts, fear and even depression. However, because of that experience I have never doubted that no matter how dark my mind is, no matter how ugly my vāsanās (latent tendencies) are, Amma's love towards me will NEVER falter. I was lucky to have this firm conviction from an early age.

***

I have been fortunate to live the last fourteen years primarily in the Amritapuri āśhram, mainly doing garden sēvā. It is hard work but probably the most joyful sēvā I could imagine. Being in Amma's presence, and in the presence of so many people who are genuinely trying to become both the servants of God and one with Amma is a blessing too great to comprehend. I bow down to Amma a million times for this opportunity.

I never envisioned living in India or even in Amritapuri indefinitely. My life plan was to live here for some time and then pursue some kind of career in the U.S. But every year, it never made sense to leave. A few years ago, I finally realized that there is a very good chance that India has truly become my permanent home.

This was for two reasons: one is that my partner lives in India permanently, and I cannot imagine life without him. Secondly, though I have a thirst to prove myself by having 'success' in the world and still have worldly desires, in my heart I wasn't convinced that pursuing a career and having worldly success is actually a worthwhile way to live. According to everything I've ever heard my entire life, the only real success is merging with God, and being in Amma's presence is the most conducive atmosphere for attaining this lofty goal.

I was torn, and I spiraled into a dark hole of depression. On one hand, I felt like an inadequate spiritual seeker: I often can't get up early enough and I sleep too much; I don't do lots of sēvā; and I still indulge my vāsanās. On the other hand, it felt impossible for me as an American citizen to achieve worldly success in India. I only know how to use my skills in the U.S. I longed to succeed wholeheartedly in at least one area of my life, whether it be spiritually or by achieving a worldly goal. I wanted to attain something! I felt like I didn't have what it takes to merge with God, nor did I have the opportunity for the type of success the world values. I felt worthless as a human being.

Many times I would cry in my room for hours. Or cry for hours in front of Amma in the bhajan hall. I felt so very alone.

I expected Amma to pull me out of my depression. When the sorrow continued and I felt ignored by Amma, I would send her the most hateful letters. I have wanted to apologize to Mother for that for a long time. I am so sorry Amma.

I thought it was her job to pull me out of my negative emotions, but Amma knew that *I* had to make the necessary efforts. One day, in desperation I asked Amma a question publicly, tears streaming down my cheeks. I sobbed telling her I did not feel I was making any progress. I wanted to know if I was moving forward at all. Amma said many kind things. She said she knew my mind was like a bullock cart with the bulls pulling in opposite directions.

Amma told me she had read my letters. Then she gave me a long satsang, at the end of which she added as if it were an afterthought, "You need to learn to accept life." This simple sentence changed EVERYTHING. It did not change overnight, but Amma had given me permission to accept my life as it is. I had been so afraid to accept myself where I was, as I was, because I did not feel worthy of my acceptance.

I had been afraid acceptance would make me stagnant. But the only stagnancy that was happening was the crippling depression and fear I was living in. I understood from Amma's words not to be mad at myself for not blossoming as fast as I'd like. I should be joyful at the gradual opening of each petal, while continuing to add the fertilizer of effort, daily practice, contemplation, and mantra japa. Amma tells us over and over that we cannot force a flower to blossom or it may lose its fragrance. Accepting where you are is not complacency as long as you keep moving forward the best you can.

I pray that none of my brothers or sisters make the mistake I made, wasting time thinking they are not worthy of this path. In scripture class, the teacher said that a spiritual seeker should try to avoid both superiority and inferiority complexes, but an inferiority complex is more damaging to one's spiritual evolution than a superiority complex. This is because at least a person with a superiority complex has the confidence to move forward. Someone with an inferiority complex lacks that confidence. Isn't this true?

We need to believe in ourselves to achieve anything, whether worldly accomplishments or spiritual progress. The only time life becomes useless is when we feel we are useless and fall down and lie there crying. We are Amma's children, 'Children of Immortal Bliss.' We should never think we have no place in this world, or that our life has no worth. I have been in that state of mind and it's simply not true. Swāminī Amma (Swāminī Kṛiṣhṇāmṛita Prāṇā) tells a beautiful story in one of her books that illustrates this point:

Once, a king decided to stroll through his garden. He was surprised to see that almost every plant looked sad, forlorn, and wilted. He stopped by a jasmine flower and asked, "Why are you so sad?" The flower replied, "I am a creeper. I cannot stand without the support of a tree or post. I wish I was like the big strong banyan tree. It is so confident. It does not need to lean on anyone!" The king went to the banyan tree who also looked very sad. He asked the tree, "Well then, why do you look sad?" The banyan replied, "Look at that mango tree! It gives such sweet fruits for you and your queen to eat. I have no fruits to offer. This is why I feel sad." The king then saw a rose bush who also looked unhappy! "Rose, certainly you must be happy. You produce such beautiful flowers. Why are you so down today?" The rose said, "Yes, perhaps my flowers are pretty, but I have these thorns. No one wants to come near me. Why bother producing flowers?"

The king walked on. Suddenly he spotted a daisy joyfully dancing in the breeze. The king stopped and said, "Hey, everyone else is so sad in this garden. Why are you so happy?" The daisy responded, "I am happy because I know you deliberately planted me here. You did not want a rose, a tree, or a creeper in this spot; you wanted a daisy to be here. Therefore, I am going to be the best daisy I can be!"

Like this, God created each of us with special gifts and talents. We each have a destiny to fulfill. Our mere presence on this earth may bring joy to others that we are not even aware of. Let us not waste time comparing ourselves to others. Amma wanted a 'Sudha' flower. She wanted a 'Big Swāmījī' flower, a 'Sundari' flower and a 'Ranjini' flower. She made us all in the way she pleased, so let us not criticize ourselves or others. Let us just be the best we can be!

I would like to conclude this satsang with a line from a bhajan that is close to my heart:

> *arikil undeṅkilum aṛiyān kazhiyāte alayunnu ñān ammē*
> *kaṇṇundennālum kāṇān kazhiyāte tirayunnu ñān ninnē*
> *ammē tirayunnu ñān ammē*
> 'O Mother, even though Thou art near,
> I am wandering, unable to know Thee.
> Even though I have eyes,
> I am searching, unable to see Thee.'
>
> *Arikil Undeṅkilum*

Amma, I watch you for hours at a time but am unable to fathom your depth. I feel sure the only way to know you is to merge with you. Please bless all your children to truly know you by merging in the ocean of love that is you. And for those who have not been able to know of you or see you in this lifetime, may the purifying Gaṅgā of your grace wash over the whole world and cleanse each being of their pāpa (sins) so that this Kali Yuga, this dark age of materialism, may transform into Satya Yuga, an era of light and truth.

10

Insights on the Path to the Light

Abhijit – Austria

To begin, I'd like to share a few words about my life journey and how I came to spirituality and Amma. I was born into a typical Western 'patchwork' family. Life circumstances didn't always turn out favorable or settled for me, and I wasn't a child much taken care of. However, this prepared me to become mentally independent early on. During my childhood, I wished somebody in my family could have given me some wisdom, and I always desired something more real than my environment offered.

When I was about seven years old, I wanted to become a Shaolin monk. I begged my mother to take me there, but she said, "We are just simple people, and China is too far away. It's not possible for us to go there."

A few years later, at the age of ten, I went to a boarding school for classical and spiritual music. This institution was famous for a boys choir that is part of an old historic monastery. We had to develop discipline, and had to undergo hardships as well. For example, in the winter, our dorm was rarely heated, and there was often a layer of ice even on the inside of the window pane. In the morning we had to wash ourselves with ice-cold water since warm water was available only once a week. We were not pampered. But I liked it there because the place offered a spiritual atmosphere.

We frequently traveled around the country to give concerts in music halls and churches. It was a golden time in my life, and I was blessed to experience my first glimpses of truth. The monastery was filled with beautiful religious art made by famous artists from the past. Beautiful paintings and sculptures were everywhere. The place was like a huge museum of fine art, and I spent a lot of time just looking at it. When my time in the monastery came to an end, I felt my prārabdha karma pertaining to music was exhausted. But, influenced by the sight of so much beautiful art, I decided to become a sculptor.

At age fourteen, I entered a four-year art college to study sculpture. I remember while doing clay modeling, I sometimes became so absorbed in the work that I forgot even to breathe. After some time, my body would suddenly start gasping for air. My classmates looked at me in astonishment. They thought I might have health issues. Actually, I was in meditation, but in those days, I didn't even realize I was in meditation. Our concentration can become so intense when we do something with interest and commitment. In the field of fine art, intense observation leads to meditation. Creating art is an excellent means to develop qualities like concentration, one-pointedness, and patience. Art requires us to develop the subtle mind which prepares us for the final realization of truth.

After art school, I started to earn my own living since I was expected by my family to be self-reliant. At the age of twenty-one my mother passed away from cancer. This was the biggest loss in my life. She was the only person I could fully rely on. My father never played an active role in my life, so I was now essentially parentless. The death of my mother pushed me into an unsettled period in my life.

Shortly after however, I received grace in the form of admission to the Art University of Vienna. I was one of the rare candidates who passed the entrance examination, thereby becoming the student of a famous sculptor. Suddenly, I was in artist's heaven. Something my art master said stayed with me: "The problem with the world is that people cannot be still in a room." Just recently I found this same quotation in Swāmī Rāmakṛiṣhṇānanda's book, *The Secret of Inner Peace*. The relevance of this statement nowadays is amazing.

After finishing my education, I didn't know what to do. I didn't feel like pursuing a professional career. My direction in life was not clear. Influenced by the world, my lifestyle wasn't always healthy or wise. I didn't know how to take care of myself, and due to my ignorance, I ran into all kinds of difficulties. At the same time, I also received a lot of grace and blessings. I felt something more fulfilling was missing, and I started to take interest in spirituality. I began reading books on Eastern philosophy like the *Bhagavad Gītā* and about realized masters like Ramana Mahaṛṣhi, Śhrī Rāmakṛiṣhṇa, and about many other topics as well.

I became aware of the meaninglessness of materialistic life. When we come to understand that the world cannot give us any lasting happiness, we automatically lose interest in worldly entertainment, career, and fulfilling selfish desires. This insight was my stepping stone into the world of spirituality. I was able to give up my unhealthy lifestyle, stopped eating meat, and developed a routine of meditation practice. Reading spiritual books had already brought some changes into my life.

One day while looking out my kitchen window, I suddenly received the call of God. That inner soundless call was like the ringing of a bell...clear and penetrating. At first, I didn't know what to do. The call was clear, but I didn't know where it wanted me to go. I didn't feel like joining the nearby monastery. I thought, let me first explore the spirituality of India, since I had always felt attracted to the wisdom of the East. I wanted to understand the mystery of life more deeply.

I arrived in India for the first time in 1999. I liked the spiritual and vibrant atmosphere. I traveled across the north of the country, visiting various spiritual places like Ṛiṣhikēśh, Dharamśhāla and Vārāṇasī. Later I met people who spoke about Amma and encouraged me to visit her. So, I came for the first time to Amritapuri in August, 2000.

I immediately felt attracted to Amma and the special atmosphere of this place. It may look as if I reached Amritapuri by my own effort, but really it was the divine will of God that brought me. My first darśhan with Amma was a profound experience and I felt the ocean of love for the first time. Soon afterwards, Amma gave me permission to join the āśhram, and I settled here in 2001. I had lived a very independent life in Austria, so it was easy for me to take this step. I had no strong ties, no plans, no commitments, and nothing to lose.

In my early years at the āśhram, I did various sēvās. First, I was a pot washer in the kitchen. After that, I did sēvā at the sēvā desk, repairing equipment. I also supervised a workspace for sculpture and handicraft work.

A remarkable incident happened when I was serving at the sēvā desk. While fixing a broomstick, I was using a screwdriver when my hand slipped and cut the palm of my hand. Blood flowed out and I thought the wound would take a long time to heal. Just then, I heard the bell signaling that Amma had come out for the evening satsang. I rushed to the temple holding a handkerchief against the wound on my hand. A friend of mine was standing at the temple entrance as if waiting for me. He told me he had set out a mat on the floor for me near Amma. I was surprised because no one had ever done that for me, either before or since then. Therefore, that day I was able to sit close to Amma, holding the handkerchief against my hand the whole time.

When Amma left after satsang I checked the wound. To my utter surprise it had completely healed. There didn't seem to be even the slightest scratch on my hand. This proved to me Amma's all-knowing and all-healing nature.

Amma created many circumstances through all my sēvās to make me aware of my incompleteness and shortcomings. I wasn't good at handling difficult situations, and I discovered how restless my mind was. I got easily irritated with even minor details. I wasn't very confident, and I used to run into all kinds of problems.

When doing sēvā, conflicts, misunderstandings, and confusion can easily occur. We may hurt others' feelings, knowingly or unknowingly. To apologize and forgive is important because conflicts can generate irritation, anger, or even hatred. When we behave egotistically, we tend to dominate people and then we forget the heart; we forget compassion. If our mind is already agitated, even a small disturbance can make us react in an unconscious manner.

When we react too quickly, it shows that we are not attentive to the gap between our thoughts that allows awareness of the divine to shine through. Too often we don't try to empathize with the mental conditions and difficult situations others may be experiencing. We fail to understand when people act in a confused or unpleasant way. To apologize and forgive is important for maintaining good relationships. It shows that we take responsibility for our actions.

During my early years in the āśhram, I faced many difficulties and challenging situations. Once I sculpted several Gaṇēśha idols to be sold on Amma's foreign tours. Unfortunately, almost all of them got broken during transportation. For me, this was a disaster. I became very dejected about this loss. So much work for so many months, with everything getting destroyed in the end.

Amma says that in life we are always confronted with the dualities of success and failure, gain and loss, praise and blame. This is the nature of the world. Understanding the impermanent nature of the world helps us to accept things as they are. We may complain about many things when we hold on to our expectations. Our senses become attached to all those external conditions, and along with that, we become excited or disturbed. Then our emotions bob up and down like a yo-yo. Amma always tells us not to become arrogant in success or dejected in failure. Keeping inner equanimity is the true success in life.

Though we have a choice over which action to take, we have no choice over the outcome. At some point we realize we are helpless, and this helps us in the process of surrender. This realization brings humility and alertness to our actions. We come to understand that rather than us, God is the doer. Amma is always guiding us on how to remain balanced in difficult situations. Going through the tribulations of life is beneficial for our inner growth. It helps us understand ourselves in a deeper way. We need to become aware of our latent tendencies and the functioning of our mind. As we bring in that awareness, our accumulated tendencies, weaknesses, and habits start to dissolve. It's like a fire that has been lit, and continues to burn away our ignorance and attachments.

Amma tells us that we should maintain the notion of non-doership. This gives us humility and we won't feel the heaviness of responsibility as much. Then our actions don't bind us. We are neither dejected in failure nor arrogant in success. To be a non-doer doesn't mean waiting for God to do something. It means striving for a higher purpose and not for selfish gain. When we try to sublimate our selfish desires through selfless activities, God's grace starts to flow and we overcome the obstacles on our path.

When I was busy doing sēvā as a sculptor, Amma was simultaneously busy carving my mind. She keeps chiseling and molding all of us, and Amma has already created many masterpieces which are her gifts to the world. Amma is the supreme sculptress of the world.

After some years, I noticed a clear and positive change in me. Due to Amma's grace my desires, worries, and fears became weaker. I became more balanced, and felt more inner happiness, peace, and bliss. Amma has always been a loving guide. Even at those times when I couldn't always live up to my highest standards, Amma has shown me so much patience and understanding. Through her example, developing spiritual qualities becomes easier.

By 2010 I felt strongly that I should return to Austria. I didn't even say goodbye because I thought it would be just a temporary break. Once we are firmly focused on the goal, we are like a released arrow that can't be stopped; we are bound to hit the target. We cannot 'return' to the world even if circumstances land us back there. The learning process continues wherever we are. Back in the West I noticed a clear improvement in myself. I handled difficult situations much better. There was a wider gap between my thoughts and my actions. I tried to use my time in the best possible way, and I managed to do some meditation in my spare time.

Coming from a foreign country, it can be frustrating not being able to speak Amma's language. I tried to learn Malayāḷam but soon gave it up since I don't have much aptitude for languages. I had enough to do to learn some English. But there can also be an advantage to not speaking Malayāḷam. When we don't understand what Amma is saying, we have to learn how to listen to the silence behind Amma's words. This silence is the true language of love. As Amma recently said, "God is in the silence." The subtle quality of listening to silence can open up a new world of connectivity to the divine. Our inner connection can become deep when it's not disturbed by external words or interactions.

Bringing peace to the world is the greatest contribution a spiritual aspirant can make. The dimension of complete inner stillness is what attracts millions of people to Amma. When we search for our inner connection with God, having a Guru who only speaks a foreign language can be helpful. Higher truths are revealed to us in silence. Inner stillness leads us to sādhanās (spiritual practices) like mantra japa, contemplation, and meditation.

Before we can dive into silence, we must master our noisy minds. For this we need to have good understanding and love for the moral values given by the scriptures and spiritual masters. Observing the do's and don'ts of spirituality[44] is the key to unlocking the gate to divine union. To act morally can sometimes be difficult in challenging situations. The do's and don'ts build the moral foundation of both our spiritual practice and our worldly life. Their ultimate purpose is to purify the mind and make it one-pointed. Observing moral values helps us to live virtuously. Without developing qualities like humility, simplicity, sacrifice, and compassion we cannot become fit to penetrate into a deeper understanding of truth.

When the mind becomes still, we are able to discern which thoughts are useful and which thoughts are not. Then it is up to

---

[44] This is a reference to the 'yamas' and 'niyamas,' the restraints and observances that provide the moral and ethical basis of Yōga philosophy. They include: non-violence, truthfulness, not stealing, sexual restraint, non-covetousness, cleanliness, contentment, austerity, self-study, and surrender to the divine.

us to choose to act in a more harmonious and connected way. We are free to choose thoughts that make us and others happy. Then our true nature starts to guide us, and our mind is kept under control. As Amma always says, "Happiness is a decision."

On the spiritual path we need to have a clear understanding of what our goal is. Then we are able to ask the right questions with a pure heart and with sincerity. The divine always answers such questions. The all-knowing and all-pervading supreme being can bless us any time and in any place.

I have always seen Amma as a profound teacher of Advaita Vēdānta.[45] She doesn't need to speak much about it. She knows that those sublime truths can only be conveyed in silence. We can read the theory in books. But only great incarnations like Amma can give us the actual experience of our divine nature. It is connection to Amma's stillness that conveys those sublime truths to us. We can feel the happiness derived from contemplating Vēdāntic principles. Advaita Vēdānta keeps reminding us that the spark of truth lies dormant in everyone. Only through spiritual practice and grace can we enter this dimension of oneness with God.

We need to develop a pure mind through devotional practices like prayers, chanting, bhajans, meditation or service. Our vāsanās continually drag us down to identification with the impermanent. Whenever we forget divine consciousness, which is our true nature, then māyā (the great illusion) keeps working on us. Māyā is illusive and tries to keep us identified with our body, mind and intellect.

We yearn to find something permanent in the material dimension of the world, and try to become happy in it. Finally,

---

[45] 'Not two.' Non-dual philosophy that holds that the jīva (individual soul) and jagat (universe) are essentially one with Brahman, the supreme reality.

we become disillusioned when we realize that the world cannot give us lasting happiness. That is the point when we turn towards spirituality in the hope of escaping the endless misery of saṁsāra (cycle of repeated births and deaths). Self-knowledge begins with the disidentification with body, mind and intellect. Holding on to the awareness of our true nature is the compassion we need to have at the beginning of our spiritual journey. By discovering and stabilizing in our true nature, we slowly become free from the miseries of illusion. As long as we think we can be happy in māyā, there is no question of going beyond it.

At present, our mind does not do what we want. Instead, we follow the dictates of the mind. Surrender to God means letting go of our expectations and accepting what life brings. If we cannot accept what we cannot change, we are bound to end up in unhappiness. The goal of a true seeker is to accept success and failure with an equal mind. Amma tells us to have equanimity of mind in all circumstances of life, in success and failure. This is the essential teaching of the *Bhagavad Gītā*.

We need alertness to gain control over our mind and senses. This leads to awareness of our real nature, and we learn to be the witness of all our actions: physical, mental, and intellectual. We develop a 'mental gap' which enables us to get out of the trap of uncontrolled thoughts, emotions and actions. Then we are in a position to observe ourselves and our circumstances from a broader perspective.

It is a rare blessing to be able to spend time in Amma's physical presence, but that's not possible for everybody. To visualize the image of Amma is another way to tune in to Amma's presence. This devotional practice helps us to understand in a deeper way what Amma's physical presence means. When we constantly contemplate on her form, we can achieve a state of connectedness. This tuning in to Amma is essential to receive the benefit of her infinite wisdom, bliss and stillness. Concentration on the iṣhṭa dēvatā (beloved deity) always gives the aura of peace and a feeling of oneness with the divine.

When we have equanimity of mind, we learn to embrace both happiness and unhappiness equally. Then we are able to enter the dimension of tranquility and go beyond the trap of our illusions. What remains is serenity, a state where nothing can touch us. Abiding in that serenity, we give up chasing selfish desires, and instead dwell in the supreme dimension of fullness, peace, and bliss.

I'll conclude with a short prayer: may all beings have the grace of God to go beyond the state of illusions. May all beings live in the constant awareness of the divine. May all beings be fulfilled, happy, and peaceful.

11

Divine Love Speaks in Silence

Amritapushpa – USA

Silence is the language of prēma bhakti, divine love. Amma says that God talks to us in the language of silence. When the mind becomes calm, we will constantly hear the melody of God residing within us. I wish I could have written this talk in words of silence for that is where we can most experience Amma.

Sage Nārada in the *Nārada Bhakti Sūtras*[46] describes loving devotion as 'supreme love for God,' and 'of the nature of immortality,' and that it is 'impossible to describe divine love.' As Amma sings in the bhajan '*Mauna Ghanāmṛita Śhāntinikētam*' — 'it is the abode of peace found in perfect silence.' Amma says Brahman, the Absolute, is love, and that bhakti is the practical way to get rid of sorrows. It is faith that removes darkness from our hearts.

The purest example of divine love is the devotion of the gōpīs of Vṛindāvan to Lord Kṛiṣhṇa. The culmination of their love was total identification with Kṛiṣhṇa. Once, the gōpīs decided to test Rādhā.[47] They gave her scalding hot milk to drink saying Kṛiṣhṇa asked her to do this. She drank the milk without hesitation, but the blisters appeared on Kṛiṣhṇa's tongue instead! This conveys that they were not two, but one!

Love for God is not an emotion. It is an immaculate love that springs not from our mind but from our true Self, the ātmā. The

---

[46] Sage Nārada's aphorisms on devotion.

[47] Gōpīs are the milkmaids of Vṛindāvan where Kṛiṣhṇa spent his boyhood years. They are considered some of the greatest devotees of Kṛiṣhṇa, with Rādhā chief among them.

nature of ātmā is eternal, pure, and free. Bhakti flows from us to God and from God to us. This energy flow from God to us purifies and divinizes us. Bhakti has to be combined with the knowledge that creator and creation are not two but one. This knowledge should awaken compassion within us. Amma says we should not be like people who go to the temple to pray, then come out and kick the beggars sitting outside. Devotion to God and compassion for the world are two sides of the same coin.

Amma says, "True happiness is when the love within us finds its expression through external activities." Amma's words to practice compassion are simple and practical yet create a profound transformation. I had a wealthy friend who had everything but was not happy. I told her about Amma, and how Amma said that giving one sāri to the needy when you buy a few for yourself can create so much happiness. She decided to give each of her household help an expensive silk sāri from her collection. She later told me, when she saw their joy she felt a hundred times happier than when she bought the sāri for herself. Eventually she became fully involved in their lives, sponsoring their children's education, and helping them become financially stable. Implementing this simple teaching created a huge ripple effect. Amma's divine influence graced her, and also transformed the lives of the other women. Through teaching her how to share, Amma gave this lady the priceless gift of compassion and contentment.

In my case also, love for Amma opened my eyes to opportunities to help others. I organized fundraisers along with students to help at-risk children, like troubled teenagers. We became Amma's instruments to serve these children for twelve years. Actually, they helped us more by giving us the chance to serve selflessly!

We can see oneness in Amma's relationship with all of creation. She loves all! Once during a chai stop on the U.S. Tour, a bee sat on Amma's head. We wanted to remove it, but Amma said no. She let it sit on her head the entire time because Amma said the bee had a bond with her. It flew away only when Amma stepped into her car.

Recently, we were sitting with Amma when a monkey came to visit. Most of us screamed, but Amma offered the monkey prasād biscuits. This monkey was also her beloved child. Such an equal vision is mentioned in the *Bhagavad Gītā*, Chapter 5, verse 18:

> *vidyā-vinaya-sampannē brāhmaṇē gavi hastini*
> *śhuni chaiva śhva-pākē cha paṇḍitāḥ sama-darśhinaḥ*
> 'Whether a Brahmin endowed with learning and humility, a cow, an elephant, a dog, or even a dog eater, the enlightened one perceives all with equal vision.'

This vision of oneness, the elevated state of true bhakti that Amma embodies, is the real Vēdānta.

Some benefits of bhakti are described in Sūtras 4 – 6 of the *Nārada Bhakti Sūtras*. Sūtra 4 says, 'On attaining this devotion one becomes perfect, immortal, and perfectly satisfied.' Sūtra 5 declares, 'Gaining this, one wants nothing, laments over nothing, hates nothing, does not delight in fleeting happiness, and is not obsessed with anything.' Sūtra 6 says, 'Experiencing this devotion one becomes overjoyed beyond measure, perfectly still in body and mind, and revels in his or her own blissful nature.'

We see this in the lives of saintly bhaktās like Mīrābaī, the princess devotee of Bhagavān (Lord) Kṛiṣhṇa, and in Prahlāda, the devotee of Viṣhṇu Bhagavān. Both were completely immersed in divine love and oblivious to worldly sorrows. Their beloved God always came to their aid, and their devotion neutralized the poison the world had given them. Devotion to Guru/God is like a kavacham — an armor that always protects us!

Even Ādi Śhaṅkarāchārya, who established the path of Advaita Vēdānta, or non-dual philosophy, eventually wrote the devotional hymn *Saundarya Laharī* praising Goddess Tripurasundarī. He declares in his text *Vivēkachūḍāmaṇi*: 'Devotion is enquiry into one's own Self.'[48] In the hymn *Bhaja Gōvindaṁ* he assures us that one devoted to the Guru will be liberated from saṁsāra. Sage Vyāsa compiled the *Vēdas* and the *Brahma Sūtras*, but was content only after writing the *Śhrīmad Bhāgavatam* which glorifies Lord Kṛiṣhṇa's life. Śhrī Rāmakṛiṣhṇa Paramahaṁsa also says, "Unalloyed love of God is the essential thing. All else is unreal."

Amma says true bhakti is based in knowledge and knowing the difference between the eternal and the ephemeral. We should have the discrimination and strength to discard what gives us pain, and embrace what gives us eternal happiness. Only the Self is lasting and dependable. We have Amma, the Self in physical form, to worship, love, and depend upon. Idealizing anything other than the Self is a big mistake. That's the lesson God is trying to teach us through our sorrowful experiences.

Even if we have this discrimination intellectually, it is very difficult to practice. Fortunately, Amma's grace can propel our mind upwards if we perform regular spiritual practices and sincerely try to apply her teachings to our daily life.

Amma finds many ways to correct me if I become lazy. One day after wasting time, I picked up a book, and a clipping from

---

[48] *'svātmatattvānusandhānaṃ bhaktirityaparē jaguḥ'* — '...others call inquiry into one's own Self as bhakti.' (Verse 32)

Matruvani[49] fell out of it. It said, 'Daughter, spiritual practices are your only treasure!' That jolted me right out of my inertia. Last year, again I was neglecting my practices. One day in front of the Kālī temple, a lady stopped me and said, "Sādhanā," and left. I thought, maybe she thinks my name is Sādhanā! When the same lady said this a second time, I got nervous. When it happened for a third time, I realized she was Amma's messenger, reminding me to focus on my spiritual practices! Amma the master, is always teaching us. She says her love is not to spoil us, but to make us grow!

A person with bhakti develops a strong connection with God who cannot ignore their prayers. Once in Toulon France, Dēvī Bhāva was ending. A young boy was standing next to me along Amma's path. He told me he admired the tour staff and felt sad that he didn't have as much dedication or devotion to Amma. He pressed his hand to his hurting heart and started crying. I tried to console him saying Amma knows his heart.

A few minutes later Amma came down the steps and stopped right in front of that boy! Her smiling, brilliant eyes were full of compassion. Saying, "My son, my son," she rubbed his heart, hugged him, and left. The boy was speechless. Tears filled his eyes. He asked, "How did she know?" His innocent devotion and spontaneous yearning connected him to Amma. She felt his pain because all of our thoughts run through her — the cosmic Self. Amma is the Kṛiṣhṇa of our age. Chapter 13, verse 14 of the *Bhagavad Gītā* describes her omniscience:

sarvataḥ pāṇi-pādaṁ tat sarvatō 'kṣhi-śhirō-mukhaṁ
sarvataḥ śhrutimallōkē sarvaṁ āvṛitya tiṣhṭhati

---

[49] 'Voice of the Mother.' The āśhram's flagship publication, dedicated to disseminating Amma's teachings and chronicling her divine mission. It is currently published in 17 languages (including nine Indian languages).

'With hands and feet everywhere, eyes, heads, and faces everywhere, and ears too in all places, He exists pervading everything in the universe.'

***

Other than temple worship I knew absolutely nothing about spirituality. I hadn't looked for Amma, but it was she who came to find me halfway across the world in the United States. One winter morning in 2003, I had a dream as real as sitting here speaking to you! A divinely beautiful, majestic lady wearing a white sāri was seated on a stage in a school in Bangalore. She was surrounded by people. I was sitting in front of her, also wearing a white sāri, weeping uncontrollably.

She looked into my eyes and said, "Daughter don't cry, I will heal the sorrow of your heart!" Then turning to a sage sitting near her, she gave him instructions to make something. He returned and handed Amma a silver glass. Reaching out, Amma held my chin in her left hand, tilted my head and poured a thick brown sweet liquid into my mouth, like a mother feeding her child. Even today, I can vividly feel the touch of Amma's hand on my chin. I woke up feeling full of light! A devotee later told me that my vision had happened while Amma was giving darśhan in Bangalore.

I attended my first Amṛitakuṭuṁbam[50] gathering on Guru Pūrṇimā a few months later. When I heard Amma's aṣhṭōttaraṁ (108 names), I was overcome with a longing so intense, nameless, and mysterious that I burst out crying. Being very reserved, I was horrified at this display of emotion in front of total strangers. But a giant wave had washed over me. We call it pure love, Amma etc. — but in truth, it is beyond all names.

[50] 'Family of Nectar or Immortality.' Amma's initiative wherein devotees meet regularly to sing bhajans and hold satsang.

After the pūjā was over, I walked into the living room and saw Amma's altar, beautifully decorated with a pair of silver Guru pādukās (sandals). I prostrated. When I complimented the hostess about the altar and pādukās, she looked at me as if I were crazy! She had no idea what I was talking about. I took her to the living room to show her, but the pādukās had vanished! I realized with gratitude that Amma had compassionately manifested her sacred pādukās on Guru Pūrṇimā to awaken love and faith in me.

That same year I met Amma in her physical form in New York. As Amma walked into the hall, I recognized the sage from my dream. He was one of Amma's swāmī's and was following Amma into the hall. I don't remember much about my darśhan, but afterwards Amma asked me to sit next to her. The swāmī was sitting there as well, and I gathered the courage to tell him about my dream. I asked him what the sweet, brown liquid was that Amma fed me. Referring to Amṛit, the nectar of immortality, he smiled mysteriously, and said, "She is Amṛitānandamayī[51]!" Amma had fed me the sweet healing nectar of her divine love with her own hands.

When I reflect on what my sorrow might be that Amma promised to heal, I realize it is not the mundane sorrow of life or mental creations. It is the deepest grief of the jīvātmā (individual self) feeling separate from the paramātmā (supreme Self). This sorrow ends only by merging with God. Devotion is the path to oneness.

***

After my dream darśhan my life changed dramatically. I fell straight from my intellect into my heart. I used to be a

[51] Amṛitānandamayī means 'full of immortal or nectarean bliss.' The name by which Amma is universally known.

workaholic and so-called intellectual, studying for a second graduate degree and other certifications. I lost interest in anything not connected to Amma. I started my day with archana before going to work. The lighting of a lamp at sunset, and short prayers I had done mechanically before, now became a celebration. I didn't know many mantras, scriptures, or traditional pūjās, but I imagined that I was doing everything with Amma. I talked to her in my heart, played with her, dressed her, fed her, sang and danced with her. Most of all I cried to her. Crying for Amma became my main sādhanā for years.

Once my inner world began to change, my outer world brought me books like *Vivēkachūḍāmaṇi*, the *Upaniṣhads*, Ramaṇa Mahārṣhi's teachings, Nisargadatta Mahārāj's *I Am That,* etc. The ṛiṣhis' exalted vision; the psychological and physiological deconstruction of the human being; descriptions about the nature of the world and the Self; were all very helpful. They supported devotion with knowledge. Still, nothing made me cry like reading Amma's or Śhrī Rāmakṛiṣhṇa Paramahaṁsa's books. Philosophy is essential, but the center point will always be love.

As a teenager and young woman, I easily became nervous and scared. I was introverted and shy. My best friends were books and nature. Once when I was fourteen, my teacher forced me to participate in a debate. I stood before the audience, opened my mouth to speak, and fainted! They had to carry me out of the hall! However, I learned that I couldn't escape my karma. Public speaking became the profession that chose me.

I would have liked to live forever in my shell, but life had other plans. I left home at twenty-one. I traveled from India to Europe to study, and finally to the United States. There, facing many challenges, I learned to do everything myself tapping into strength I didn't know I possessed. All the challenges were

Amma working on my ego and making me mature, changing from a scared kitten to a fierce lion cub!

Amma says the real Guru can only be known through experience. I learned Amma's teachings not just in theory, but in practice. Some of Amma's lessons for life are: nobody loves you for your sake, but only for their own happiness, and the mind is the cause of both bondage and liberation. Amma says that when we are alone, we are alone, and when we are in a crowd we are also alone. As long as I remained detached, I was saved from sorrow. I always pray to Amma to help me interact with others in a detached way as Amma sings in her bhajan, *Chintakaḷkantyam Vannen.*

> *gandhavāhanan pōle bandhichhu sarvattilum*
> *bandhamillātte vāzhān uḷḷil nī vasikkaṇē*
> 'Dwell within me that I may live like the breeze, that touches everything but doesn't get attached.'

Amma tells the story from the *Mahābhārata* where Yama, the god of death, asked Yudhiṣhṭhira, "What's the most wonderful thing in the world?" Yudhiṣhṭhira replied that although countless people are dying every day, the rest of humanity still thinks they'll live forever.

In 2010 I had major surgery which made this teaching on mortality very real for me. After complications and five hours of surgery, I survived. Amma however had performed the real surgery on my mind. While I was recovering, I wondered where was this 'I' during those hours? Where was this world? How fragile is 'reality.' When the brain, which allows the mind to function is sedated, 'I' the perceiver, and the perceived world vanish.

Now, when a cremation urn is placed next to Amma during a funeral service, I reflect on the perishability of this body. Just as someone who travels a lot always keeps a suitcase packed, a part of our mind should be prepared for this final departure. Amma says we should be like a bird on a dry twig, ready to fly at any moment. Death is the reality. Only the ātmā is eternal. Deep sleep is like death. When you wake up it is like a new life. Amma says this is how we should reflect on death.

This experience put my life, regrets, worries, desires, aspirations, and everything else in perspective. Amma says all these are mere bubbles that can burst at any time. When my mind is out of control, remembering this helps me refocus.

Here's a funny example of how synchronicity and the miraculous coincide around Amma. I love Indian sweets. Sometimes I vow not to eat any sweets unless it is Amma's prasād; then I can control myself. One afternoon, I was craving Rasmalāī.[52] The more I tried ignoring it, the more Rasmalāī floated before my eyes. I said to my mind, "Stop it! If Amma wants me to have Rasmalāī she will place it before me!" I forgot that Amma, the indweller, is always listening!

Two days later, we were preparing dinner at our Amṛitakuṭumbam. A devotee came and placed two huge packets of Rasmalāī right in front of me! I almost fainted. I asked, "Is this your favorite sweet?" She said she'd wanted to bring mango ice cream but couldn't find any. Instead she brought Rasmalāī! Internally I laughed so hard. Only Amma has such a sense of humor! She rewarded me for keeping my vow and spoiled me like a child with Rasmalāī.

***

I remember the first directly-spoken spiritual teaching Amma gave me. During Amma's U.S. programs her pīṭham was placed on the floor and we sat close to her. One day, everyone was

---

[52] A sweet delicacy made from cheese and milk.

meditating when I felt Amma watching me and opened my eyes. She looked straight at me and said, "*Iṣhtāniṣhtam pādilla*" — You should not have likes and dislikes, and said a few other things. Then she went back into meditation. I'm ashamed that I didn't understand the importance of her words then. My mind was full of likes and dislikes, and I failed many of Amma's tests that followed!

Another time I was doing line sēvā[53] near Amma during Dēvī Bhāva. Suddenly Amma's hand landed on mine. I became fully aware and alert. Then she looked at me and said, "Ellām mayam, brahma mayam." — Everything is pure consciousness, pervaded by Brahman. Yes, for Amma everything is divine consciousness or God. This is the ultimate truth. The lesson was to imbibe this teaching and apply it in my life.

This is almost impossible because we identify with the mind, body, and intellect. Amma sees unity in diversity, and we see diversity in unity. We perceive ever-changing, unreal names and forms but are unaware of the substratum. We see only the ornaments and not the gold! Amma sings about this quality of the mind in the bhajan '*Manassoru Māyā Marīchika*' — 'Our mind itself is māyā (illusion).' When we look at the world through the filter of an ignorant mind, we see the world as māyā.

Amma tells a story about how devotion to the Guru's feet can defeat this māyā. There was a little fish who never got caught in a fisherman's net. When asked how she managed this, the fish said that when the fisherman casts his net far and wide, instead of swimming away from him, she swims straight to his feet and hides there, escaping the net. If we swim to Amma's feet when in danger, and fill our heart with her image, māyā cannot trap us. Chapter 7, verse 14 of the *Bhagavad Gītā* says:

---

53 Assisting people waiting in line for Amma's darśhan.

> *daivī hyēṣhā guṇa-mayī mama māyā duratyayā*
> *māmēva yē prapadyantē māyām ētāṁ taranti tē*
> 'This divine illusion of Mine, made of the three guṇas (the three modes of nature), is difficult to overcome. Those who take refuge in Me alone, cross over this māyā.'

Amma says, "My children, it's only through devotion that one can melt away the ego and other impurities." I learned that the only way I could reduce my negativities was by replacing them with devotional practices like archana, japa, meditation, and talking to Amma in my heart. I also practiced asking myself what Amma would do in certain situations and tried to follow that.

Many of my negativities have been reduced not through Amma's direct instruction but merely by her physical presence. The strong spiritual vibrations emanating from Amma's divine form can weaken and change our saṁskāras or mental impressions. This is the great advantage of living with the Guru. Once we learn to tune in to this presence, we can reach Amma even in her physical absence.

How lucky we are that divine-director Amma has come down to be among us in physical form. She reminds us that life is only a play, māyā's dance of light and shadow. Do your best, but don't take anything to be the truth or everlasting. In the end, we all have to play our part and leave.

Amma is Śhrī Kṛiṣhṇa, the very life breath and love of Rādhā, and much more! She has incarnated on earth as 'Amṛitakṛiṣhṇa' to reestablish dharma and harmony. Amma's promise to me in my dream darśhan was, "Daughter, don't worry. I will heal the sorrow of your heart." Amma has made this promise to all beings who are her children. She takes us singing, laughing, dancing, praying, and crying on the path of love to reach knowledge and liberation.

Amma says again and again that what will make her happy is if we truly recognize that we are embodiments of pure love and supreme consciousness. We should honor her monumental sacrifice and endless patience by opening our hearts, and reaching out to take the priceless diamond she offers us.

12

Amma's Amazing Rescue

Devadath – The Netherlands

First, I want to thank Amma for letting us stay here during the pandemic. In 2017 Amma talked about how travel would be difficult in these years. I prayed that I could be with Amma during that period. I forgot about this prayer, but Amma didn't. In December 2019, we came to stay for three months which turned into two years.

When thinking about my topic for this talk, I remembered numerous stories about my experiences in Amma's loving presence and the lessons I've learned.

God's Most Consoling Promise

I grew up in a small fishing village. My father was a carpenter and my mother a secretary. We went to church on Sundays and I went to a Christian school. I had a strong belief in Jesus. Before bed I would pray for forgiveness of my sins and for the long life of my family. I remember asking why people didn't live by Christian values. Nobody I knew turned the other cheek when being hurt like Jesus said, let alone love their neighbors. I drifted away from Christianity. Why follow it if no one lives by its principles? As I matured, I became active in social movements and left wing politics. However, I soon learned that progressive ideas don't always go together with human values like respect, love, and compassion.

Finally, I just wanted to free myself from all dogmas. In the West we learn that fulfilling desires equals happiness and freedom. If you're unhappy, then you're not pursuing your desires effectively. Little did I know that satisfying desires only makes you jump to the next desire. This leads to unhappiness and exhaustion.

Nisargadatta, the great advaitin (non-dualist) from Mumbai, used to tell a story based on the *Rāmāyaṇa* about the monkey army of Hanumān. After they liberated Sītā from the demon king in Laṅkā, Lord Rāma wanted to reward them, so he asked them what they wanted. Now monkeys are very clear on what they like: lots of food, lots of fighting, and lots of sense pleasures. So Lord Rāma granted them the boon to all be reborn in the West in the 20th century! (Maybe that's where my monkey mind comes from.)

Feeling disconnected from the world, I thought something was wrong with me and went into therapy, until I recognised my depression was a longing to reconnect with the source — with God, with my highest Self. Then it became my spiritual journey.

In the *Bhagavad Gītā*, Chapter 4, verse 8, Lord Kṛiṣhṇa says to Arjuna:

> *paritrāṇāya sādhūnāṁ vināśhāya cha duṣhkṛitām*
> *dharma-saṁsthāpanārthāya saṁbhavāmi yugē yugē*
> 'I manifest time and again to protect the righteous, to destroy the evil-doers, and to reinstate righteousness.'

Kṛiṣhṇa promises to be there for the world and for us as well, dwelling within us. This is God's most consoling promise. I needed help to protect the divine spark in me, and to weed out the bad and become a better person. Amma not only gives hope and consolation, she inspires us to make the best of our lives, for ourselves and for the world. Amma brings us in touch with our innermost Self. That Amma is really with us is the greatest miracle and the highest consolation. Amma often says during darśhan, "Don't worry, my child."

Meeting Amma

Amma rescued me twenty-five years ago in 1996. I saw the Dutch version of Amma's biography in a bookstore. I was struck by Amma's cover photo, but I didn't buy the book. That would be silly for a rational person like me. Some weeks later, someone told me about this 'hugging mother in Kerala.' I somehow knew it was the same Amma. Then I saw a poster that Amma would be coming to a venue nearby. Even for my rationality, three times in a row felt like a call.

At the program, I had no idea what to expect. People sat on the floor. There were no darśhan tokens. Everybody just queued up, waiting their turn. There was Amma, clad in white. Around midnight I was finally held in Amma's arms. I don't know what happened, but it was deep and profound and strangely familiar...so very normal.

Next day I stood in the hall as Amma walked in, and tears welled up the moment I saw her. For weeks after, I felt as if I was in love and thought of following Amma to India. Slowly my rational mind started doubting. What about my job and my mom? I was afraid if I went to India I would never come back. "The mind is a thief," says Amma. It took four more years before I could get to Amritapuri.

Don't Interfere with the Divine

In 2002, I was helping with Amma's program in the Netherlands. It was a busy Dēvī Bhāva day. My sister-in-law and three-year-old nephew had a time card.[54] The boy got restless waiting and

[54] Time cards are given out to people wishing to have darśhan. They can be traded for a darśhan token when these become available.

was soon crying, making his mother desperate to leave without getting darśhan. This cannot happen, I thought.

Then I saw a darśhan token on the floor. Jai Mā! Divine intervention! My desperate-to-help ego was foolish enough to take them to the front of the darśhan line. I handed the token to the darśhan line assistant who was standing next to Amma. Looking at me she shot back, "That's yesterday's token!"

I felt so embarrassed. Then Amma noticed and started apologizing saying she was giving darśhan as fast as she could, that it was such a busy day and she really wanted to see everybody. I wanted to crawl under the carpet. I hadn't learned the lesson yet that everybody gets whatever helps them progress on their path.

Amma's Play in Three Acts

For many people, certain themes keep recurring. Some specific karmic pain and burden knocks on the door asking for release. In the first half of my life, one major theme was about not feeling seen or welcome. As a kid I wasn't one of the 'cool guys.' I was bullied a lot which made me alert to how people reacted to me. I tended to please and could easily feel hurt and rejected. This pain also came up in my relationship with Amma. Did she really love me? Could I handle her testing me? Amma's testing unfolded like a three-act play with a happy ending. The first act was in Amritapuri around 2007. For years I longed to swim with Amma, but I was never there at the right time.

Finally, I had a three-week vacation from work. The first week in Amritapuri, I bathed in Amma's grace and joy. Then my vāsanās said, "Hi!" and I got really restless. Fed up with myself and āśhram life, I thought I would spend some time at the beach in Varkala, a nearby vacation spot. The first night there, I went to an internet café and read that Amma had gone swimming with the residents that very evening! It was like getting hit with a brick. How could I have missed this? What was I doing in Varkala? The fun was over and next morning I took a train back to Amritapuri.

As I walked into the āśhram a devotee saw me looking glum. Feeling very sorry for myself I told her what had happened, hoping for some sympathy. She smiled and shrugged and said, "Well, you went swimming without her; she went swimming without you. What's the big deal?" A few hours later I went for darśhan and told Amma my story. First she laughed right in my face seeing that I had failed the test and triggered all my old pain of feeling left out. Then she looked at me so lovingly I can still feel it in my heart.

The second act came some weeks later. Amma was in Munich, Germany and I was asked to help with the webcam-livestream that night. During Dēvī Bhāva the webcam was connected to a laptop that Amma used to look at her children in Amritapuri and other centers. Towards the end of Dēvī Bhāva the person operating the webcam got to hold the laptop close to Amma. Suddenly, the internet connection failed. I was told to find someone to fix it.

After searching and not finding anyone I hurried back, but by then someone else was holding the laptop for Amma. At first I thought, "No big deal." Five minutes later I was sad and disappointed. Why was I left out again? Ten minutes later I was pretty irritated. I decided to go for darśhan and just lay my frustration at Amma's feet. Surely she would pity me.

As I got closer, Amma was speeding up and I was only briefly in her arms. Amma looked at me and said, "You eat a lot? Pffff!" and she showed me how fat I had become by opening her arms wide. Did Amma just call me fat? I was in shock. I had gained some weight, but did she really say I was fat? How dare she! As I walked off the stage, angry steam was coming out my ears; I was furious. Two weeks later Amma would be in the Netherlands. I thought, "Well she can take her program to another lōka (world). I won't be there!"

Everybody bathed in the Dēvī Bhāva flower-petal shower while I stood angrily in the back of the hall. It took me some hours to come to my senses and realize that this was the power of māyā (illusion). Amma had given me all this love and had graced me with so many beautiful experiences. One little tease and I wanted to throw everything away. That is the power of the mind. This was a big lesson.

The third act of Amma's testing happened when we were in the Netherlands. Because of my sēvā, I was invited to sit near Amma at the end of Dēvī Bhāva. It was a beautiful chance to see Amma up close while she gave babies their first solid food and conducted weddings. I was sitting there for only a few minutes when Amma asked me, "Did everybody get darśhan? Please search the whole venue in every room to find anyone who didn't get darśhan."

"Here we go again," I thought. "Just as the fun is starting, I get sent away." But then I realized I was being tested. I straightened up, put on a smile and joyfully searched every room in the building. Of course I found nobody, but I managed to keep my mind under control. Amma wasn't gonna get me this time! When I got back, the stage was packed with people. No chance this two-meter body could get anywhere near Amma now. Instead, I stood on the top of the steps. Almost immediately Amma's attendant waved to me saying, "Amma wants you to sit next to her now." Finally I got the lesson, and Amma's reward came immediately after.

Amma's Amazing Rescue

The most amazing example of Amma's incomparable protection and grace fell upon my wife Marieke and me when we had a very serious car accident five years ago. The accident itself was horrible and (according to astrologers) unavoidable. But the whole accident and everything that happened after overflowed with Amma's grace.

We both had worked hard organizing the Netherlands program that year. After the clean-up and a long night's rest we planned to join the rest of the Europe tour in a small, rented camper. As we drove into Germany, the weather turned bad. It was evening and the highway was pitch black. After driving for three hours, Marieke decided to rest on the bed in the back of the camper. I was happy to continue driving. I felt like I could drive all night.

A little later, a bang shook the camper. I tried to control the steering wheel as the vehicle went into a skid. I hit the breaks, but the camper rolled over. We hit a tree, and the camper ended up lying on its side, next to the road. I was hanging sideways in the seatbelt and fell as I unbuckled it. I tried opening the door above me, but it was blocked. I tried kicking out the shattered front window, but couldn't. I called Marieke but heard nothing. Everything was black and dark. Finally I managed to crawl out through the rooftop window.

I called Marieke again. This time she responded saying she was in pain and had difficulty breathing. The camper was totally wrecked. A big tree that we had crashed into lay across the road. By now other vehicles had stopped to help. Soon the police, fire department, and paramedics arrived. They cut open the vehicle to free Marieke. I later learned they had already intubated Marieke because she had collapsed lungs and was suffocating. The paramedics said they were taking Marieke to a nearby hospital because her condition was critical.

I had to wait for another ambulance, and a policeman asked for my papers and driving license. Everything was in the wrecked camper. He left and miraculously, returned moments later with both of our phones and laptops. Immediately I thought, "I must call Amma." I managed to reach Swāmī Śhubhāmṛitānanda who was on stage with Amma. When I told Amma what had happened, I heard her repeat three times, "You did nothing wrong. It was not your fault." With Amma's grace, I've never felt guilty about the accident, even though weeks later I realized I must have fallen asleep behind the wheel. Amma asked us to keep her informed about Marieke's condition.

In the hospital, Marieke was now in a coma. Her ribs had pierced her lungs, she had multiple fractures in her shoulder, nine broken ribs and a shattered wrist. I asked how serious it was on a scale of one to ten. It was a nine. The next seventy-two hours were critical.

Despite the severity of Marieke's condition, grace flowed in big waves in the days that followed. Marieke was in one of the top three hospitals in the country that specializes in lung injuries. A devotee living nearby came and took care of everything with the police and insurance. The next day, Swāminī Śhrī Lakṣhmī Prāna's brother and his wife came to bring Amma's prasād and clothes for me. A lovely couple living nearby offered free accommodation so I could stay near Marieke. Within twenty-four hours, pūjās in Amritapuri were offered for Marieke. The Dutch Amma Center and satsang groups all over the world were praying and chanting. There was so much support from our entire Amma family. We believe that Marieke survived only because of Amma's grace and all of those prayers.

Five days after the accident, the police released the wrecked camper that they'd impounded as part of their investigation. Two devotees drove me to the police impound lot to pick up our personal belongings. On the way, we passed the site where the accident had occurred on the opposite side of the road. It was easy to spot because the tree we'd knocked down showed the exact location. We would be passing right by it on the return trip. When I got to the camper, I could see that the tree had smashed right through the passenger seat. if Marieke had not been sleeping in the back, she surely would not have survived.

Driving back, I was anxious to go past the accident site. As we approached it, my phone rang. It was Swāmī Amṛitaswarūpānanda. He said, "Amma is giving darśhan in Paris and she wants to know how your wife is?" Then Amma spoke to me right when we drove past the accident site. As we were driving on the German highway at high speed, this was amazing. Amma's grace is not just endless and ever-flowing, but her timing is also impeccable...to the second.

When Marieke came out of her coma after seven days, she tried to talk. She was still on a breathing machine, so I held my laptop in front of her and she slowly typed: "Long trip to AIMS." Marieke had had such strong experiences of Amma being with her while in the coma, that she was convinced she was at AIMS hospital in Cochin. I hope one day Marieke has the opportunity to speak about these experiences herself.

Twelve days later, Amma was in the German āśhram, about a two-and-a-half-hour drive from the hospital. Amma sent Swāminī Śhrī Lakṣhmī Prāṇā and Swāmi Śhubhāmṛitānanda to visit Marieke. They brought Amma's prasād and a pair of Amma's socks for Marieke. By then Marieke was out of danger, so I went to see Amma for Dēvī Bhāva. Amma promised that Marieke would be dancing again in the Spring. Her recovery went very fast, to the amazement of her doctors. Amma called every few days until she returned to India.

Miraculous Beacon of Hope

Amma was so close to us during the most dramatic moment of our lives. This is Kṛiṣhṇa's promise, and Amma fulfills this prophecy profoundly. What an amazing blessing to witness this 'Amma Gītā' unfold.

Amma is a miraculous beacon of hope in this Kali Yuga world. This is my greatest consolation and restores my faith in God and in life. Amma actually lives the teachings of the Jesus that I heard about in my youth. As Yolanda King said, "She walks the talk." Thank you Amma for saving us and holding us close.

U bent Schepping en ook haar Schepster
You are Creation and Her Creator

U bent Waarheid, kracht achter alles
You are Truth, Force behind Everything

Het heelal is uit U geschapen
The Universe is Created from You

Oorsprong van alles en ook het einde
Origin and End of Everything

Sṛiṣhtiyum nīyē sṛiṣhtāvum nīyē
Śhaktiyum nīyē satyavum nīyē
You are Creation and Creator
You are Divine Power and Truth

U bent het Allerhoogste bewustzijn
You are the Highest Consciousness

En u bent ook de vijf elementen
And You are the Five Elements

Sṛiṣhtiyum nīyē sṛiṣhtāvum nīyē
Śhaktiyum nīyē satyavum nīyē
You are Creation and Creator
You are Divine Power and Truth

Dutch version of Amma's bhajan *Sṛiṣhtiyum Nīyē*

13

Self-Confidence

Dr. Vidya - USA

Before returning to Amritapuri after two years, I had replayed over and over in my mind the moment I would see Amma. It would be perfect, and I would be filled with joy. Amma would gaze into my eyes when I got there, and it would feel like the past two Covid years had never happened, and I would move along with my life, happy as can be. When I finally saw Amma at bhajans, I was shocked. I was actually filled with a deep sadness. I began reflecting on the past two years and felt like somewhat of a failure. Amma's presence jolted me out of a delusion I had been experiencing for the past two years. It felt like I suddenly woke up. The Divine Mother is here!! Have I been focused on her?

Sure, I was busy, but how many times did I think of Amma daily? I watched the webcasts, but was it with śhraddhā (attentive faith) and bhakti (devotion)? Did I do sēvā lovingly, with a smile? I was so afraid of feeling sad to be away from Amma that I had shut myself down, and I began to feel like Amma was not with me. Once international tourist visas came back, my first thought was to book a flight immediately, but part of me wondered, "Is it worth it? Will Amma even interact with me? If Amma doesn't see me or give me darśhan, I may be more depressed than if I stay here." As I observed these negative thoughts, I was a bit shocked. After all these years, how could I imagine not running to my dearest Amma because I was afraid of not getting any physical attention? What was my goal after all? Why was my faith so weak?

The problem was I forgot about the one whose opinion matters most. AMMA! Surely, she missed me and wanted to see me? So, I came. Whether we realize it or not, that small thought, "Amma wants to see me," is an incredible blessing. It is a blessing expressed in Self-confidence. If we reflect on the times we feel closest to Amma, we realize that in those moments, we are blessed to believe with every iota of our being that Amma is *our* mother, and we are *her* child. Just as I had to remind myself that Amma would want to see me, we all must remind ourselves that Amma is our biggest cheerleader and supporter. Ultimately, she loves us more than anything in this world. This feeling of closeness can be summed up in one word: Self-confidence. When I say Self-confidence, I do not mean our "little" ego-self. I mean the Self, (ātmā) that which is all-pervading.

Amma says:

> "Children, never lose your Self-confidence. It is like a booster rocket. It helps us break free from the impurities and bondage of the mind and allows us to soar to the heights of spirituality. It is like fuel giving us the power to forge ahead."

Self-confidence is the understanding of our true nature. It is deeply knowing that we are one with Amma, though we do not see it yet. Our limited intellect struggles with this concept, but we can find Self-confidence in Amma by fervently believing that we are Amma's children and Amma is always with us. With every action we perform, we can ask ourselves, "Would this make Amma happy?" This question not only makes life more straightforward, but also makes it a celebration. Self-confidence begins in faith and ends in compassion and service to others. Only when we develop Self-confidence can we strongly face any situation.

Almost all problems in life boil down to not having Self-confidence. Because of my lack of Self-confidence, I've hurt others with my words or actions. For that I'm sorry from the bottom of my heart. How many times have we made a small comment that created unintended ripple effects? Why do we do it? Perhaps to feel closer to others, or to feel better about ourselves. Actually, it is because we did not have the strong conviction that we are Amma's children. If we have such a conviction, actions that hurt others naturally fall away. If Amma is with us, and we want to make her proud, surely, we wouldn't perform such actions, right?

In Chapter 2, verse 15 of the *Bhagavad Gītā*, Lord Kṛiṣhṇa says:

> *yaṁ hi na vyathayantyētē puruṣhaṁ puruṣharṣhabha*
> *sama-duḥkha-sukhaṁ dhīraṁ sō 'mṛitatvāya kalpatē*
> 'O noblest among men, that person who remains steady in happiness and distress, who is verily undisturbed by these, that person becomes eligible for immortality (attaining liberation).'

Amma constantly teaches us not to be disturbed by the ups and downs of the world. I am reminded of one instance: one summer I flew in for one night to attend a Dēvī Bhāva. I already felt a little insecure and lacking confidence as I was alone and did not have my usual tour setup and schedule. I decided to try to get a good seat down on the 'musical magic carpet'[55] as some of us call it, to calmly enjoy the end of Dēvī Bhāva. Before I knew it, someone yelled at me in front of everyone to get up as I had taken their spot. Already feeling sensitive, I was furious and upset.

---

[55] Carpet placed in the seating area directly in front, facing Amma during the Dēvī Bhāva program where the musicians sit as they play bhajans (devotional songs).

I let it fester, then finally told Amma what had happened. I expected Amma to tell me lovingly not to worry and to console me. But Amma clearly explained to me that person's side of the story. I was a little taken aback. Was Amma mad at me? Did I actually do something wrong? I suddenly spiraled down into "I disappointed Amma... She must not love me... etc." If I had focused on my confidence in Amma, I would have understood that she was using this as a teaching moment.

Now, I realize this was a big lesson from Amma to see things as they are and to focus on my Self. As Amma says, "We should see an elephant as an elephant, and a frog as a frog. If we understand the nature of the world, we will never take such situations personally." Knowing that Amma is our biggest supporter doesn't mean we can do anything we want. Rather, it means we understand that our unshakeable bond with Amma will give us the strength to see things just as they are, to understand the nature of this world, and to move forward without getting affected emotionally. Self-confidence also makes us fit to receive such teachings, knowing that Amma as our biggest supporter will do everything to make us stronger and progress on the path.

It is lack of Self-confidence that makes us feel distant from Amma. If we were convinced that we are Amma's children and that, as she says time and again, she is always with us, our thoughts would turn into excitement and joy knowing that Amma is in our heart. To reflect on this, we can think of our joyous memories of Amma and how she brought us into her fold as her own.

***

Though I don't remember it, I met Amma at the Universalist Church in New York City in 1997, just a few blocks away from my home. My mom had heard about Amma for years but was never in town at the right time to meet her. By Amma's grace, that year we were there. It was Dēvī Bhāva. My mom says that my dad really did not want to go. He was so confused and grumpy. "Why would we go meet someone in the middle of the night? We have a two-year-old." However, he reluctantly came along just to look after me.

We met Amma and my mom was mesmerized. She got a mantra and an Amma doll (that would become mine) that very same night. Every year thereafter we would meet Amma when she came to New York. I have vague memories of running up for darśhan at the beginning of Dēvī Bhāva with all the other kids to sit on Amma's lap, with Amma blowing on my tummy and affectionately holding me. The funny part about being a child around Amma is that you really don't understand then how lucky you are, but Amma creates an indestructible bond.

In our house, my mom always played Amma's bhajans and other devotees' music while we did chores. From reading *Amma Comics*, to watching old āśhram kid videos, I would remember Amma throughout the year. My mom was a musician, and she often wrote songs, sometimes for Amma too. One day we sat together and made up a song we called 'Help me Amma.'

The song goes:

> 'Help me Amma, help, help me Amma,
> You're so red, you never go to bed.
> You're so green, you love all the trees.
> You're so true, you were born blue.
> You're so sweet, you give us Hershey treats.'

I was super excited about the song. Then one year, we were also able to go to Michigan after the New York program to see Amma for Thanksgiving. My mom says she was in line at the snack shop when she suddenly heard a little girl singing our song. I barely remember it, but what I do remember is running up to Anu Chēchi[56] and Swarna Chēchi on stage and singing the song for them to learn so they could accompany me on tablas and keyboards. From then on, I always sang our song for Amma. Amma would talk to me about the song in every darśhan. I would even gather other little girls to sing songs with me. This was Amma's infinite grace. Ultimately, it brought me closer and closer to Amma.

My mom told me that one day Amma mentioned that the other women on tour should have confidence like me. This was a lesson to always keep child-like innocence and confidence. I had no doubt then that Amma would always want to hear me sing — whether that was true or not. As I grew older, each year Amma asked me to sing the song if I hadn't done so already. In fact, she told me to study music too!

Then came the pre-teen years when most of us start to feel more self-conscious. Suddenly the confidence that Amma had praised me for became fear. I started to feel a bit embarrassed about my song. Sometimes I actually hoped Amma wouldn't bring it up as I wanted to be a big grown up and not do such childish things.

By Amma's grace, during these years I began to intensely reflect on Amma and my life. When I was thirteen, I started watching Amma more closely. While in line for my last Dēvī Bhāva darśhan of that tour, I wished I had been closer to Amma through all these past years. It seems silly for a thirteen-year-old, but I felt sad that I had traveled to so few cities with my mom and didn't know many of the other kids on tour. I also strongly felt that, though I had been with Amma my entire life,

---

[56] Chēchi is the Malayāḷam word for 'older sister,' which is used both respectfully and endearingly.

perhaps I didn't appreciate the value of it. The AYUDH[57] group was singing bhajans for Amma at that time, and I felt sad not to be part of the group.

Scared that I was too young, I just told Amma in my mind that I felt bad for not being involved for these many years. Tears welled up within me. As I reached Amma, she gave me a BIG hug and pulled me back exclaiming, "Amma always remembers your song and thinks about you. What's going on? Why are you not singing with AYUDH? You should go sing with them. And sing your song!"

She gave me so many kisses and so much love and affection. I was still a little shocked. She knew my exact wish to be part of the AYUDH group. I went and sang with them, and Amma lovingly smiled from the stage. This experience instilled in me a strong desire to travel with Amma whenever possible, and also to do sēvā for AYUDH. Years later, Amma gave me the chance to help coordinate our AYUDH Americas youth summits which welcomed more than 250 youth as well as renowned speakers from all over the world to M.A. Center Chicago.

This story is a highlight of my many years with Amma. Like with so many stories, when we take a step back to think about the big picture, we realize that something as small as singing a song for Amma can be so much more. We like to think we know what is best for us, but only Amma sees the bigger picture. Would any part of me have thought, "Oh yes, singing this song for Amma would be good for me." No. Only Amma knew that. As many of our stories of meeting Amma have shown, Amma knows the big picture and her plans for us are much more than we can envision. I remember this important lesson when I feel frustrated with Amma for not saying or doing something I

57 'Amrita Yuva Dharmadhara' or 'Amma's Youth for Unity, Diversity and Humanity' – the youth wing of the Mata Amritanandamayi Math.

expect. When we reflect on how Amma pulled us to her, we find more than enough reason to have everlasting confidence that Amma is always guiding our life and holding onto us.

When I reflect on doing so many tours with Amma, I notice that after that one final time of singing my song for Amma, she never brought it up again. I did sing it a few more times, but she never commented about it to me again. Probably because as a child, I sang it with so much innocence, but as I got older my ego grew. This also made a strong point about the 'big picture' that I clearly did not understand then. I am sure all of us have had such situations with Amma. Let us be confident that we are ever hers and make her proud.

***

Amma says, "It is safer if the mother holds on to the child's hand. If it is the other way around, the child may run away unclasping the hold." May we always be like toddlers on this path, ever confident that Amma is holding onto us. But how do we do it? How do we develop such Self-confidence?

One blessing of growing up in Amma's arms is the incredibly strong conviction that Amma is ours. When I was around five years old, another little friend I grew up with told me she had a secret. She said whenever we feel like it, we can stand right behind Amma and give her a massage. This became my favorite thing to do. One day Swāmījī told me I should take a little break from the arduous massage I was giving Amma. Suddenly Amma looked back and told me to pay him no mind, as he was just jealous. I don't recommend walking up to Amma and randomly massaging her, but when we innocently embrace our inner Amma as ours, she cannot help but keep us close.

One example that has struck me is how she encourages all of her children to perform their dharma (duty in life). She showed me the value of Self-confidence in school. Growing up with Amma, we all knew school was always *top* priority. The one year I took off from school between college and medical school, Amma asked me almost every time she saw me, "*Vacation kiṭṭiyō?*" (Did you get vacation?). Or if I didn't have class, "*Class illē?*" even though I had already informed Amma. I started to wonder if Amma didn't want me there because I should instead be studying to make her happy?! It makes Amma so happy to see her children study and work to empower themselves to help the world.

Studying became my connection to Amma when I couldn't be around her physically. Every year, I tried my best in school and would come and tell Amma all of my grades and any accomplishments I had achieved – solely due to her grace. She would carefully listen and excitedly tell others. This became my offering to her. While performing my duty, I constantly thought about how happy Amma would be when I told her my latest news. My focus on informing Amma, followed by her excitement and unwavering support throughout the years was my source of Self-confidence. Even when I failed, I knew Amma had confidence in me so I could put it in perspective. I told myself that this happened to make me stronger and more focused or else I might have gotten lazy. I didn't take it personally. I looked at it as an opportunity to grow.

Amma gave me many opportunities to learn this, too. During my medical school interviews, I stayed in Amritapuri for some time. I wasn't receiving any responses from medical schools, even though others around me were. I was so stressed that I couldn't sleep at night (which helped me wake up for morning archana). I constantly thought about whether Amma's plan for me would be put into motion. I really began questioning myself.

Although Amma gives us the opportunity to come to her with all of our problems, I always question whether I should go tell Amma something; but this time the stress was eating at me. I went for darśhan and told Amma about the situation. Amma lovingly cuddled me like a little child, and asked, "What are you stressed about? You are Amma's daughter."

I will never forget these words. Though simple, we should always hold onto this conviction. Amma constantly flows towards us. We have to open our hearts and receive her. With Amma's grace, I not only received interviews, but I also received a scholarship. The scholarship came out of the blue. The dean of admissions told me he had a 'certain feeling' about me during the interview. Only I could know who caused that feeling. It was my Amma. My best friend.

When I gave my kaimaṇi (hand cymbals) for Amma's blessings as a teenager, she said, "If you play with enthusiasm and with a smile on your face, I will always see you." This attitude can be brought into every action we perform. We can do everything with a smile and happily tell Amma.

Just as I excitedly told Amma every step along the way of my schooling, I pray that I can do this with every action. I imagine running to Amma and saying:

> *"Amma... guess what?!?! I did my archana this morning. I was ever immersed in your form, and I prayed that the whole world felt such peace!!*
>
> *Amma... today one of my patients was feeling so lonely. I sat with her and held her as she cried. I gave her as much love as I could and counseled her to be strong. Amma, you would have been there holding her too.*

Amma... though this person hurt me, I was able to realize that they too were suffering and had their own perspective and are your child. I forgave them, forgot, and moved forward."

These are the things Amma wants to hear from us. If we open our hearts to her, we will not only feel more confident, we will transform our faith in Amma to serve in this world as her instruments.

- Self-confidence means not hurting others.
- Self-confidence means seeing things as they are and not getting affected by the world.
- Self-confidence is not about what others think of me and their acceptance. It is about what I think of myself and the trust I have in me.
- Self-confidence means always focusing on Amma.
- Self-confidence means transforming that focus into compassionate acts that wholeheartedly serve society.

With confidence in our most beloved Amma, every action we do will become pūjā, and all that we receive will become prasād. No need to worry or stress. Amma is always watching over our actions, and the more we confidently act as her children by performing compassionate acts, the closer we get to merging in her infinite love and compassion.

Amma wants us to be strong. She says:

> "Through spiritual thoughts, we cultivate inner strength and a strong mind. God represents all good qualities such as self-sacrifice, love, and compassion. Faith will allow the Satguru's (true Guru's) constant flow of grace to reach you. Mother is more than this body. She is all-pervading and omnipresent. Have faith that Mother's Self and your Self are one."

I pray that we all focus on Amma and make her proud of our every thought, word, and deed. I pray that confidence in our Self allows us to emerge victoriously as instruments in Amma's hands. I pray that such an attitude never allows us to stray from the path.

14

Amma Is My Shade Tree

Navaneet – Belgium

I met Amma in Belgium in 1995 when I was nine years old. My only memory from that time is running to sit on the stage by Amma for meditation. My first real memories are from a few years later when I started doing sēvā. I spent hours working for the Indian snack shop and yelling, "Chai Chai Chai! Onion Bhajji! Laddu!" to the people waiting in line for Dēvī Bhāva tokens. I was very energetic and enthusiastic and sometimes my supervisor would scold me when that excitement messed with my śhraddhā (attentiveness). For example, I would absentmindedly stick the greasy serving tongs right in my supervisor's face, as I gesticulated while giving someone directions. My supervisor thinks he was a strict teacher, but mostly he taught me by his example. He made everyone laugh and had a smile for every customer, no matter what was happening or how long his shift had been. People's faces would light up when they came to the snack shop. I still try to emulate his behavior when doing my sēvā to this day.

In those days, I floated from sēvā to sēvā. When the snack shop closed, I went to the GreenFriends[58] table. When they suggested I go see Amma, I would go to veggie chopping or pot washing instead. I was a small child so I must have looked pretty funny washing pots twice my size. Once all the kitchen work was done, I would go back to the snack shop and start the entire

[58] An international environmental initiative launched by M.A. Math in 2001 to promote environmental awareness and to inspire people to take up activities that protect and conserve nature.

cycle over again. I love doing sēvā, but truthfully in those days I kept busy partly because I was struggling emotionally and it was hard for me to connect with Amma.

In my teenage years I was bullied at school and was really depressed and even suicidal. Amma's Europe Tour was one of the few times a year that I felt safe and could be myself. The love and friendship I received from Amma's tour staff, as well as from the local staff; the hot chai Swāmī Rāmakṛiṣhṇānandajī gave me to warm me up after a cold night of pot washing; the food one of the kitchen coordinators would give me because I was too busy to eat at mealtimes — all these things and more sustained me. They made me feel that maybe the bullying was not my fault and people could actually like me. Amma says: "God doesn't have any hands or feet of his own. He works through us, through our eyes, ears, and hands." Even though I was unable to connect to Amma then, she kept me close by surrounding me with loving people.

Then one day, I think Amma decided it was time for me to come back home to her. Generally I was not interested in darśhan, only sēvā. But I would always go for darśhan on Dēvī Bhāva. Once, I sat in the back of the darśhan line and for some reason that's beyond me, while watching Amma give darśhan, I just started crying. Tears were running down my face. I did not know why, but I couldn't stop crying. I got to the stage, and someone gave me a tissue to wipe my face. Then, as I got closer and closer to Amma, various people gave me tissues to wipe my face, but to no avail. When I got right up to Amma, my face was again drenched.

Just before my darśhan, someone gave me a big flower mālā (garland) to offer to Amma. I put the mālā around Amma's neck and knelt down. She tenderly wiped the fresh tears off my face and hugged me tightly. Something inside me shifted with this darśhan. I continued my sēvā, and I still wasn't completely sure about what to think of Amma, but I knew there was more to her than my eyes could see. I started looking forward to darśhan. As I started to pay more attention to Amma, slowly my relationship with Amma evolved.

Besides all the kitchen sēvā, I began helping with darśhan sēvā on the stage. A new position was created for guiding people's hands to grasp the arms of Amma's chair so they would not instead grab on to Amma during their darśhan. My first shift went very well. I would gently place people's hands on the arm of Amma's chair before their darśhan even started. Amma was in a joyful mood and Amma's darśhan attendant was leaning on my shoulder and translating Amma's jokes for me.

I felt great! I was really good at this sēvā! I was helping to protect Amma! My ego was getting big boosts! The next day, I was told men should only be on Amma's left side, so I was moved to that side. I quickly realized this side was a lot harder. People had flowers or photos or gifts for Amma in their right hand, so I wasn't able to position their hand correctly before their darśhan started. As a consequence, people started holding on to Amma with their right arm; but it was my job to protect Amma!

As I mentioned before, I was a very energetic and enthusiastic child. I started pulling people's arms away from Amma and placing them on the arm of the chair. Suddenly, Amma with Kālī[59] in her eyes slapped my hand and said something in Malayāḷam. I froze with fear for what seemed like hours, but remained, unwilling to abandon my post. Finally someone tapped my shoulder to relieve me at the end of my shift, and I bolted like a rabbit being chased by a hound. Amma once said, "First I heat you up with love, and then I beat you into shape with a hammer!" Years later, when I was brave enough to try

[59] The fierce aspect of the Divine Mother.

another stage sēvā close to Amma, I always made sure not to get proud of what a good job I was doing.

My depression however continued. I realized that I could never act on my suicidal thoughts without hurting my family and making them feel guilty, so I was determined not to act on those thoughts. But the thoughts didn't go away; they just morphed into an intense desire to die. I hoped every car I saw would swerve and hit me. I imagined jumping in front of the train I took to school. Hiking in the mountains, I hoped an avalanche would crush me. I went through life living along the path of absolute least resistance. I started smoking *a lot* of cigarettes to give myself an air of self-confidence. I hoped the phony look of self-confidence from smoking would translate to real inner self-confidence, and all the while I kept hoping for death to come and find me.

***

I finished high school, got a bachelor's degree, and started working. But none of it was for joy, or to ensure my future. I was just waiting for death. In 2012 I finally decided that if death meant to take me young, surely it would have done so already, and if I was going to have to continue living, I didn't want to do it with these constant thoughts of death.

I decided to ask Amma for help. I went to Swāmī Śhubāmṛitānandajī, asking if he could help me get a question to Amma. He instructed me to keep it short — write down two or three sentences maximum, as Amma was very busy. Once I started writing I filled a whole page. I tried to cut it down but got stuck. Every sentence felt important for providing the full context. I ended with, 'Please Amma, I don't want to live, but if I have to live, I want to *want* to live.'

When he saw this long letter, Swāmī Śhubāmṛitānandajī shook his head and said, "Didn't I tell you to keep it short?" I implored him to at least read it. After reading the letter, he became a lot more serious and told me to get in the question line. When I reached Amma, Big Swāmījī translated my letter. The whole time, Amma was rubbing my chest and caressing my face and I was crying. Once the full letter was read, Amma told me two things:

"Go to therapy; this will help you. And come to Amritapuri. This will also help you."

As I left the stage, I was committed to following both pieces of Amma's advice, and I suddenly realized that Amma had already answered my prayer. My thoughts of suicide and death had disappeared. It felt as if Amma had physically cut the neural connections that triggered those thoughts.

I remember Amma saying that she is like a tree in the middle of the desert and all we have to do is choose to step into her shade. That day, I took full advantage of her shade. My depression was not suddenly magically cured. That took many years of both therapy and spending time in Amritapuri and on Amma's Europe and U.S. tours as a volunteer staff member.

For anyone struggling with bullying, depression, and suicide, and for all those who are told that the teens or twenties are the best years of your life, I would like to say, "I also often thought things would never get better and life would always be like this." But as Amma says, "Illusion (māyā) does not mean something is not real. It means it is impermanent." This also applies to depression. Things do get better. With our sincere effort, professional help, and devotion, Amma's grace will flow, and things will get better. I tell you this now, as I wish someone had told me when I needed to hear it.

A few years later, on Amma's Europe Tour, I was having an especially hard time. Mostly, on tour I try to remember how blessed I am to travel around serving Amma like how Hanumān served Lord Rāma. But for that particular tour, I just wasn't feeling it. I felt like I was just 'doing a job,' clocking in and clocking out. When Amma called the staff for darśhan after a few stops on the tour, I got excited. Surely Amma would put me in the real tour spirit. While I was in line, I prayed, "Please Amma, put me in the real tour spirit. Surely, I deserve at least that much?" — *bad* idea. For the first time ever, Amma did not look at me during my darśhan; she was talking to someone else.

Amma never even glanced at me. Though Amma's darśhan is always a blessing, when she didn't give me the attention I was expecting, I was devastated. Over the next few days, a lot of negative thoughts came up like, "Why am I doing this, volunteering in the rain and cold? I must be crazy to do this... and not even one small smile from Amma, what's the point?" In this way, my mind tortured me while I went through the motions of my sēvā.

One night, all these thoughts came to a head. We were at Amma's āśhram in Germany, where I ran into a friend of mine who was walking to the neighboring building that served as the bathhouse. I remember that though it was quite cold, he was wearing only a towel. I started talking to him about all these thoughts: "Why am I doing this? If I want something in return, is it really sēvā? If Amma never ever looks at me again, would I still tour? And if not, if I need something from Amma in return for my sēvā, can I really honestly call it sēvā?" My friend stood there in the cold, listening patiently, until I came to my own conclusion, "Amma saved my life. She is the Divine Mother of the universe. I owe her my life. I will serve her even if she never looks at me again."

That same night I went for darśhan as it was my birthday. Remembering when someone gave me a flower mālā to give to Amma, I bought a flower mālā and garlanded Amma with it, resolving to work on my expectations and attitude. Coming off the stage from darśhan it suddenly hit me: touring with Amma was about learning and growing. Amma 'ignoring' me during my previous darśhan caused me to grow, so she had in fact granted my prayer to put me in the tour spirit...just not in the way I had imagined. We may not understand Amma's intention, and sometimes the things Amma does don't make sense to us, but ultimately, each and every one of Amma's actions is for our benefit, whether we can see it or not.

***

For many years, I had heard many beautiful stories about how people got their name from Amma; how she doted on them; how she discussed different name options with them; how she spent a long time looking through a book of names. So in search of my own beautiful Amma name story, every year I would ask Amma for a name. The first few times, she just laughed and pinched my cheeks. After a few years she would either say, "Later," or ignore me altogether.

Then in 2015, one of my friends came up to me and asked if I wanted to get in the name line? I had to think about this for a bit. Going into a name line didn't seem like the start of a great story, but then I realized that after nine years of asking, maybe I should stop pursuing the 'big' story, and just ask Amma when she was actually giving names. I felt that getting a name from Amma would mean a deeper commitment to her...a way of saying, "You are my Guru and my mother."

I got in the name line and waited. I had overcome my desire for a sweet story, but my second big desire was to get a

Śhiva[60] name. I'd always thought of myself as a reserved and stoic person, so thought a Śhiva name would suit me well. As I got closer to Amma, and afraid that if I got too attached to a specific name, she would send me away without one, I thought to myself, "Ok Amma, if you do not think a Śhiva name is right for me, I will accept that." Suddenly it was my turn. Amma looked at a few pieces of paper in her hands. She dismissed the first two and then handed me the third one. It said, "Navaneet." It instantly felt right. I realized once I got over all my preconceived notions, Amma was able to give me a name. An hour later, someone called for 'Navaneet' from across the hotel kitchen and I instantly responded. There was no need for an adjustment period.

Not six months after giving me my name, Amma tested me to make a deeper commitment. I had built myself up as the tour 'smoker guy,' and used that image to protect myself and to appear strong. One day after a very late night of running snacks for the snack shop, I walked into the staff room. As I was pouring a cup of fresh coffee, another one of Amma's children said, "Oh, you are one of those people that need coffee in the morning just to wake up. Don't you think Amma would be concerned about this?" I said, "If Amma is concerned about anything, it should be the fact that I smoke two packs of cigarettes a day." I would soon find out exactly how concerned Amma was about that.

One day I was doing 'stool' sēvā, where you steady a little stool for people to sit on who are not able to kneel for darśhan. Suddenly Amma looked at me and said, "It is so dangerous for you to smoke right now. Your throat is in such a bad state

---

60 The Lord of destruction in the trinity of Brahmā (Lord of creation), Viṣhṇu (Lord of preservation), and Śhiva. He is the destroyer of ignorance.

because you smoke so much. I have known you since you were a child, and your voice is changing because you are smoking so much and your throat is in such a bad state." I was taken aback.

Amma finished hugging that person, so I moved back to the waiting position. Shortly after, another person needed the stool. During their darśhan, Amma continued, "It is so dangerous for you to smoke right now. Your mother had cancer, so it is very dangerous for you to smoke right now." I started thinking, "I always tell people I come on tour to learn and become a better person. Amma is telling me something very important about my health, completely unprompted. If I do not listen to Amma now, how can I say I go on tour to learn from Amma? I have to choose – either I go home and forget all about this tour business, or I quit smoking right now."

I handed Amma my rolling tobacco, which was always in my pocket during my stage shift. Amma's tone changed from very stern warnings to sweet pleading. "You are really going to quit now, right? You won't start again?" "No, Amma. I will really quit," I said. My mind was panicking. "How am I going to do this? I can't just quit cold turkey while on tour. How will I function?"

Then I remembered, "At least I still have my nicotine vaporizer!" The next person needing a stool came. I sat in front of Amma again, without realizing that my nicotine vaporizer was sticking out of my pocket. Suddenly, Amma's darśhan attendant took it and gave it to Amma. Amma looked at it and asked, "What is this?" "Ooooh noooo," I thought. "I can't lose this too; I really don't think I can quit cold turkey. I have to play it cool." I said, "It's something that can help you stop smoking Amma, like nicotine patches only you breathe it in." Amma said, "This is sooo bad for your throat right now," and she passed it off to an attendant sitting behind her. I don't think I could have quit if I had kept that vaporizer.

Some years later, remembering Amma's focus on my throat, I decided to ask my doctor if I should get tests on my throat and lungs. Together we calculated my 'pack years,' meaning how many packs per day times 365, times the number of years I smoked. I smoked two packs of unfiltered, self-rolled cigarettes every day for fourteen years. Based on this, my doctor concluded that if I had continued to smoke for just another three to four months, I would have been in a high-risk category for cancer. Because I had quit before that, she didn't see the need for a screening. Once more Amma saved my life. Amma says, "The Guru brings out the divine essence in the disciple." In my case, Amma coaxes this child towards better habits.

Another year, another stool sēvā shift. The person I had just helped up tripped and almost fell down. Amma shot me an angry look. Scared to get scolded as I had that time so long ago, I decided to move myself and the stool far back enough so that I would be out of Amma's direct line of sight, thinking if she couldn't see me she wouldn't scold me. Suddenly Amma leaned forward on her chair and made a beckoning motion to me. I moved forward towards Amma. "Don't try to hide from me!" she said with a big smile on her face. Still smiling Amma added, "Now don't get stressed out and start smoking again!"

I'd like to conclude with a prayer: may I never try to hide from Amma's lessons, nor forget what she has taught me. May I learn to serve truly selflessly, and always live in gratitude for all Amma has done for me.

15

It Is Amma Holding My Hands

Purnima - Germany

Amma has given me the precious gift of living in her abode. How to appreciate it properly? I have discovered several ways: to strive sincerely for the goal; to recognize māyā — the divine power that veils the truth and then lets us mistake untruth to be truth; and to respect everyone and everything.

How many times did Amma catch me just before a huge disaster was about to happen, to prove to me it is not me holding Amma's hands? It is Amma's grace that she holds my hands and doesn't let them go. To realize this, we need to be sincere. We may have many good saṁskāras and we might have acquired knowledge through our striving, but this plane of ignorance that most of us are experiencing now is not a place to stay and relax. We have to overcome it.

Even if we feel ok, we are a fraction of what we could be as beings of divine origin. Why is there so much suffering? How many human beings are exploited, starved, raped or depressed, and how many animals are tortured? Swāmī Vivēkānanda said, "If we feel the world is not right, but we are, then why should we be here?" If everything is interconnected, then we are part of it. There is a connection between our state of mind and what is happening outside.

If even the smallest trace of impurity exists in us, it will grow mountain-like if we don't pay attention to it. So, we should purify our actions and turn them towards healing. That is called karma yōga. According to the karmakāṇḍa, the ritualistic portion of the Vēdas, everything is connected to karma, even our attempts to meditate.

Once a man was meditating peacefully high in the mountains. It was very cold, so he kept a fire to warm himself. After some months of retreat, he packed his bag and left his cave to return to the valley where he lived. On the way he saw a snake half dead from the cold. Its body seemed frozen. The man, whose heart had become expansive after his long silence and meditation in the mountains, felt sorry for the animal even though he knew very well that it was poisonous. as he descended the mountain, soon it got warmer, and suddenly he felt a terrible pain in his neck. The warmth had awakened the snake, and remembering its nature it bit the man.

We usually try to make our life comfortable, even on the spiritual path, as that is our natural inclination. We may feel undisturbed by our present situation. It's like living peacefully in the mountains and meditating. However when we get challenged, our negativities show up to trouble us. That's like the moment when the snake awakens.

Here is a verse from the *Kaṭhōpaniṣhad*, where Lord Yama (the lord of death) tells Nāchikēta about the two paths available to human beings:

> *śhrēyaśhcha prēyaśhcha manuṣhyamētaḥ*
> *tau samparītya vivinakti dhīraḥ*
> *śhrēyō hi dhīrō'bhi prēyasō vṛiṇītē*
> *prēyō mandō yōgakṣhēmādvṛiṇītē*
> 'The good and the pleasant will both approach a human being.
> Discriminating between them, the wise will prefer the good.
> Whereas the fool, out of attachment to his body and mind, will prefer the pleasant.' (1.2.2)

Even if we get a taste of the 'good,' value it and get some good results, our memory easily gets scattered. The truth is veiled and twisted again because our habitual patterns drag us down. Becoming weaker and weaker, we take refuge in 'the pleasant' that are short-lived pleasures as nothing else seems available to us. Even with this golden opportunity of living near an enlightened being, māyā's intention seems to be to prevent us from rising.

It is also significant that at the end of the first section, Lord Yama tries to prevent Nāchikēta, an eight-year old child who proves himself to be firm in faith and detachment, from learning the truth. Lord Yama says:

> *ētattulyam yadi manyasē varaṁ*
> *vṛiṇīṣhva vittaṁ chirajīvikām cha*
> *mahābhūmau nachikētastvamēdhi*
> *kāmānām tvā kāmabhājam karōmi*
> 'Decide to ask for another boon equal to this one,
> be it wealth or long life, I will grant it.
> I will make you the greatest king on earth
> and I will fulfill whatever you desire, O Nachikēta.'

Why does Lord Yama not want to tell Nāchikēta the secret of life? Nāchikēta had asked him before to tell him what happens after death, which shows that he knows there is more to life than fulfillment of desires. This scene from the *Upaniṣhad* shows the knot that every seeker has to untie.

Death is our closest companion. From the moment we are born, death is our destination. Yet, we usually think it happens only to others. What do we not want to see? Maybe we wishfully imagine we won't die because we know deep down that we are in fact immortal. However, enslaved by the senses, we die again and again. Lord Yama has to test Nāchikēta because the greater the worldly pleasure, the further the separation from real freedom and real peace. In his compassion, and being a real Guru, Lord Yama wants to make sure that Nāchikēta won't fall prey to temptation.

As most of us have problems digesting pure non-dual philosophy, we should remember to approach it with devotion and childlike innocence. We should melt in love for God. We should use our imagination and cry for God, talk to him and offer everything to him. Remembering the Lord at all times helps us give equal value to each activity we do, be it work, meditation, helping someone, or cleaning the house. We will find that our beloved constantly talks to us through every situation. Devotion is like the glue that keeps the memory of our goal and how to reach it alive. Also, we become useful for service. Not everyone may want to cry for God and that's ok. But crying can help us to become soft and flexible.

A very powerful way to talk to the beloved is through bhajans. The fact that Amma sings with us every day shows how important it is. Some bhajans also present Vēdāntic truths that we can approach just through our feelings. Treating music respectfully and attentively helps us to hear the teaching. It invokes sound as the medium of connection. All we have to do is give ourselves to it. Even if we are not Indian-language speakers, we can read the simultaneous translation of the lyrics displayed on the screen and understand what we are singing. With time and Amma's grace, we will get closer to our source which the bhajans point us towards. By this sādhanā many have even awakened their ability to sing.

The same depth that can be reached while studying the *Kaṭhōpaniṣhad* can also be reached by singing bhajans. Some songs open us up as we sing God's names and glories. Some describe enchanting scenes of Kṛiṣhṇa and the gōpīs, and may inspire us to more remembrance of the divine in our daily life. When we sing about spiritual truths, they can sink deep inside us. In the Malayāḷam bhajan '*Manassoru Māyā Marīchika*' (the mind is māyā, an illusory mirage) we learn the truth about the nature of the mind. Māyā deludes us whenever we stop being attentive to her presence.

> 'The mind is an illusionary, limitless mirage. When we are unaware of the mind, it follows us like a shadow. When we are aware of it, it is merely a mirage.
>
> The mind causes sorrow, joy and thousands of experiences. We are not the objects of sensory experience, nor are we the ones who experience. The mind is merely a mirage.
>
> The mind revels while immersed in the worldly pleasures. It burns in the fire of renunciation. It is the cause of bondage yet also the straight path to freedom. Our mind is merely an illusory mirage.'

Māyā distorts our perception of the world in such a subtle manner it goes unnoticed. Once we recognize how strong māyā is, we realize how careful we need to be with every step we take, especially on the spiritual path. No matter what lifestyle we follow, we need to let go of our clinging or possessiveness to anything in this world, from material objects, to people, and even the faculties of our body and mind. This is also mentioned in the second verse of the bhajan that talks about how to surrender our grip on the objects of this world. By respecting and worshiping everything with an attitude of service we can understand and cultivate this renunciation.

***

My own story shows how Amma pointed out a way to purify myself in order to become receptive to her grace. I grew up in a small village in northern Germany. The people I knew there were atheists except for the family of my aunt whose husband was a preacher. When I was three years old, my father died while working in Africa and my mom and I had to return home. After his death, for a long time my mother became so sad that she spent most of her days in bed. She said that I was the only reason she continued to live.

When I was seven, a stepfather came into my life who started showing resentment towards me after he came to stay with us. Slowly I became aware that anger was a constant guest in our house. After some years I visited my aunt, and she told me about Jesus and gave me a 'Bible for Youths.' I started to talk with God and apologized to him for the smallest transgressions, like even when I just drank a Coca-Cola. For a while I wanted to become a nun, but then I saw the beautiful, slim girls on television. Wanting to be like them, I slipped into anorexia and severely reduced my food intake. This turned into bulimia — I ate a lot, and then vomited it all out. I became very thin.

Through excessive eating I covered up a terrible emptiness, and the vomiting took up several hours of my time each day. Due to my artificially-induced starvation, I lost a healthy relationship with food. I would get hunger attacks, couldn`t stop eating, and then vomited to make space for more. I would feel numb for some time, and in that way the sadness couldn't reach me...but then the sadness would return, and the whole cycle would repeat itself. When I was sixteen, I became suicidal. I started smoking marijuana because I wanted to have a divine experience but at the same time felt unworthy, thinking I couldn't have such an experience without the help of intoxicating substances.

It goes without saying that ganja was not the solution. Actually, I overcame bulimia because my body was exhausted and I often fainted. At the same time, my thirst for meaning had become so intense that I looked for it in everything I did. I searched for the Lord in every moment.

I didn't know about mantra or other kinds of traditional worship or about any spiritual groups. But I knew I had to remember God all the time. In 2006, Amma decided to intervene. I met Amma in Munich. The touch of motherly love, well-known but long forgotten, reached my heart. I remember the train journey back home. With a relaxed mind I could still hear the bhajans reverberating in the hum of the train engine. How I missed Amma! I had to go to her next program too, and then in 2007 I came to India.

What struck me about Amma was that she fully accepted me as I was, and I knew that she understood me. At that time, I didn't pay much attention to her teachings. I needed time to separate myself completely from my unhealthy lifestyle. In 2009 in Munich, I again went to Amma. For the first time I felt reverence, gratefulness, and an openness to listen to Amma's message. I realized that I was the one who benefitted from that reverence.

From then on, I did volunteer work and tried to give my life to society. That often seemed impossible as I was still depressed, but Amma always protected me and gave me strength. Even though I experienced most people behaving in an unfriendly manner towards me, once I understood that their behavior was triggered by my inner discomfort, I stopped reacting. I endured a lot and tried to give back love.

I studied Amma's teachings from the book *Lead us to Light* and tried to imbibe all of it. That is how Amma's divine touch slowly lifted the shadows from my heart. Amma showed me that true happiness lies in serving others. Since that revelation from Amma, I never had to undergo such mental suffering again. I am convinced that every mental imbalance can be fixed by developing the right attitude. Working on our anger and trying not to hurt others helps to save us from all kinds of fear, and even lost mental health can be regained. Also, if we learn to love others, we will never have to worry if we are loved in return.

***

In the *Bhagavad Gītā* Lord Kṛiṣhṇa describes the qualities necessary to become dear to the Lord:

> *advēṣhṭā sarvabhūtānām maitraḥ karuṇa ēva cha*
> *nirmamō nirahaṅkāraḥ samaduḥkhasukhaḥ kṣhamī*
> *santuṣhṭaḥ satatam yōgī yatātmā dṛiḍhaniśhchayaḥ*
> *mayyarpita-manobuddhiryō madbhaktaḥ sa mē priyaḥ*
> 'The one who is free from malice towards all beings, who is friendly, and compassionate, free from feelings of 'I' and 'mine,' even-minded in happiness and distress, and forgiving, ever content, steady in meditation, self-controlled, having firm resolve, and with mind and intellect dedicated to Me, that devotee is dear to me.' (12.13 – 14)

The twelfth chapter of the *Bhagavad Gītā* describes the essence of bhakti yōga (yōga of devotion). The qualities of a bhakta (devotee) begin at the level of consideration for those around them. This quality has the potential to solve all of the problems of our modern world. If we start paying attention to the qualities that exist as expressions of our essential nature (i.e. pure love), but that may be covered by our acquired nature (i.e. latent tendencies), we can break the bondage of saṁsāra — the cycle of birth and death, and attain freedom. If we cultivate the attitude of love, it will eventually become natural. Feelings of hatred, jealousy etc. are merely the result of habitual thoughts based on previous choices. Love gives us innocence, and in innocence the rays of grace can enter.

Amma says, "Love is the only solution for our problems." This doesn't mean we can ignore our thoughts. Though we cannot control our first thought, after that first thought, we can choose to shift our attention. Instead of finding fault with others and blaming them because of our own pain, we can take responsibility for whatever happens to us. This is not easy, but by it the ego crumbles.

Sometimes our mind will refuse and confuse, but in the heart sweet divine love ever flows instead. Once we have understood this, it becomes easy. Tracing our issues back inside, we regain the kingdom of our soul. When we start working for the whole, we can experience that the whole universe supports us.

When we realize the immense grace that our Guru Amma has showered on us, we will wish to give something back to the world. We will understand that we are born to be instruments of the divine. We ourselves should become the offering. As we are all unique expressions of the divine, the message each of us has to share will add beauty and color to this world in a different way.

Our ancestors all over the world and not just in India had a vision of fullness — pūrṇam. It is found in the ancient philosophies that our ancestors lived by. They knew that they were complete. They lived inside divine consciousness. They didn't ask, "Which came first, the chicken or the egg?"

Whatever anyone can think of already exists. It just becomes manifest or unmanifest. Everything has always been there. If we meditate on this, all fear must disappear because we then realize that we are never alone. We know that whatever we need is with us. We are whole. So naturally all competition, jealousy, and doership fall away. Let this be our goal. We won't achieve it overnight, but with effort we can slowly wake up. Let us embrace Sanātana Dharma, which is the truth and the heart of this universe. It is the eternal teaching of unity.

16

Sēvā — Amma's Transformative Path

Amar Gressel - USA

I grew up in a moderately observant Jewish family. We attended our synagogue (place of worship) and observed rituals and holidays. I learned all my prayers by age thirteen, the age a Jewish person becomes an adult. I led the congregation in prayer services, gave a satsang, and chanted from the Torah, the Jewish Bible. To this day, twenty-three years later, I remember by heart every single prayer I learned then. My Jewish faith provided me with a community full of love, but there was no teacher to explain the mystery of the world we live in.

My high school years were filled with an overwhelming sadness, but I did not know why. Once in the gym locker room, two boys put me in a headlock, then threatened to beat me up if I did not give them my wallet. This scared me, but surprisingly did not anger me. It saddened me. Now I understand that I was witnessing suffering; I saw confusion and anger. I saw others searching for happiness in places where they could never find it. However at that age, I didn't have the vocabulary or understanding to explain what I saw. I searched, but didn't know how to look. And frankly...I was a bit lazy.

In 2003 when I was eighteen, Amma found me; I did not search for her. First, I saw her photo in a newspaper and simply thought to myself, "She seems nice, I'd like her to bless me!" But I took no initiative. I simply went on with my life. Months passed. Then I saw her photo again, this time on a friend's desk. I took the opportunity to ask questions, then asked my friend if she could bring me to meet Amma.

By Amma's grace, in November 2003 my friend brought me to the San Ramon āśhram and I received Amma's darśhan. We arrived late at night, well after the satsang, bhajans, and meditation had ended. Amma was giving darśhan in the temple. I remember entering the darśhan line. At some point I started to cry uncontrollably with tears streaming down both cheeks. People brought me tissues from the side of the darśhan queue.

As I neared Amma, I did not want to cry. I wanted to be presentable, so I tried to pull myself together, taking deep breaths, drawing my emotions inwards...controlling myself. As Amma held me and whispered into my ear, I heard the words, "More, more, more." *Now* I know Amma was saying, "*Mōn, mōn, mōn.*"[61] But then I thought Amma was telling me, "Open your heart son, open it more, more, more." Following her instruction, I tried to open my heart, to open myself to Amma. A tear began to form in the corner of my eye, and in that *exact* moment Amma pulled back and my darśhan was over.

I was struck by Amma's incredible precision. It felt like my heart was a flower bud, and Amma knew it had just cracked open. For the moment, her work was done. Over the next four years of college, I would slowly transform from a very tāmasic[62] and lazy boy who liked to smoke, drink alcohol, and play video games as often as possible, into someone who wanted to live by Amma's teachings, with Amma. Each summer and fall, I would visit the San Ramon āśhram to be with Amma during her programs. Each time, I'd return home with a little more knowledge and desire to change. By the time I graduated university my only goal was to join Amma on her summer tour.

---

[61] 'Son' in Malayāḷam.

[62] Of the nature of 'tamas,' one of the three universal qualities (guṇas) characterized by dullness, lethargy, apathy, inertia, staleness, etc.

I had realized something very important. Other people could teach me how to be the best martial artist, to be an excellent musician, or to gain a PhD and faculty position in a prestigious university. However, only Amma could teach me how to always be happy. Somehow, ever since I graduated university in 2007, I have spent nearly all my time either on tour with Amma, living in Amritapuri, or living in the San Ramon āśhram.

The Practice of Sēvā

Amma's 2018 New York City program was held in a five-star hotel located in Times Square in Manhattan, which is perhaps the busiest place in the whole United States. Buildings tower hundreds of stories high. Each building has gigantic LED billboards attached to them that make the LED screens in the darśhan hall look like telephone screens by comparison. These LED screens advertise the sensuous pleasures of the world non-stop. It is full immersion; a barrage of unending external stimulation. Amma's darśhan was on the seventh floor of this fancy hotel, right in the middle of all that madness. All day long droves of people found their way into Amma's arms to receive her blessings.

My sēvā was to recruit volunteers to help clean dishes, chop vegetables, and serve food. I will never forget one person I met. He was tall, strong, young, and seemed to be your average young American guy. He came to see Amma because his friend had dragged him there. He didn't really have much interest in being there. He saw our sēvā-sign saying that we needed help washing pots and he decided to volunteer. He wasn't sure about the rest of the program, but he was ready to wash pots! The contrast between the front of the hotel, where the guests visit, and the back of the hotel, where the work happens, is dramatic. The guest area of the hotel is magnificent. There is beautiful carpet, polished wooden tables, expensive art hanging on the walls, and luxurious decor.

The moment you enter the 'back' of the hotel through the 'employees only' door, you are in another world. The kitchen is steel and tile. The walls are white. It smells of industrial strength cleaner mixed with burning gas, oily food, and cooked meat. It is choreographed chaos. People hurrying in all directions, zigzagging carts full of food. A sense of urgency fills the air.

The pot washing room is the lowest place in the hotel kitchen. The workers there are the least respected, lowest paid, and least cared for. The room is often wet and slippery and without air conditioning. The moment you step into that room, you realize that you will not leave dry. You put on an apron and gloves, then stand mostly alone or sometimes with other hotel workers, and you start scrubbing, cleaning one dirty vessel after another.

This man seemed totally fine just washing pots. I left him with our tour staff without thinking much of it. Hours later near the end of my sēvā shift, he emerged from the kitchen looking totally different. He was beaming. Where before he seemed lost, restless, and confused, now he was full of light with a glowing smile.

The next day was Dēvī Bhāva, and he returned for the program. Again, he did another long shift in the pot washing room. Afterwards, I encouraged him to get a seat for the pūjā and Amma's satsang. He obliged and waited in the queue for hours to get a spot in the hall.

The ballroom was completely packed during the ātmā pūjā.[63] I had a seat at the sēvā desk outside the hall. Suddenly, in the

---

[63] Ceremonial worship (pūjā) created by Amma honoring our true Self, the ātman.

middle of the satsang, here came my friend. He simply said, "Listen, I'm just not really into this stuff. It's fine, whatever. I'm sure it's good. Amma is wonderful. But can I please just wash some more pots?" I was flabbergasted. "Are you sure?" I asked. "Yes, please. It's what I really want to do."

Now, I ask you...what causes someone to only want to wash pots in the basement of a fancy hotel in the middle of Times Square? For no pay? From the materialistic world-of-duality perspective, this is insanity! Yet, I completely understood him. Personally, I have had the same experience doing sēvā. My first moments of lasting happiness and peace near Amma came *only* when I began to do sēvā.

The Joy of Sēvā

Why does sēvā cause lasting happiness? In the *Bhagavad Gītā*, Chapter 3, verse 10 Lord Kṛiṣhṇa says:

> 'In the beginning of creation, Brahmā created humankind along with yajña (sacrifices), and said, 'Become prosperous by performing these yajñas, for they shall fulfill all of your wishes."

Lord Kṛiṣhṇa tells us that humankind was created together with yajña, meaning actions performed considering the needs of others over one's own. Kṛiṣhṇa further explains that it is through selfless service that all our desires will be granted. This is a statement about the true nature of life; the way we were intended to live. Amma says:

> "In nature, every animal and being lives in constant sacrifice and harmony. All of nature lives according to this inherent divine nature — to live in service to the world. The bees and ants live in service to the world.

> It is only we humans, blinded by our ego, who live selfishly always taking more than we give."

When we look beyond our egoistic likes and dislikes and evolve as humans by living for a purpose higher than ourselves, we begin to experience a more permanent happiness. By doing sēvā, we begin to see ourselves in others, and this expansion of our mind and heart also purifies all the mental garbage we have accumulated over many lifetimes.

As Amma says, "We are born, live and die searching for love." To reach a spiritual master like Amma, you most likely have a strong desire to understand this transient world of pain and suffering, and a desire to find lasting happiness. With this desire in our hearts we do sēvā, and suddenly we are filled with a truer experience of happiness. In the *Bhagavad Gītā*, Chapter 3, verse 19 Lord Kṛiṣhṇa says:

> 'Therefore, remaining unattached, always do what should be done; for by performing actions without attachment man certainly attains the Supreme.'

The moment you become attached to the fruit of your action, whether it's your job, sēvā, or hobby, you invite suffering into your life. Recently we conducted an enormous rice packing sēvā. When I was simply chanting my mantra and trying to be present in the moment, it was wonderful. The moment I began to think, "How many more bags? How much longer will this go? Why is he packing it that way? It would be much better if he did it *this* way" — all my peace and happiness evaporated. Then I would remind myself, "Your duty is to be here and do your part. You aren't responsible for any of this," it would immediately become a joyful experience again. Whenever we dedicate our actions without attachment to a purpose higher than ourselves, we are doing sēvā.

One of my first sēvā experiences was washing dishes at night in San Ramon. The cleaning supervisor asked if I could help clean the cooking area with a large push broom. I said, "Sure." After twenty minutes I felt frustrated. I thought, "I'm sweeping this whole kitchen alone! This will take forever. I'm not a slave! I'm not getting *paid* to do this." My frustration built for probably five minutes, and then I gave up.

I told the supervisor, "Hey, sorry but I'm done, I need to go now." I braced myself for a negative response since I clearly had not finished sweeping. I will never forget her response, "Ok! Thanks so much for all your effort and sēvā. Have a great night!" She said this with a beaming smile and twinkling eyes. I was free. I stepped into the gravel parking lot under the night stars. Free at last! Yet now I felt empty and sad..."I could do more." As soon as I recognized I was not being *made* to do the work, I realized I would not mind doing more.

That moment has stuck in my mind because I understood for the first time that sēvā is voluntary. We are not obligated. It is an offering from us to the world. Further, it wasn't my 'job.' It was simply what I could offer then. When we are not required to do something, then the burden of 'how will I get this done?' is lifted. I didn't have to clean the whole kitchen. Whatever I offered was enough. Suddenly I had the energy to do more.

Now you may think, "Sure, that's true when you sign up for just a random shift at a program. What about when you are the coordinator? What about when your duty is as sēvā coordinator?" The answer is the same. It isn't on your shoulders. It rests on Amma's shoulders! There is a famous saying: 'The graveyard is full of people who could not be replaced.' The same is true for sēvā. Except for Amma, everyone in this entire āśhram could be replaced tomorrow. Your duty is only to the action, not the results. The creed of sēvā is, 'Do your best and God will manage the rest.' However, the action of sēvā alone is not enough. We must also do our sēvā with the correct attitude.

On Sēvā Attitude

The ninth verse of the *Īśhāvāsya Upaniṣhad* says:

> 'They who worship avidyā alone fall into blinding darkness; and they who worship vidyā alone fall as though into even greater darkness.'

According to the accepted commentary by Ādi Śhaṅkarāchārya, avidyā here means karma (action) and vidyā means spiritual knowledge and meditation. My understanding of this śhlōka is that pursuing only actions without spiritual knowledge, even if done with the attitude of selflessness, leads to darkness and conversely, pursuing spiritual knowledge without selfless action leads to even deeper darkness. Both are needed to achieve the goal; one without the other will lead to failure.

Let me tell a story about action not grounded in knowledge. On the 2007 Europe tour, my sēvā was pot washing in the Indian kitchen which was a tent attached to the side of a truck. The Munich program was extremely cold as it snowed the entire day. Everything felt like slow motion. Every pot was more difficult to wash. We wore knee-high rubber boots that were excellent at keeping our feet dry. However, they had no insulation, which meant our feet quickly grew very cold. Our toes were so numb we couldn't feel them. We would stomp around trying to warm up our feet.

The cooks would bring large pots to clean, and sometimes, if we were lucky, one would be full of very hot water left over from boiling potatoes. Our job was to empty the pot and clean it. These pots were not as big as āśhram pots that you can stand in, but they were big enough to sit on the edge and immerse our waterproof boots with our numb toes in the nearly boiling water! It was a perfect foot warmer. Our cold feet would get warm, and we could feel our toes again. This went on throughout the day.

At some point Swāmī Śhubhāmṛitānandajī visited all the sections in the kitchen, offering kind words of support. He looked shocked when he saw our foot warming break. We happily explained our strategy and he shook his head in wonder. Later that night, when we finished the final cleaning of the kitchen and closed up, I discovered that Amma had just left the hall. I was crushed because it had been such a long day, and I had spent so much energy facing the bitter cold. I was completely exhausted, and wanted nothing more than to sit in a chair in the warm hall and gaze at Amma giving darśhan.

Instead, I got to watch Amma's car drive by the kitchen as I locked the doors. What could I look forward to now? A floor where my sleeping bag lay. Then I would wake up in the morning and face more pots. I looked around the kitchen and I began to think, "I spent all day cleaning this place. Why? So people could stuff their faces with samosas and dosas and indulge their vāsanās! My bones are weary; my feet are numb. I can barely stand. For what? One more samosa. What is the point?" My mind was going on and on. I was miserable. In retrospect, it's clear to me now. Due to my ego, I had pushed myself too hard to prove to myself and others that I was a hard worker capable of superhuman efforts.

I did not take proper breaks or ask for help or even eat properly. Still, immersed in that entirely miserable mindset, Amma, the real superhuman, lifted me up. At that moment, Swāmī Śhubhāmṛitānandajī came walking by the kitchen and stopped me. He said, "I told Amma how you were all washing the pots in the cold, and how you were sitting on the edge of the pots to warm your feet in hot potato water." I stopped.

"What did Amma say?" Swāmī Śhubhāmṛitānandajī looked at me carefully and said, "Her eyes filled with compassion, and she said, 'My children are suffering so much for me.'"

Amma said I was suffering for her?! This shocked me and melted my heart. All my frustration and anger vanished. Hearing those words, I remembered why I was there in that kitchen. It wasn't to clean pots for others. It was to purify myself. Through Amma's compassionate words I immediately found enthusiasm to continue my sēvā with excitement and happiness. I understood I should not do sēvā for others' approval, admiration, or my own pride, but as an offering to the divine.

Who benefits from sēvā? Does Amma benefit? No. That would be like a candle offering light to the sun. Do the people who eat the food benefit from my sēvā? The cooks who need the clean vessels? Yes, in some mundane sense they do, but not compared to the benefit I receive. The one who does the sēvā is the one who benefits first and foremost from it. Action without knowledge leads to darkness. In egotistically attempting to prove to everyone that I was a super-duper worker, I did not understand what I was doing. I exhausted myself and was miserable. When I understood *why* I was doing sēvā, my entire experience transformed from the 'blinding darkness' I had fallen into, to light.

A Final Anecdote

On the 2008 U.S. Tour in Albuquerque, I was mopping the floor after Amma's prasād meal during the retreat. Again, I was in a horrible mood. (You'd think I'd have learned my lesson in this matter, but I'm a slow learner.) That kitchen was directly next to the darśhan hall. You could hear Amma's bhajans in the kitchen. I was mopping the hallway thinking, "Everyone ran off to bhajans. We had fifty people cleaning, and not one realized we still had to mop the hallway. Now I'm mopping here alone.

Why? Because I'm the only responsible one. I can't just leave it and maybe come back later. The hotel employees will think, 'Amma's people don't know how to clean up after themselves.'"

In my bitterness, I continued to savage the floor with the mop. I thought, "I have to mop it alone. I always get stuck with it. I'm the only responsible one. Everyone is enjoying bhajans but me..." and on and on.

Then a miracle happened.

Suddenly, like the snap of a finger, or a clap of thunder, or the clouds parting, I had this thought, "Amar, thinking these thoughts doesn't make them true. This mental loop in your brain doesn't accurately describe the reality that exists outside of yourself. You are choosing to think like this and make it your reality. You are embracing this pain." This hit me like a thunderbolt. Tears streamed down my face. For the first time I realized that thoughts aren't reality. My thoughts are creating an illusory reality.

So I created a different reality thinking, "Amma, thank you so much for giving me this sēvā and for allowing me to notice that we had forgotten to mop the floor. By your grace I didn't fail in my duty to clean the kitchen properly before leaving. By your grace I have this chance to do sēvā. In fact, if I went into the hall right now, I would likely fall asleep because I am so tired. This way I can do sēvā and listen to your bhajans. I am so lucky."

At that moment, I saw the fraud of my mind and I could control it. It wasn't a game. I wasn't 'faking it until I make it,' pretending to have good thoughts in order to suppress negative ones. For the next ten minutes while I mopped the floor, I was able to control my mind. I felt free, joyful, and feather-light thinking good thoughts while happily mopping a floor — something I sincerely enjoyed!

Amma has always been able to sculpt me through sēvā and teach me to change and improve. I feel incredibly blessed and grateful for all the opportunities to live in Amma's āśhrams and do sēvā in her institutions. I can only bow down in gratitude.

17
Seeds of Wisdom

Madhurima - Austria

Many of these satsangs have made me laugh, and many have moved me to tears. One of them made me firmly decide to join the āśhram as a renunciate. Another encouraged me to plant some mango trees. Another satsang inspired me to be more careful and alert when cutting a new roll of fabric for Covid hospital suits. What I want to say is that all these satsangs have an impact when we hear the glory of Amma, the power of living in Amritapuri, and all of these touching first-hand experiences.

There is only One

Amma normally begins by mentioning the highest truth. When she addresses an audience, she begins with, "Amma bows down to all of you, whose true nature is pure love and supreme consciousness." Afterwards she explains in more detail and illustrates these points with many stories.

In Chapter 10, verse 20 of the *Bhagavad Gītā,* Lord Kṛiṣhṇa says:

> *aham ātmā guḍākēśha sarvabhūtāśhayasthitaḥ*
> *ahamādiśhcha madhyaṁ cha bhūtānām anta ēva cha*
> 'I am the Self, O Guḍākēśha, abiding in the hearts of all beings.
> I am the beginning, the middle, and the end of all beings.'

All creatures are his divine body only. Lord Kṛiṣhṇa addresses Arjuna as "Guḍākēśha" — the one who has conquered sleep.

This is the 'sleep' of ignorance. On a deeper level, it can mean that Arjuna has reached a level of awareness necessary for receiving the greatest gift we can receive from our master: the knowledge of our own true nature. As Amma says, "Creation and creator are not two. Dance and dancer cannot be separate from each other."

Amma often mentions that it is difficult to wake up those who pretend to be asleep. Intellectually we know the truth, but we are not willing to practice it. Amma can place food in our mouths, but she cannot chew it for us. Generally, we listen to Amma's instructions and then bend them to fit our capacity to follow them. We cling to the belief that we are our limitations. It is a long journey from this state of 'sleep' to waking up to our real nature. I once heard Amma say, "Many people are slow, but most are very very slow."

Waking up is a long process that we could call a yōga practice. It's an attempt to step out of our idea of being a limited being, and towards the higher consciousness of our true existence — to awaken to the awareness of our oneness with the whole of creation.

***

I grew up in a very beautiful rural village in Austria, 200 km from our capital, Vienna. My father was a forestry manager, hunter, and fisherman. Therefore I can say I grew up as a modern Austrian forest dweller! At the age of nine I was entrusted with an air gun to train my shooting skills and to hunt sparrows sleeping in the grain storage. At the age of eleven, compassion began to grow within me and I soon abandoned this kind of activity.

Family life with a husband and children was always unthinkable for me. At the age of twenty I found an ideological home in the women's movement where I found unconventionally brave role models. One of them inspired me to learn cabinet making. With a battery drill, a Japanese saw, and a hammer, I began a multi-faceted career as a carpenter.

About faith

Even as a child I daydreamed of India, and it was always my favorite country. I imagined it to be surrounded by a magical aura. When I was twenty-two I met a psychologist and astrologer who prescribed books by well-known, Indian spiritual teachers to 'treat' my many negative thoughts. Through these books I discovered the sages from the East. One teacher greatly attracted me. I hardly understood his teachings but I loved his books very much. I was absolutely fascinated by his life story. However, one day I heard someone speaking badly about him and his lifestyle, and I believed this malicious gossip. Thus, my love for him ended. My heart was filled with sadness when I thought that I would never meet a living master.

We can have a peaceful and harmonious relationship with something or someone until our trust is tested and shaken. A few windy words blowing across our path are often enough to shatter our ideals. This is illustrated by the famous Purāṇic story of the churning of the ocean of milk which produced gems and other treasures, as well as the deadly poison 'Halāhala,' which Lord Śhiva swallowed to protect all beings, causing his throat to turn blue. Our minds can be like this ocean, revealing incredible wealth as well as poison. Churning agitates and releases the poison. We cannot swallow it, so it sits in our throat waiting to be spat out as toxic words. Only when we develop the qualities of Lord Śhiva can we begin to control our speech. Words can be a highly potent treasure, even medicinal. Words can also be a most potent poison and weapon.

Amma please bless us with perfect awareness of our speech. In one of the last room darśhans Amma held during the Covid pandemic, Amma said, "Negative words have great power. They work on the gross material level." She mentioned that when we hear from a doctor that we might have cancer, it can have a serious impact on our health. We tend to take negative statements very seriously. They settle into our judgment and multiply quickly like a virus.

Amma says, "Doubt is your number one enemy; faith is your best friend." My journey to Amma was not straightforward but it was certainly guided by Amma. At the age of forty, I found a spiritual home with the shamans. With sacred plants and mushrooms I came closer to the soul world than ever before. I experienced that everything was alive. This touched me deeply and widened my heart, and I wanted this path for myself and others. I dedicated holidays and weekends to exploring this fascinating world.

Then, one Sunday I came across a YouTube link: 'Amma is Embracing the World.' I wanted to find out which 'Amma' was about to 'embrace the entire world.' The first thought that came to my mind was, "If what I see here is true, then my life will change completely." An invisible dam broke, and streams of tears poured down my face. This happened in the spring of 2009.

She attracts the whole of creation

Amma had finally found me with the help of a YouTube link. Now it was up to me to seek her out. On November 1st, 2009, I traveled to Munich, Germany for the Dēvī Bhāva program. I had no idea what to expect but everything was perfectly directed by Amma. Even the fact that I came on the third day of Amma's visit..

That day was filled with auspicious messages. I joined the long token queue in front of the hall. It was 'All Saints' Day,' the Christian day dedicated to holy beings. This was already a promising omen. An incredibly huge swarm of swallows flew circles over the hall. This was another omen. The time spent waiting for darśhan passed quickly. The program was remarkable. It felt like I met many long-missed brothers and sisters. Apart from this, everything was strange to me. Amma ensured with dramatic orchestration that I did not leave the hall without a mantra. There was no logical explanation, but I could not stop the flow of tears.

> *ōm sauśhīlyādi guṇākṛiṣhṭa jaṅgama sthāvarālayē namaḥ*
> 'I bow down to her who attracts the whole creation by her noble qualities.'
>
> *108 Names of Amma, 28*

This mantra from the 108 names of Amma reminds me of this most special day of my life. Sliding from chair to chair in the mantra queue, I noticed Amma gazing at me. When our eyes finally met, I felt as if Amma knew all that could be known about me, and our bond had been built over infinite lifetimes in an infinite number of worlds. I am one of the 'countless people who were able to quit drinking alcohol and smoking since receiving Amma's darśhan for the first time.'

Giving water to the roots

Two years later, again in Munich, many questions were on my mind. How could I manage to spend more time or even the rest of my life with Amma? What about my job? Was it right to give it up? Can I do that? Was it following my dharma? My sēvā during the program limited my free time, so unfortunately I wasn't able to get a token for the question line. Following Amma all over Europe, hoping for another chance to ask Amma, was also not an option at all.

Towards the end of the Dēvī Bhāva program, I was standing in line for darśhan. As I moved from chair to chair, I developed some plans to ensure that Amma somehow answers my main questions:

Plan A: During all my darśhans, Amma had always whispered exactly three times in my ear, "*Meine Liebe, meine Liebe, meine Liebe*" ('my darling' in German). This time, if she says it an even number of times, and more than three times, for example four or six times, this would mean: "Yes, you can quit your job and YES, you can come to Amritapuri." After a few moments of introspection, I had a doubt. "Was I really able to decide something so serious just depending on Amma's darśhan, without asking her verbally?" NO. Something more must happen.

Plan B: Amma should give me an apple! That would definitely be a clear sign, wouldn't it? Or even better...

Plan C: Please Amma, tell me somehow, "I am your *baby*," then I can go on my journey to Amritapuri — the city of eternal bliss, with a clear conscience.

Finally, I had darśhan. Amma certainly said "My darling" more than three times. It felt like six times, but I could not say with confidence how many times Amma whispered this mantra into my ear. She did not hand me an apple. Nor did Amma whisper anything about a baby. I feared that all my questions would remain unanswered.

Then Dēvī Bhāva was almost over. Suddenly and unexpectedly, I was given the incredibly special sēvā of bringing the remaining fruit that Amma gives to people during darśhan to the stage for Amma's blessing. I brought up two full baskets of apples. This allowed me to watch Amma give darśhan for a long time. Finally the fruit I was carrying received Amma's blessing, and Amma also stuffed a jelly candy into my mouth.

It took several hours before I realized that through this experience, Amma had answered my questions — it was Amma's blessing, Amma's "yes." All the elements from my plans A, B, and C were satisfied during darśhan, giving me my answer:

1. Plan A was satisfied by the number of mantras she whispered in my ear.
2. Plan B was satisfied by the two full baskets of apples I first gave to Amma to bless, and that she returned to me.
3. Plan C — the "you are my baby" message was satisfied as the jelly candy Amma fed me is usually reserved for small babies only!

Grace alone

After so many hours of sēvā and all the excitement, it was clear to me that there was no way I would be able to drive a car. However, a friend who came with me felt awake enough to take us home to Austria, about three hours away. Tired but bathed in bliss, I contemplated what Amma had told me in those beautiful, subtle ways. Like this, I fell asleep while my friend was driving. Not long after, there was a terrible noise as the car crashed into a crash barrier. My friend had fallen asleep too!

After this, all that followed was a fascinating and incredible sequence of grace alone. It was a busy time on the highway, around 11:00 a.m. in the morning. But miraculously, at the moment the accident happened there were no cars near us. There was also an emergency lane. An emergency or breakdown lane is a paved shoulder alongside the roadway reserved for vehicles to exit onto in case of an emergency. This is a real rarity on these highways. This is where the car came to a halt, safely out of the way of any traffic, however the car was totally wrecked.

We sat in the car in shock and silent amazement. We were unharmed. After fifteen minutes an ambulance showed up.

They asked us if we were all right. Within another fifteen minutes a patrol car stopped by. Two extremely friendly police officers asked us about the accident for which we only received a warning. In Germany, falling asleep while driving is a serious traffic offense. The police arranged for the car to be towed.

It was evening before we reached a car repair shop, and it was on a Sunday. To our surprise an employee was there, so we were able to turn the damaged car over to them. This may not be remarkable in India, but it certainly is for Austria, where normally car repair shops are supposed to be closed. The car was well-insured. As a result, the insurance company gave me the same money for the completely wrecked car as I would have received had I sold it. This was such a relief since I really had been thinking about selling the car for quite some time.

Finally, even after months no bill ever came from the government for the damaged crash barrier. The following six months were just as exciting. Amma was the charioteer of events. Amma took the reins firmly in her magic hands for all the next steps. Everything was seamlessly guided and managed so that in 2011, I finally arrived in Amritapuri without any obstacles blocking my desire to live there.

Surprises

The sēvā-information board at Amritapuri regularly posts requests for help in the carpentry department. Though I had several years of professional experience in carpentry work, I used to regularly ignore this posted request. However, Amma was about to catch two flies in the blink of an eye, as we would say in Austria.

First: she took the opportunity to teach me about my own preconceptions. The contact person's name was 'Sulma.' I ignored the posting because I assumed Sulma was a guy.

Second: Amma used this sēvā to give me a position in Amritapuri that was meaningful for me.

In February 2013 I eventually had a surprise encounter with Sulma. Someone whispered in my ear, "This is a VIP, she's a carpenter," As if stung by a tarantula, I jumped after her and introduced myself. Sulma was excited, and she can be quite infectious with her enthusiasm. She invited me to interview for a position in the carpentry training program for the 'Women's Empowerment Project' at Ammachi Labs[64]. After the interview I was overjoyed. It felt fantastic to be able to work on such a project.

But that day held one more surprise for me. Two hours after my interview, I found out that my brother Wolfgang in Austria was about to die. I was shaken by the news. Before lunch I was floating in heaven from the interview. In the evening, I had to deal with the question of staying in the āśhram or going back to be with my brother. That same evening I took part in a pūjā for my brother. However by then, Wolfgang's eyes had already closed forever. It had been less than two months since I had moved my life into the āśhram.

Questions tormented my mind: "Do I really have to go home to my family? Is that my responsibility now? Do I have to support my mother? She had already lost her husband and now her son...and her daughter (me) was far away. How could I tell Amma?" (Amma was on tour somewhere in India.) The next day I received a call from my mother in Austria. Her first sentence was, "You don't need to come home." This phone call was my answer.

---

[64] AMMACHI Labs is an academic and research center at Amrita Vishwa Vidyapeetham that brings an interdisciplinary approach to addressing societal challenges. AMMACHI Labs creates innovative educational tools and skill development solutions to help uplift entire communities, especially women and girls in rural villages in India.

Also, I now had a good reason to stay in the āśhram because of that very special sēvā project that came to me out of thin air right before I heard the news about my brother. My mother visited me some years later in Amritapuri together with my brother Wolfgang's son, and she also came once to Switzerland and received Amma's darśhan there. Since her visit to Amritapuri, I feel many doubts she had about my way of life have disappeared.

We have heard countless stories about how Amma's grace becomes so visible. Events happen like lightning strikes. On one hand, a turn for the better, and on the other hand, with completely unexpected results that are mostly beyond what we had imagined. Amma creates incredibly special moments for everyone. Once we have met our Guru, we begin to experience the meaning of 'I am the Self, seated in the hearts of all creatures.' — what a great gift.

We have heard it many times, but I want to repeat it: it is an incredible gift to obtain a human body. It is said that only in a human body do we have the faculties needed for the realization of our true nature.

Not only that, we have the invaluable wealth of being guided and protected by the Divine Mother herself in human form. If we look at the rarity and the preciousness of this extraordinary gift, we can arrive at the following conclusion: all celestial beings, like the earth, the moon and the sun, are part of our larger body. All visible and invisible elements, objects and beings, like water, light, air, and space, are inseparable from our existence. Each and every single one of us is woven from these cosmic threads, from the greatest to the subtlest; from the largest to the smallest; from the beginning, in the middle, and also in the end.

If we cannot see everything as our own, we may be able to see that we exist only because of the whole. Understanding this relationship we can see that we have a natural obligation to all beings in creation. We have to repay this through our effort in the form of awareness, respect, and compassion. What higher purpose could māyā or 'divine creation' have if not to lead us to the deepest truth, to realize the oneness of creator and creation.

18

You Prepared Us for This

Priyan – Lebanon

Amma is our mother, our Guru, our friend, our 'shaker.' She patiently works with each one of us, slowly and gradually molding us in her masterful ways, cleaning us from our limitations despite our many resistances. For this, I can only say, "Thank you, Amma! A simple thank you..."

Amma, I don't know if you are satisfied with our progress, but I hope and pray that our attachments and our needs do not block your work on us too much, over and over again...especially our need for an identity which gives us a feeling of security, or rather the 'illusion' of security — emotional security. Our ego is like a little child, always finding ways and justifications to get what it wants, and to avoid what it doesn't like or want. Is this why you call us 'children'?

Those who are 'away' might put too much emotional focus on whether they are physically in Amritapuri now or not, especially because 'away from Amritapuri' so easily translates to being 'away from Amma.' Over the last two years, for long periods of time, I personally have been both physically present in Amritapuri as well as away. I would like to remind those who are sad and seriously affected about not being in Amma's physical presence of the following:

Hasn't Amma repeatedly said many times for many years that happiness is a decision that we should and can make? Keep the attitude: I *will try* to be happy in any situation; I *will be* happy in any situation; I *am* happy in any situation. In this way, real happiness doesn't depend on our circumstances, like being in Amritapuri now or not. Real happiness depends on our attitude, our choice. Then why waste any time not being happy? Unhappiness is like poison that slowly eats us.

Still, I will be honest here. I say this with a heavy heart, because whenever I am away from Amritapuri I have to follow Amma's programs behind an electronic device, exactly like so many of you are doing now. But who says that actually at a deeper level, I won't be in Amma's presence? Who says that you are not with Amma now? With your heart, with your soul, through your love of Amma, you *are* with Amma! Just close your eyes for a moment, keep a pure heart and you will get the confirmation! Your heart will tell you, and maybe some innocent tears will tell you too.

My heart is also heavy because in Lebanon, the country of my birth, daily life for everyone at this time is filled with helplessness, misery, pain, despair, and hopelessness.[65] Economically, it is in extreme crisis. Everything is eighteen times more expensive than it used to be. Eighteen times! For example, if something used to cost one rupee here, it now costs eighteen rupees. If something used to cost one dollar or one euro, it now costs eighteen dollars or eighteen euros.

A rough and tough reality. Hard. Very hard to bear. Harsh. Very harsh. Even getting bare necessities is a painful daily struggle. Finding basic food and essential medicine is hard enough, but then being able to afford it if you can find it is even harder. The government now allocates only two to four hours of electricity per day. People survive with whatever little money family members or friends working abroad are able to send them.

---

[65] This satsang was given in December 2021, a time when Lebanon was facing extreme economic and political upheaval.

I have made some life resolutions over the past few years: to accept and adjust to whatever situation comes and to not complain; to always smile and share with others the love that Amma has sowed in my heart and soul; to try to be positive and patient and centered on goodness, whatever comes. That's what I have understood from Amma's teachings and guidance for practical daily-life spirituality.

The Mumbai Hotel and the Slum

A few years back, a day of private darśhans was arranged for Amma in Mumbai. She was invited to a nice hotel in the outskirts of the city where she spent the day meeting influential people from society there. I was part of a small team with Amma taking photos and welcoming the guests. Everything was nice and pleasant, until I looked out the window of the upper floor where we were and was struck by what I saw! A very large slum was almost touching the hotel's walls. It was a vast expanse covered by huts made out of corrugated tin. Humans, dogs, and pigs shared the same space. A ditch filled with dirty sewage water was running down the middle of those miserable shelters.

What a contrast! What unfairness! How can some humans enjoy such a 'self-built, self-protected comfortable heaven' while right down below other humans are crushed, having to live like animals without basic dignity? Only Amma's example and inspiration can reach the souls of those who dwell in protected five-star hotels to sound the alarm of their conscience, to open their hearts to compassion. Amma has traveled throughout India to reach the poor, the sad, and the underprivileged. She has traveled to all the corners of the world to reach out to the oppressed, and to those who need her healing compassion, her support, and her protection.

Grace and Joy with Amma

From the early days when I first met Amma back in 1992, my time with her has always been full of the grace she has generously showered on me. It has been a time of joy; a time of singing and serving; loving and caring for others; with a cheerful smile here and there, and a kind word. All this is actually nothing but an expression of the love that Amma has sowed and nourished in my heart.

Therefore, for the rest of this satsang, I see it as my duty to reconnect with that energy and to share it with you all. The joyful way I connect with Amma and express my learning and assimilation of her teachings, as well as recounting the lessons she makes us go through to be learned well and absorbed better, has been to express my feelings and 'discoveries' through poetry. Playful poems that come to me on their own when they wish, often with a tune — a melody. They become songs that carry the mood of a moment, what I have experienced — with humor and some teasing too! Let's enjoy some of these songs. Each song had its own bhāva (mood) and was linked to a certain period of *learning* with Amma.

Songs

When I was learning Amma's 'living in the present' teaching, accepting changes in life and letting go of attachments, the *Bird on the Twig* song came:

See the bird in the sky, flying low and flying high.
Playing with the wind he is, free and happy, as he is.

Moving from tree to tree, moving easily, moving free
Gliding in the open sky, landing on a twig so high.

See the bird on the twig, he is swinging with the twig.
Hear the bird on the twig, he is singing like a jig.

Watch the bird on the twig, he could take off very quick,
If the bird on the twig, feels a shake to the twig.

If the twig shakes, so the bird flies.
If the twig breaks, so the bird flies.
If the wind blows, so the bird flies.
If the rain falls, so the bird flies.

Like the bird on the twig, we should be ready to fly,
Any moment to take off if it gets shaky and rough.

Like the bird on the twig, no attachment to the twig.
He enjoys it for a while, but his home is the sky.

When I was getting a taste of my first hard lessons with Amma, and feeling that she was ignoring me or didn't love me anymore, it was the song *You don't look at me anymore!* that everyone related to and even adopted back then:

You don't look at me anymore!
You don't smile to me anymore!
You don't talk to me anymore!
You do neglect me more and more!

What can I do? What can I say?
I have to accept that this is Your way!

By Your silence, you deepened my love.
And in that love, I found my silence!
Now I close my eyes, I pray, and I cry...
When there are no lies, I see Your smile!

Don't look at me, I don't mind...
Don't smile to me, I'll be all right...

I'll do it my way, left all alone...
I'll find my way, walking alone...
I won't feel sad, don't see my tears...
I won't feel bad, just close Your ears...!

But if You look at me, from time to time,
If You smile to me, I won't mind!
So... please look at me, from time to time,
please smile to me. I won't mind...

During this same period, I was enjoying with others discovering Amma's ways of sometimes saying 'yes' and sometimes 'no,' and changing her instructions at any time. So came a song praising Amma's 'special compassion' and trying to describe it in 'teasing' ways:

Amma is love,
Amma is only compassion.

Amma is love, Amma
Amma compassion, Amma
Amma compassion, Amma
Amma confusion, Amma
"Confusing-Compassion", Amma

Then:

Surrender, to Amma
Surrender, to Amma

When Amma started emphasizing making the firm decision to always be happy, the Smile, Smile, Smile song came:

Amma wants you to be happy.
Amma wants you to smile.

Amma wants you to be happy.
Lighten up and smile...

Smile, smile, smile,
Smile and be happy.
Smile, smile, smile,
Smile, be worry free.

Smile! Like the sun in the sky.
Smile! Like the bird, the butterfly.
Smile! Like a dolphin in the sea.
Smile! Like the flower and the bee.

Smile! Don't take life too seriously.
Smile! Why to worry endlessly?
Smile! Especially, if you are sad.
Smile! Especially, when you are mad.

And... if you cannot smile,
ask Her: why no smile?
If you cannot smile,
remember Her smile!

Smile with your face,
Smile with your eyes,
Smile with your heart,
Smile from inside.

Amma wants you to be happy.
Amma wants you to smile.
Amma wants you to be happy.
Show... Her... a... Big... Smile...

I have many other songs, like the *Question, Answer* song or the *Your Eyes* song, or the most 'famous' one which is in Arabic,

'*Uttruck kulla chay'en*' (Leave everything and follow me), etc. There is even one song that I never had the chance to sing in public, as it came at the beginning of the Covid period: *You Prepared Us For This.*

You prepared us for this
Because you knew all of this.
So, we are strong,
It can't go wrong.

You prepared us for this.
Spiritual practice from virus.
So, we are strong,
It can't go wrong.

We have no fears. We keep our courage,
Shraddha/Awareness, and yet more courage.
Discipline, and add some prayers,
Self-control, and more, more prayers

We pray for Grace,
For those who left us,
and we pray for their families...
With Love!

And we pray for the doctors,
for the nurses, and all health workers!

You prepared us for this,
And even for much more than this.
So, we are strong,
It can't go wrong.

We are all One, interconnected,
With your Grace, we are protected.

With a pure heart, we close our eyes.
We send white flowers to heal the world.
Lokaaaaha...Samasthaaaha...Sukhinoooo...Bhavantu...

Maybe my most precious song is *You took me by the hand*. It is one that has not been sung often, and it is one of my very first songs, describing my coming to Amma. I sang it for the first time on the newly built stage of the Delhi āśhram back in February 1995. It was a Śhivarātri[66] night. I was on the stage directing the āśhram kids in a small play that Amma was enjoying. Some of those 'kids' are sitting here in the audience today.

However, the play finished very quickly and the program coordinator rushed over to me saying, "Priyan, Amma is waiting for more. What else do you have?" I said, "That was the only play we had ready, nothing else. Shall we repeat it again?" He said: "No! something else, something different!" I had no idea what I could do to save the situation. Do a clown act on stage? So I told the coordinator half-jokingly, "Well, I could sing a few of those songs that I sometimes sing in Amritapuri." He agreed, and two minutes later I was sitting alone on the small stage facing Amma and the audience. I closed my eyes mechanically so that I wouldn't get distracted by my surroundings, and so that I could fully 'feel' the songs, as though I were singing alone.

I sang two or three of the usual songs, and I opened my eyes. Everyone was still sitting and Amma was fully gazing at me with immense love coming from her face. I will never forget the glow on her face and her eyes that were tearing up. I closed my eyes again, and decided to sing the more private song: *You took me by the hand...* a song that describes the early days of my meeting Amma for the first time:

---

[66] The 'Night of Śhiva.' A night in the winter season, usually in February/March, dedicated to the worship of Lord Śhiva.

You knew that my life had lost its aim,
So, You came to me, and You took me by the hand.
And You know how much I needed You Mother,
How much I missed You, how much I cried...
Now no one but You will lead my life,
My Amma! My Amma!

The days were passing, hard and useless.
So much energy was lost in vain.
Then I heard Your voice singing through the oceans
My heart went crazy, I ran and came to You.
It felt so nice when You took me in Your arms,
My Amma! My Amma!

I'd like to conclude with a prayer: Amma, please help me, despite these difficult and sad times, to never lose my original childlike innocence and expressivity, that innocence that brought me to you, and that you asked me on several occasions to always remember and to always keep alive, to make it my number one priority on the spiritual path. Thank you.

19

Devotion in Duality

Yati – USA

In oneness, when we have merged back into our Self, there is no differentiation or identity. Only when there are two can we experience and enjoy the sweetness of devotion. Without duality, who is there to be devoted to? And who is there to relish that devotion?

Sage Vyāsa felt great dissatisfaction even after he'd composed the *Mahābhārata* and compiled the *Vēdas* to uplift mankind. Sage Nārada diagnosed his unrest. He said:

> 'Knowledge, characterized by purity, does not shine with dazzling brilliance if it is devoid of the fervor of devotion to the Supreme Being. What then to speak of mere karma, with motive or even without it, if the karma is not dedicated to the Lord.'
>
> *Śhrīmad Bhāgavatam* 1.5.12

Nārada then instructed Vyāsa to write the *Śhrīmad Bhāgavatam*, which extols the supremacy of devotion.

Once Śhrī Rāmakṛiṣhṇa Paramahaṁsa had a vision of Lord Kṛiṣhṇa while listening to a recitation of the *Śhrīmad Bhāgavatam*. Luminous rays beamed from his lotus feet in the form of a rope, which first touched the Bhāgavatam and then Rāmakṛiṣhṇa's own chest, connecting all three — God, scripture, and the devotee. After this, he often said, "I came to realize that Bhagavān, Bhāgavata and Bhakta (God, scripture, and devotee) are really one and the same."

Amma asked Swāmījī what he wanted for his 50th birthday. The last Dēvī Bhāva here in Amritapuri was the fulfillment of his wish. One devotee asked Swāmījī why he didn't ask for mōkṣha (liberation), but that's like offering ice to an Eskimo. He doesn't need it; he's already got everything he wants. Just as Amma sings,

> *ānandam vēṇda ārōrum vēṇda*
> *nirmala prēma bhakti tarū*
> 'I seek neither bliss nor anything else.
> Give me only pure love and devotion.'
>
> *Anantamāyi Paṭarunna*

Along similar lines, Śhrī Śhuka tells Rāja Parīkṣhit:

> 'Wise men who try to relieve themselves of the heat of saṁsāra (the cycle of birth and death) bathe in the nectar of God's love. The bliss arising from that devotional experience is such that they reject even mōkṣha, which comes automatically as a result of their devotional discipline. Rather than merging in him, they prefer to continue in the bhakti experience — the consciousness that they are the Lord's own.'
>
> *Śhrīmad Bhāgavatam 5.6.17*

Whether we seek mōkṣha or prēmabhakti (highest love for God) is our choice. Either way, we can't deny the value of cultivating bhakti on the spiritual path. By sharing a few stories, tonight I'll talk about some qualities that are essential for devotion to flourish.

Amma says in *Awaken Children 7*:

> 'A true devotee or disciple will have great humility, and because of this he will also possess a certain spiritual beauty. The beauty of spirituality lies in humility.'

Being the humblest devotee in the āśhram, I can tell you all about humility. First of all, that was just a joke. I'll share an experience where I was lacking in humility and how it was brought to my attention.

The Western Café in Amritapuri loses many dishes because people take them to their rooms. To prevent this, some years back we started a sēvā called 'Dish Police.' The 'officer' on duty would sit in a particular place to stop people who were trying to take a café plate or bowl from the Western dining area. The 'officer' would nicely tell the thief that they could either eat their food in the dining hall or buy a tiffin and take it out.

I had the habit of collecting my breakfast and returning to my room to continue my meditation. Sometimes you don't want all your food mixed together, so I often took a café bowl back to my room. I was pretty good at hiding the bowl under my tiffin as I walked past the Dish Police Officer. I justified my actions because I always returned the bowl the same morning. One day a new Dish Police Officer caught me. She politely told me what I already knew, but I quickly escaped to my room, slightly irritated.

Days went by. Every morning I went down anxiously anticipating a conflict. Doesn't she know I will return the bowl? I've been doing sādhanā (spiritual practices) all morning. I shouldn't have to waste my time defending myself.

One morning, as I snuck past her thinking I was clear, I heard, "*Namaḥ Śhivāya*!" Ugh. Mentally prepared for battle I turned around. Before I could speak, she said, "Amma put it in my heart to get you this." Saying that, she handed me a brand new bowl that she had purchased herself. With one simple act of kindness my perceived enemy won the war I had created.

If we can stop and step back and observe our own behavior without identifying and getting defensive, sometimes we'll see it's pretty silly. Embarrassing might be a more accurate description. I was going to return the bowl. I just wanted to get back to my sādhanā. I was stuck on '*I*.' The sēvite[67] however, identified the problem and offered a solution, just like Amma so masterfully does. Just buy a bowl! Why didn't *I* think of that? When ego clouds our mind, to think clearly is like trying to see the bottom of a murky lake.

Did I behave like a humble devotee? No. I wanted to get to my room to do more sādhanā. But what good is sādhanā if I don't respect the āśhram rules and residents? I sincerely apologize and thank that devotee who gave me the bowl and the priceless lesson that came with it. In *Awaken Children 6*, Amma says, "Without renunciation and humility one cannot be content. A true devotee has both of these qualities." This brings me to the second quality, tyāga (renunciation).

Ever since Amma gave me my name, there's often been some confusion when I meet new people. You see, there's *the* Yeti — the abominable snowman, that lives high in the icy mountains. And there's me, Yati who can hardly bear cold weather. While I assure you we are two separate entities, I admit that when I got the name, there *was* a slight resemblance. To complicate things further, I will introduce a character from the *Bhāgavatam*. King Yayāti will show a contrast between the meaning of my name and his character.

'Yati' means sannyāsī (renunciate). The Sanskrit root '*yat*' means to strive, so 'Yati' is one who strives to renounce attachments and direct his mind toward the highest ideal. Why should

---

[67] A person who does sēvā, selfless service.

we forsake lesser pleasures or enjoyments? To gain something far greater. Amma sings:

> *ellā bhāgyaṅgaḷum maṛaññāl mātram*
> *kiṭṭunna saubhāgyammē*
> *ellā saundaryavum maṛaññāl mātram*
> *kiṭṭunna saundaryamē*
> 'You are the real fortune which is obtained when all fortunes are discarded,
> the beauty one beholds when all other attractions are forgotten.'
>
> *Ānanda Rūpiṇiye*

This verse answers the question: "Why practice renunciation?" By letting go of small, temporary enjoyments, we can attain what is eternal and truly satisfying. When we give up everything except our pursuit of God, love and devotion will flourish unimpeded.

In contrast to that attitude of renunciation, here's King Yayāti's story in brief:

King Yayāti had five sons from two different women, Dēvayānī and Śharmiṣhṭhā. After being cursed to grow old and unable to enjoy himself as he always had, he received a boon. If someone was willing, he could trade his old age for their youth. He asked each of his sons for their youth. The first four said, "No, we've also got desires," but the youngest one, Puru, agreed to give his youth to his father.

Yayāti went on indulging for another thousand years. Finally, he realized how far he had fallen. When this awakening came, he lectured his wife Dēvayānī, the very woman he'd been enjoying himself with, about renunciation. Despite the hypocrisy, a few verses from his sermon are especially potent:

- Desire is never satisfied by the enjoyment of its objects. Like fire fed with ghee (clarified butter), it only flames up all the more.
- A man who seeks his own good, should at once abandon his desire for sense-enjoyments, which evil-minded men find difficult to do. It (desire) does not decay even when he himself decays through old age.
- For a full thousand years I have been having every kind of sensuous enjoyment, but instead of subsiding, the craving for them comes with added force whenever situations arise.

Śhrīmad Bhāgavatam, Skandha 9, chapter 19

How many times have we heard Amma tell us these same points about the nature of desire? Whenever she's asked about lust, she responds that even a 98-year-old man may still have desires, and that indulging desires never quenches them, but rather reinforces them. It's no wonder that she chose, '*tyāgēnaikē amṛitatvamānaśhuḥ*' for the āśhram logo. Taken from the *Kaivalya Upaniṣhad*, it means 'By renunciation alone is immortality gained.' Amma says in *Eternal Wisdom 2*:

"Children, even if someone who is engaged in acts of tyāga doesn't find time for japa (mantra repetition), he will still attain the immortal state. His life will benefit others like nectar. A life filled with tyāga is the greatest form of satsang because others can see and emulate it."

That's Amma. A perfect living example of complete renunciation. Amma's life is her message of selflessness and it's for us to strive to emulate it. A true devotee of Amma will do their best to share that message through their own actions.

***

Amma tells a story about Kṛiṣhṇa and the gōpīs[68] in all her satsangs. Here I will follow her example in a small way with a modern, fictionalized story:

One day in Vṛindāvan, the gōpīs were happily doing their usual household work, immersed in thoughts of Kṛiṣhṇa. They imagined his yellow silk cloth while washing their clothes. As they milked the cows, they dreamed about catching him trying to steal the freshly churned butter they had just made. During their work, a few of them noticed a new girl moving into a vacant hut near the edge of their village.

In the coming days she met the other gōpīs and they welcomed her, and she caught a brief glimpse of Kṛiṣhṇa. She understood right away why the other gōpīs could speak of nothing else. Like the others, the Lord captured her heart, and her mind became fixed completely on him.

After a few days some gōpīs noticed something strange. This new gōpī would hang a pot of butter so that it seemed safe from thieves but was just accessible enough to tempt Kṛiṣhṇa to steal it. The strange thing was...*she didn't have any cows.* Where did her milk come from? The gōpīs hadn't noticed any missing from their own stock, and she seemed quite innocent. They decided to spy on her while she prepared the butter.

Early next morning, a few of them hid together where they could watch her. The new gōpī sang as she prepared her ingredients.

Kṛiṣhṇa Kṛiṣhṇa Mukunda Janārdhana
Kṛiṣhṇa Gōvinda Nārāyaṇa Harē

[68] The milkmaids of Vṛindāvan where Kṛiṣhṇa spent his boyhood years. The gōpīs are considered some of the greatest devotees of Kṛiṣhṇa, with Rādhā chief among them.

She was completely absorbed in her offering and her sweet song until one of the hidden gōpīs sneezed, and the new gōpī heard it. She found them and asked them what they were doing? The gōpīs had to confess. They said, "We've seen you hang butter for Kṛiṣhṇa to steal, but where are you getting the milk from? You have no cows."

The new gōpī laughed and said, "Oh, I don't use milk. I'm vegan. I make margarine for Kṛiṣhṇa." The gōpīs were stunned and thoroughly confused. They had so many questions. Butter without milk? What's a vegan? What's margarine? After a long, uncomfortable discussion, the gōpīs accepted that the vegan gōpī was simply not interested in learning how to make real butter. They thought, "Surely Kṛiṣhṇa won't like this fake butter. It must taste horrible."

That evening, Kṛiṣhṇa broke the vegan gōpī's pot and ate all the margarine. Later he was resting, fully satisfied and content. The gōpīs ran to him and asked, "Lord, did you really eat all that margarine? There's no way it could have tasted good. She didn't even use milk!"

Kṛiṣhṇa answered: "The item offered matters not. What counts is how much love's put in. Butter with or without milk, I'll even eat your margarine."

He continued, "Oh, dear Gōpīs, when I eat your butter, I'm not noticing the creamy texture or the sweetness. I'm relishing the love that you put in while preparing it. That's where the real flavor comes from."

Lord Kṛiṣhṇa makes this point in the *Bhagavad Gītā*, Chapter 9, verse 26:

patraṁ puṣhpaṁ phalaṁ tōyaṁ yō mē bhaktyā prayachchhati
tadahaṁ bhaktyupahṛitam aśhnāmi prayatātmanaḥ

> 'Whoever offers me a leaf, a flower, a fruit, or water with devotion, I accept it, the loving gift of the pure-minded.'

Innocent devotion attracts the heart and the grace of the Lord. There's nothing we can give God, as everything is already his own creation. Kṛiṣhṇa is telling us that, regardless of wealth or lack of wealth, high or low caste, knowledge or lack of knowledge of the scriptures, anyone can offer any item to God. If our heart is innocent, He will accept our offering as a most precious treasure. Our attitude is what pleases God.

Like the vegan gōpī offering her margarine, or like one of the little āśhram children teaching scriptures to a calf,[69] where there is pure innocent love, God can't stay away.

As important as it is to cultivate good qualities like humility, renunciation, and innocence, it's equally important to do our best to remove our negativities. The scriptures talk about the six main enemies:

- kāma – desire (lust)
- krōdha – anger
- lōbha – greed
- mōha – delusion
- mada – arrogance (pride)
- mātsarya – jealousy (envy)

All forms of negativity derive from these. But how can we overcome them? In the *Śhrīmad Bhāgavatam* (6.3.24), Śhrī Śhuka explains to Lord Yama how Ajāmila was saved and got mōkṣha by merely uttering the name, "Nārāyaṇa" one time when

---

[69] Little Niranjan was very keen to give spiritual discourses like the great teacher Ādi Śhaṅkarāchārya. Amma told him to teach the cows — and so he did for several weeks with inimitable enthusiasm. His favorite disciple was a little black calf named Śhyāma Kuṭṭi.

facing death.[70] What is the use then of performing devotional practices regularly like chanting the divine name with faith and love? Śhrī Śhuka says, "Such practice alone can efface all evil tendencies, and generate deep-rooted prēmabhakti which is even higher than mukti (freedom from saṁsāra)." Simply chanting the divine name with faith and love can remove our vāsanās and generate devotion.

***

Many years ago, during a Dēvī Bhāva in Holland, I went for darśhan. I had been feeling very disturbed by my negativities and was praying for Amma's guidance. When my darśhan came, Amma reminded me many many times that I am her darling son, and she kissed my forehead over and over and over.

Tremendously relieved, I sat in the prasād queue still wondering what to do when negative feelings rose up in me. As I was sitting next to Amma to pass prasād to her, a woman having darśhan was showing Amma her mantra paper. It seemed she was having trouble with the pronunciation. Amma, helped this woman and simultaneously answered my doubt. Amma slowly and clearly repeated the mantra for her...and for me. Of course, it's no surprise that this woman's mantra was the same one that I received from Amma years before.

Her message was clear. Amma has given us a simple, yet effective tool to conquer negativities — our mantra. The *Śhrīmad Bhāgavatam* says, 'No vow or austerity purifies the heart of man so effectively as devotion engendered easily by hearing and uttering the names of the Lord.' (6.3.32) So much power is attributed to chanting God's names. What to say about our

[70] In previous births, Ajāmila had accumulated a lot of punya (merit) which enabled him to attain liberation after just repeating the name of the Lord one time at the moment of death.

mantra given by Amma, the greatest incarnation the world has ever seen? By its immense power and Amma's saṅkalpa (divine resolve), our negativities don't stand a chance. There's no obstacle that we can't overcome. With unshakeable faith and by chanting Śhrī Rāma's name, Hanumān accomplished amazing feats.

What can stop us if we have firm conviction and Amma's mantra? Is Amma any less than Rāma? Certainly not. Are we any less than Hanumān? We may think we are, but we don't have to be. With sincere dedicated practice, we can all rise to that level.

Amma's senior sannyāsīs faced daunting circumstances in the early days. And we can see now, how through their persistence and faith, Amma has transformed them from iron into gold pieces. They are like a bunch of Hanumāns, ready to take on any task fearlessly, and with devotion to carry out Amma's will. This unfathomable bond between Guru and disciple brings me to one final story:

Amma says that the love we receive from our grandparents is uniquely special. I had the very unusual good fortune of having all four of mine alive and living nearby. They showered their love on me, not just as a child, but even as I grew into an adult. It was only after I turned thirty and was already living here that the first of them passed away. They each lived for at least ninety years, and they left this world together. My mother's parents died only ten days apart, and my father's parents died about a month apart. It's amazing how two people can be so deeply connected that, when one goes, the other follows soon after. If ordinary people can be so bound in love to their life partners, what about the unparalleled relationship between God and her devoted children?

In 2008, Guru Pūrṇimā[71] was celebrated during Amma's Boston program. I guarantee that anyone who was there will never forget it. Swāmījī read Amma's message aloud. When he read the story about Lord Kṛishṇa leaving Vṛindāvan and the gōpīs never seeing their beloved Lord again, he broke down crying. Everyone broke down crying. Hundreds of people there were inconsolable imagining never again seeing their Lord.

What would be our state if Amma left us like that? Amma stroked Swāmījī's back for some time and encouraged him to continue with the satsang, but it was impossible. Finally, Swāmī Śhāntāmṛitānandajī finished the rest of the talk for those who could focus on it. When we can weep out of love and longing for God, where is the desire for liberation? Surely, it will happen due to our intense one-pointedness. But a true devotee desires bhakti alone. The true devotee simply loves God for the sake of loving God. In one of his lectures, Swāmī Vivēkānanda says:[72]

> 'When the whole world will vanish, when all other considerations will have died out, when you will become pure-hearted with no other aim, not even the search after truth, then and then alone will come to you the madness of that love, the strength and the power of that infinite love which the gōpīs had, that love for love's sake. That is the goal.'

Just imagine the gōpīs and how it must have been thousands of years ago in Vṛindāvan. Thousands of years from now, seekers will read about Amma and think, "Oh, I wish I could have seen her. I wonder how it was to live in her presence." They will try to imagine what we experience with Amma every single day.

---

71 The full moon day in summer, dedicated to worshiping the Guru.

72 *Vivēkānanda, The Complete Works*, Vol. 3, 1955 Edition, p. 260.

Without a doubt, we are the most blessed people ever, in all the worlds.

I pray that all of our hearts melt upon hearing your name, Amma. I pray that every time you incarnate, you bring me along as your devotee, fluent not only in the language of love, but also in whatever language you speak.

20

Child #9,800,012

Nityanand - USA

Thank you, Ammē Jagadambē,[73] mother and master, for incarnating on our beautiful planet in the midst of massive delusion. Thank you for searching the world for your children; for working tirelessly to uplift us out of the mess we've placed ourselves in; for constantly showering us with the cool radiance of your love. Thanks to this lineage of mahātmās dating back to time immemorial; to my elder brothers and sisters who have been mother's arms and legs, making her mission on Earth possible. Thank you again and again to this holy land, 'Amritapuri,' to this holy land, Mother India, and to this holy land, Mother Earth.

I beg forgiveness for any joke that's not funny and for any point that misses the point. Anything that sounds wise or profound, I plagiarized from Amma; anything off base or ridiculous, I own. Amma please guide this moth child of yours straight into the blazing inferno of your innermost being.

The opening quote of my archana book says, "Just as a child would come to his mother without any hesitation, so you can come to me, your own mother." Well, I just happen to be your Child Number 9,800,012 and I have found it difficult to run to the outer Amma when my diapers need changing or when I need milk.

Fortunately, Mother has lots of ways of giving us the milk of her love, for Mother is an ocean of love-milk. Everywhere she goes becomes the Milky Way. Her presence turns hotels,

---

[73] Mother of the universe.

casinos, and football stadiums into the highest of temples. Even just thinking of her produces this milk. Milk is currently flowing from laptops around the world (because of the livestreams of her programs). Her milk indeed flows to all corners of reality, but we need subtle tongues to taste it. Though any tongue can tell you that the closer you get to Amma's physical body, the thicker and more delicious the milk becomes. At the back of the hall, it might be skim milk, at the front — milk coffee, up on stage we are swimming in heavy whipping cream, and darśhan is like bathing in butter. It is the milk of her love that calls us, binds us and transforms us.

I don't speak Malayāḷam. In eleven years I have not traded eleven sentences with Amma, yet I feel closer to her than to my own skin. Why? Because she speaks a language my heart understands. The language of divinity. A wordless language that bypasses the mind and makes the heart ache with longing. A longing to love God, love Truth and love Love.

One year at the beginning of the U.S. Tour in Seattle, Amma entered the room, sat down, and asked for a joke. Humans are suffering from many pandemics, one of the worst is a chronic pandemic of seriousness. Dēvī wanted a joke. It so happened that I had woken up that morning laughing from a very funny dream. I did not share the dream then because I was terrified of talking to Amma. Today, as proof of my spiritual progress, I shall:

It was the beginning of Amma's World Tour, and I had been chosen to lead the very first archana of the tour. I was walking towards an enormous radio tower where the archana was to be blasted to every devotee all over the world.

"Axi!" A Western renunciate was calling to me, using the name people call me in America. "Axi, we are all very happy you will be offering the first archana of the World Tour. We have only one tiny concern. A concern about the addition to the archana."

"The addition?" I asked confused. "What addition?"

The renunciate frowned and said, "The addition of the 'seven names of Axi.'"

These 'seven names of Axi' are my greatest enemy. They are the pegs on which all my likes and dislikes are wrapped. They are the sum total of who I think I am, a separate soul looking for praise and validation on the world stage. Amma says, "To become a hero, you have to become a zero." So, she renamed me Nityananda, which means 'The unchanging bliss.' Or, as I translate it: 'The eternally happy nobody.' For happiness is what is waiting for us when who we think we are finally dissolves.

A devotee once asked me, "What are the names of Axi?" The first and foremost is: "Sri Sri Sri Me Me Me." Then comes more mundane names, "Father," "Artist," "Potential Messiah," "that funky clown from New Orleans," and.... "Mysterious Spiritual Shaman Dude." And of course... "Mr. A Little Bit Better Than You," which was a name that Amma annihilated in Madurai.

It was South India Tour, 2016, I had finished evening sēvā and was sitting on the stage a few meters behind Amma. Suddenly, my least favorite devotee sat next to me. I don't remember who this person was or what negative comment I thought to myself but Amma, in the middle of darśhan, turned around a full 150 degrees and gave me a look of revulsion so intense it made my mind whither. She caught me doing the nastiest thing I could do — judging another devotee. I felt like a pile of garbage a mile wide. What to do? I made an intense vow to never ever think like that again.

Arrogance is a heart-closing demon of the first order — a miserable thing that delivers misery to those we judge, and brings double misery to ourselves. In a single gaze Amma incinerated it. Like Kṛiṣhṇa, she guided the Arjuna of my awareness to shoot an arrow into the heart of the beast. Now, demons do tend to re-sprout heads, but I never want Amma to look at me like that again, so whenever I notice one of those heads beginning to sprout, I 'sudarśhana chakra'[74] that menace.

I first met Amma when I was twenty years old, in 1998 in Washington, DC. I went because a cute girl told me a saint was in town, gave me a ride, walked me to the door, and then evaporated into the crowd. I didn't know anything about India at the time and was prepared to dislike the whole event, but the music was good, and the feeling was happy. In those days we went for darśhan on our knees, and it surprised me how much I liked that. It felt humble. I had never tried humble before. Being hugged by Amma was like being hugged by the ocean. I had heard this saint was considered to be the Divine Mother, so when she said some baby sounds in my ear, I said some baby sounds back. "Gaga googoo gaga mama Amma." She laughed uproariously and threw flower petals on my head. I walked away dizzy...and forgot all about her.

I wasn't ripe enough. I hadn't suffered enough. I wasn't subtle enough. I was enjoying Amma's candy shop too much. I grew up in a city of jazz with parents who were artists and poets. I had a street theater company that performed cosmic clown dramas. I always attempted to have two girlfriends at the same time, (It was a family tradition that went back generations). I grew up with the values of a bohemian — a mixture of reverence, irreverence, indulgence, and humor.

However, I was simultaneously searching for the divine. The search for God led me from New Orleans to Mexico, from Brazil to Peru, and finally to the Pacific Northwest. I went from Sufism to Haitian Voodoo, from mushroom shamans to the Pachakuti

---

[74] The divine discus that Lord Viśhnu uses to lop off the heads of demons.

Mesa. I worshiped the ocean, the mountains, lightning, and hummingbirds. I had many teachers, from many traditions, but no masters.

Amma says worshiping many different gods is like digging many shallow holes in search of water. I felt like I was digging in the same hole, just exploring different digging tools. Some spiritual paths were like sturdy shovels, others were like using chopsticks. Amma is a twenty-story crane with a drilling rig attached. Painful perhaps, but the hole becomes very...holy.

After thirteen years of apprenticing in diverse spiritual traditions I was more subtle. I had more discipline and devotion to the living universe, a universe that responds to prayers and sends messages through synchronicities and dreams. I knew that inner transformation was the path to God, yet I was still angry, still lustful, still lying, still arrogant, still delusional, and a little lazy.

In 2011 at the age of 33, I was in school, had a nineteen-month-old baby, and my wife and I were fighting constantly. Although life was full of blessings, I wasn't seeing them. I was waking up every morning weeping for God, wondering why I was alive.

Our family had to fly to the East Coast to visit my wife's dying mother. The night before we left, a friend let us borrow *Awaken Children 1* to help uplift our spirits. During the visit I had three vivid Amma dreams. We flew back to Portland, and that same afternoon there was a knock on the door. A friend we hadn't seen in years was standing on the porch, dressed all in white with a suitcase. We had no idea she had become an Amma devotee. She said she was planning to fly to Amritapuri, but due to a number of coincidences she moved in with us instead. Within minutes Amma music was playing in the living room,

Amma pictures were on the walls, and Amma was smiling at me from my phone.

Five months later we arrived in Seattle on the weekend of my daughter's second birthday. We received an early token for the morning program, and as Kālī willed it, we received our family darśhan at 11:35 a.m., the exact minute of our daughter's birth.

The next morning, I was sitting alone in the first row of chairs during the program. Amma was giving darśhan on the floor below the stage, with the musicians singing on stage above her. I was very close to her but had no view due to the large swarm of devotees buzzing around her. Swāmī Amritātmānandajī was about to start the *Lalitā Sahasranāma*. I thought it would be a brief chant, perhaps ten or fifteen minutes long, so I made a vow to sit in lotus posture for the duration of the chanting.

Around name #330 my legs caught on fire, though by wild grace, by name #500 the fire had been put out. Around name #750 the pain came back doubled. By name #850 the pain had tripled. By #950 it was so excruciating I was screaming to myself on the inside. By #990 I was on the verge of fainting, but I held on. In response to my holding on, Swāmījī slowed down. He started savoring each name. Oooommm Shriiiiimaaaat Triiiiipuuuuraaaaaa Suuundaaaaryaaaai Naaammmaaahhhaaaaa (#997).

It was interminable. Agonizing. Finally, it ended. I could relax. I had to lift one leg over the other to let the blood pour back in. I looked up, and Amma was parting the devotees that were swarming around her. She leaned forward and gave me a huge smile with a big thumbs up. I was dumbfounded. Shocked. No one was behind me. She had congratulated me on sticking to my insane mental vow. I was hooked. I swallowed not only the bait, but the hook, the fishing line, the fishing pole, and the boat. I'm still trying to swallow the fisher-lady.

God had answered my prayers. I was back on the path...and yet my life got worse. God's presence made everything hotter. More intense. But now I had a focus for that intensity — Amma. The next two years held many small miracles, many Amma dreams. My wife also became a devotee, but we did not stop fighting. My family was breaking apart. I felt like I was losing my mind. So we went to Amritapuri. For the first time in years, I felt peace. Life made sense again. Here was a place where everyone lived for God.

On the last day of my first trip to Amritapuri I went to give prasād. During the entire two-minute sēvā Amma was laughing with some devotees. As I watched her, completely relaxed and enjoying the moment, a thought bubbled up in my mind. "It's so easy to be happy." At that very instant Amma turned and looked at me, giving me one of her most radiant and twinkliest of smiles.

"Happiness is a choice," Amma says. I found it hard to penetrate that teaching until I flipped it around — Misery is a choice. Ah, that I got. I had become habituated to being miserable. Being miserable is very hard work. It takes a lot of effort to be tense every minute of every day of your life.

Amma tells the story of a Guru who had a disciple who was always complaining about his life. "My wife... My boss... My kids..." The guru replied, "Just let go." "What! Just let go?... What do you mean, 'Just Let go?'" The Guru said, "Come back tomorrow, and I will show you."

Tomorrow came and the devotee arrived to an empty āśhram. "Guru! Guru!" he called out. In response he heard, "Help! Help!" He ran to the nearby forest and found his Guru embracing the thorny trunk of an enormous tree. Blood was pouring from his arms and chest. The devotee tried to pry his Guru off the tree, but the Guru was too strong for him. "Help!

Help!" The Guru cried out. "Gurujī," the devotee said, "Just let go."

When I met Amma I was like this devotee. I was clinging to so many things. I was clinging to my old life as an artist in New Orleans. I was clinging to my family that was falling apart. I was clinging to wanting things my way. I was being crushed by the sheer weight of all my clinging. I had no choice but to return to Amritapuri. Much to my daughter's sadness, our family separated and I came to India for three months, and later for five months, then again for ten months. I was learning to let go. As I let go, I got lighter. As I let go of what I thought was love, I got happier and could love better. As I let go of my family, I was kinder to them and bit by bit dropped my grudges and expectations.

Herein lies one of the central issues of my upbringing and that of many Americans. We don't understand love. Love is what everyone wants, love is what everyone strives for, love is what everyone is hungry for in their rush to consume things — but no one is absorbing any of the love nutrients. Why? Because it's not pure love. It's love tainted with lust and greed on one side and attachment and fear on the other. If your breakfast has poison in it, it can't be properly digested.

Discerning between love and attachment is not easy. 'Father' was one of the names of Axi, a name with lots of attachments and expectations built into it. 'Father' is a very difficult name to let die. Especially when you have so much love for your daughter.

Once during a Q&A in San Ramon, a very bold devotee asked Amma why she didn't grant him mōksha this instant. I remember Amma saying something like, "Sure son, I could do that but are you prepared to leave your wife and kids this instant?" That was a shocker! It's not that God wants to tear apart families; farthest thing from it. The ancient ṛiṣhis (sages) all had families, but they also had proper education on what love, God and the mind are. Amma wants us to unglue ourselves from the dream of the world so we can recognize ourselves as the dreamer.

The God game is all or nothing. If we want any bit of the world, we don't get all of God. But if we get all of God, we get the whole wide world as well. Quite the conundrum. No half-baked potatoes. My problem was that I never learned the rules of the game. No one taught me Vēdānta[75] in public school. I grew up with Dr. Seuss, not the *Bhagavad Gītā*. This lack of proper knowledge led to improper thinking. Improper thinking led to mental problems. Misery is a mental problem. The only cure is proper education and the grace of a divine doctor.

After ten months in Amritapuri I returned to the U.S. and found my daughter had put all her Amma pictures away and had stopped saying her prayers and her mantra. She was mad at me and mad at Amma for taking me away. And yet those ten months were absolutely necessary for me to become a good Papa. What a paradox. Life can be very complicated, and the ways of karma are nuanced. I'm sure there's a great *Bhagavad Gītā* quote about this. Unfortunately, I don't know it. But I do have a Dr. Seuss (American children's book author) quote that's kind of appropriate:

> 'I have heard there are troubles of more than one kind.
> Some come from ahead and some from behind.
> But I've brought a big bat (that's Amma). I'm all ready you see.
> Now my troubles are going to have trouble with me.'

[75] The philosophy of the *Upaniṣhads* found in the *Vēdas* which deal with the subject of Brahman — the supreme Reality — and the path to realize that truth.

When I asked Amma about my relationship with my daughter her answer was immediate and to the point. "Love her as much as you possibly can." That became my guiding compass. Love says, "Be there for your daughter, be kind to her mother, and visit Amma as often as you can." And so, like a migratory bird, I follow the magnetic pull of this love and fly between America and Amritapuri. I am still a fledgling, learning how to have both compassion and vairāgya (detachment). They seem contradictory yet are two sides of the same coin. Only surrender to a mahātmā can solve that riddle. My daughter, Raya, blessedly is blooming into a wonderful teenager, full of creativity, style, and passion. Her mother and I are close friends, both as co-parents and devotees.

A devotee told me a story once about the time he had the chance to sit at Amma's feet during a Tuesday prasād lunch at Amritapuri. Amma was eating cashews and laughed so hard one of the cashews flew out of her mouth and landed in front of my friend. He grabbed it and gobbled it up.

How I wanted to eat that kind of prasād! My desire was like a firework that shot up in the air, exploded and was gone. The very next day I went for darśhan in San Ramon. The lady in front of me presented Amma with a large bowl filled with M&M's.[76] Amma's assistant was horrified at the thought of Amma eating too much sugar and snatched the bowl away, but Amma grabbed her wrist and took the bowl back. After scooping up an enormous quantity of M&M's in her hand, Amma put them into her mouth. Her assistant got mad and scolded Amma in Malayāḷam for doing that. Amma then took one M&M and fed it to the lady who had given her the bowl, and taking another, she fed it to me.

---

[76] M&M's are little, multi-colored chocolate candies.

What kind of physics governs this? How do so many of our tiny, weird wishes come true? What is the law behind miracles? How can there be a room of 10,000 people and everyone thinks Amma is smiling at them? And they are all probably right! Like how the incredibly attractive force of a black hole breaks all known laws of physics, our Amma breaks all known laws of consciousness. The mind cannot mathematically meet the magic of a mahātmā; logic cracks. So, Amma keeps things simple:

Love and Serve.

Ammē, I am child #9,800,012. I have yet to ask you directly how I can best serve the world. My resume consists of acupuncture, clown shows, and the attempted obliteration of my ego. Once, I asked you for guidance. I said, "Amma, I have so many questions about the direction of my life. Should I explain everything to you so you can advise me? Or should I trust that when I need your wisdom, your wisdom will be there." You answered in three words: "Live in presence."

Ammē, I am yours until the end of time and beyond. I am your flute, your trombone, your one-man jazz band. Please use me to help bring your smile to the world, to help share your light, to help humankind remember humankindness.

21

Embrace Your Own Nature

Gati – Spain

When I started translating Amma's satsangs years ago, a brahmachāriṇī who has been translating for Amma for many years told me that I would start seeing life according to Amma's satsang points (her teachings). And that's what happened. I started noticing Amma's satsang points or stories in situations in my own life.

Why are we sometimes not able to integrate Amma's teachings in our lives, even after hearing them so many times? Maybe because we don't make the connection between our specific life situations and her teachings. Therefore, we may not be aware that sometimes we act exactly opposite to what Amma advises.

Amma says, "My children, use every opportunity God gives you to serve." She does not say to help according to our mood, or just some opportunities but not others. No. Amma says that every time we see a need, God himself is giving us a chance for grace. Do you mind if I cut the line in front of you? Can you help me move these boxes? Can anyone do some sēvā now? Can you run some errands for me today? This is not some theory to go in one ear and out the other. Every time we say 'no' to someone who asks for help that we can provide, we are saying 'no' to God's grace.

What makes us think we can evolve faster by doing sādhanā quietly in our rooms and attending to our assigned sēvā, rather than by helping others during our non-sēvā hours? I think real sēvā starts when our assigned sēvā is finished. I used to try to apply this idea when working in the world. It was even more challenging, because being attentive to the needs of others out there can make one feel very lonely at times. Fewer people in the world challenge their habit of making their personal needs top priority.

And what about the 'silent treatment' that we give to people sometimes when they send us a text message asking for help? Not even a "Sorry, I am busy." Just silence. What satsang point is that? Surely not 'meditation is like gold.' This silence is not the silence of meditation. Is it the 'power of words' satsang point when Amma tells us to have awareness with each and every word because our words can turn our best friend into an enemy and vice versa? This cannot be it either because there are no words!

What if someone sends me a text message and instead of going into 'meditation is like gold,' I forget about the 'power of words' and reply with some harsh comment? I am enacting Amma's 'deposits and loans' satsang point about karma.

How many times have we heard this one? Amma says, "Some people in their previous lives have deposited a large amount of good deeds into the bank of karma. However, others come into this life with an outstanding loan that now they have to repay." I may start my reply to the request for help with "ōm namaḥ śhivāya," but if my response is passive-aggressive, then I just took out a loan. I will have to repay it, and I may have just hurt someone's feelings.

***

I never planned to become a renunciate; it just happened. One morning two years ago I woke up and I realized that I was one. The only memory that I have of such a feeling of renunciation happened years before, after bathing with Amma in the Ganges during the Kumbha Mēla.[77] It was only for a minute, but I remember its sweetness. This time, the feeling popped up out of nowhere, steady and strong, maybe as a natural result of having spent the last twelve years with Amma in an intense purification process.

Because this path of renunciation revealed itself when its time was due, it shocked me very much at first, but ultimately I had no doubts about it. The only question left was, would I follow what had just unfolded, or ignore it out of fear? Amma confirmed my path during my next darśhan. She orchestrated a līlā so that I said the word 'brahmacharya'[78] out loud to her. I did not write that word on a piece of paper to be translated to her as a formal request. I wanted to respect traditional initiation into brahmacharya and all the yellow-robed brahmachārīs and brahmachāriṇīs at the āśhram. Still, saying 'brahmacharya' conveyed to Amma my relationship to renunciation and its vows.

After getting Amma's blessing, I wondered how to break this news to my friends because according to some people's perceptions, I don't seem like the renunciate type. Here are some comments I received:

> Me, to one friend: "I have some news."
> Friend: [Silence.]
> Me: "I am becoming a renunciate."
> Friend: "Are you kidding?"

---

[77] A major Hindu festival occurring every three years in one of four sacred riverbank pilgrimage places in North India.

[78] The path of the celibate disciple dedicating their life to practicing spiritual disciplines under guidance of a Guru. Once initiated, male disciples are called brahmachārīs, female disciples are called brahmachāriṇīs, and they wear yellow robes.

Me: "I have some news."
Swāminī: "Are you getting married again?"

I had very nearly gotten married more than a decade ago. It was canceled just two days before the ceremony. Swāminī helped me a lot during that time of grieving. Her joke that day reminded me of Catholic nuns whose renunciation involves taking vows to marry Jesus.

Me: "I have some news."
A devotee from my country: "Are you pregnant?"

A few years after being with Amma, I realized that I am not a silent spiritual woman who looks introspective and speaks low and little. I am more like a constantly erupting volcano. I went to Amma to ask her to please change that. I wanted to be quiet, more shy, more serious, and not to cry in bhajans. I wanted to 'look' spiritual.

We were in Toulon. First I tried to make her transform me while sitting in the front row of the hall. I started to meditate. A bhajan was playing and my tears started falling. "No, no, no. This crying thing, no more! I want to be like the swāmīs — calm, collected, silent." That was my perception of most spiritual people then. They look calm and I don't. Seeing that my technique was not working, I jumped over to sit next to Amma's chair. However, that bhajan was still playing and now... Amma was so close... my heart was fully open... tears were rolling down my cheeks again... And I'm thinking, "No, no, no! This has to stop."

When I opened my eyes looking for Amma's help, Amma was already looking at me. We were looking at each other. There was a pause. I did not know what to expect. Then Amma made a face. She pointed her index finger at the side of her head making circular motions as if saying, "You are brooding over nonsense," or "You are a little crazy right now." As if on cue, a river of tears overflowed down my face, my sweater, the plant next to me... I love God, I love this plant, I love the birds, and I love everyone in this hall... It is so nice to be a volcano!

Once I accepted the fact that Amma was not going to change my personality, I went to Swāminī for advice on how to make the most of it. I shared that I was having yet another fight with someone on tour. Some devotees saw me as 'fiery Gati' during my first years around Amma. I would fight or make a harsh comment whenever I thought I saw what felt like an injustice to me, a lack of sensitivity, no discernment or no śhraddhā (awareness). I would also critique my own flaws to the level that my awareness at the time would allow. But I got angry whenever I felt hurt or mistreated, or when I noticed others being mistreated. I knew that it was arrogant, but I could not avoid those thoughts.

I was very much into human justice then, though I didn't know what compassion for myself and others really meant. On tour, to keep my mouth shut, I would leave the hall and go outside to hyperventilate. Only Amma and the trees nearby witnessed the intensity of all this. I used to go out alone during sēvā breaks and do fast walks, sweating out my toxic energy and cursing; really cursing. Then I would throw imaginary flowers on the people's heads who had upset me as if I was doing pūjā to them. Then more cursing, and more flower offerings, until the episode was over.

In time, all my anger was replaced by the underlying sadness that was hidden beneath it. Realizing this has been a fundamental teaching for me. Every time I feel angry now, I bring out my spiritual toolbox to try to calm my mind. Once calmed, I then search for the sadness, pain, and fear that I am not connecting with. Anger is my response after feeling hurt. The hardened ego's self-defense mechanism obscures our true feelings. That harshness is what I was projecting onto everyone else in the form of judgments and opinions.

Everyone who seems to mistreat us helps us uncover our pain and fear inside. It is *on us* to stay as open as we can, and allow Amma to do her magic and heal us. I know that I cannot heal myself. I am not a Satguru; I cannot remove my vāsanās (latent tendencies). My role is to try to open a place of vulnerability inside. To give her grace a way in to transform me. I usually get to that place through tears.

So, fiery Gati was trying to get some wisdom from Swāminī. A friend had mentioned to me that a woman I was having issues with was very childish. When I shared this comment with Swāminī, she encouraged me to learn to accept and adapt to people's different natures, and not to fight them. A few days later I complained to another friend of mine about this childishness that I perceive in some of the 'grown-up' Amma devotees. I said, "I don't understand the 'It-is-her-nature' thing. It sounds like an excuse not to work on oneself. Do I also have a nature? If so, what is my nature?" My friend looked at me amused and calmly said, "Rage."

She did not have to explain to me what rage meant in this context. I felt an aliveness arise within me. She was not referring to the negative anger that destroys and hurts; the anger that makes me suffer and that I have to purify. She meant the power beneath that, that thrills with intensity and vibrancy, the creative śhakti. Amma is patiently teaching me how to control and channel this śhakti (divine energy) for my own spiritual growth and to serve others.

As Amma says, there is always someone looking at us. And since we all are beautiful flowers in Amma's garden, each one different, each one unique, it is imperative that we learn to love and accept ourselves and others just the way we are, looking to become the most beautiful work of art with what God has given us. Sometime, somewhere, a person with a broken heart may be looking to us in search of some inspiration.

Some people tell me now that I look peaceful. Writing the words peaceful and me in the same sentence is a bit shocking but it is nice. I still have a long way to go for the deep peace that I long for, but no doubt a transformation has taken place since I first set foot in Amritapuri in January 2008.

***

I had met Amma in New York the previous summer. I remember the anticipation, then getting near her, and then the 'nothingness,' not in the sense of having realized Brahman, the Absolute, but in the sense of not feeling anything, even when Amma looked at me. A while later, when we were queuing up for dinner, my heart exploded and I started to cry and hug my friends saying, "Oh, this is love."

In the fall I received an announcement about an IAM meditation course happening in New York. In the second session of that IAM course they played an old video of Amma, and suddenly I realized that she was my Guru. I was so shocked that I had to leave the place before finishing the course. In tears, I walked around the Soho neighborhood in New York City in the rain holding onto my cushion and my yōga mat with one hand and calling a friend on the phone with the other. I said, "Something huge just happened! I have a Guru!" My friend laughed and said, "But you don't believe in Gurus!" "Well, I don't know," I replied, "But I have one now. It's Amma who I saw in July."

In less than two months I came to Amritapuri to check out the āśhram and left with a mantra from Amma. The next summer I returned and got my Amma name. Then I jumped on a plane to see Amma in Europe, and then to other programs here and there. My Amma family is my strongest bond, and it is all my brothers and sisters whom I miss the most when I am away. I miss this environment where we all are striving for the spiritual goal together.

On Friday March 13, 2020 I had a plane ticket to fly to Spain. That was the day of the sannyāsa and brahmacharya dīkṣha (initiation) ceremony in Amritapuri. Of all the days that year, I had to fly on *that* morning. Since mid-February 2020, it had been clear that the world was in real trouble from the Covid pandemic. Things were terrible in Spain and not just because of Covid. I had a strong intuition that I had to be there, and not in Amritapuri. The evening that Amma picked up the mic to alert everyone about the severity of the world situation and instructed us not to leave the āśhram, I was near the ramp ready to say good-bye to her. I will never forget the way she looked at me. Her glance accompanied me and gave me strength to go through the many months ahead.

I reached Spain a few hours before a state of emergency was declared. I walked through surreal, empty airports and train stations where screen monitors displayed alerts: 'canceled' ... 'canceled'... 'canceled!' The world was closing down, and I was still running errands!

When the news of the first lockdown broke, I was alone in a coastal village picking up a few of my things. What initially seemed to be just a couple of weeks of isolation, turned into two months of no contact with any other human being. Europe was in shock. People were afraid. The army had taken over the streets of Spain. Dead bodies were stored in sports halls since hospitals and funeral homes were full. Doctors had to decide who would live and who would die on the spot since there were not enough ventilators for everyone. Old people were dying alone in nursing homes without receiving any medical treatment. Their relatives couldn't communicate with them or even find out if they were dead or alive. It felt like a state of war.

Many people in Spain lost their jobs and had no savings or insurance. NGOs and neighbors were feeding those who didn't have any food. A huge wave of solidarity arose. There was not enough medical protective equipment for doctors and nurses and some of them died in their hospitals after caring for others. At 8:00 p.m. every night, we would come out on our balconies all over the country to applaud all those heroes who were looking after us. It was Amma's blessing that I got to see and experience all this.

I was in the middle of my trial as a renunciate when I left Amritapuri. A couple of months after the first lockdown was lifted, it was clear that restrictions would continue for a while. I felt the urge to spend some time in a spiritual atmosphere while Spaniards were enjoying their summer vacation.

By Amma's grace, I miraculously ended up in a Catholic monastery in the Pyrenees mountains near the French border. During the second Covid wave I was trapped for three months with Carmelite nuns and a priest who had been a hermit for over thirty years. They welcomed me with open arms. I was immersed in Jesus, the Catholic mystics, and their sādhanā. I felt a natural affinity for Saint Teresa of Ávila and Saint Thérèse of Lisieux.

My stay in the monastery was blissful and also hard-core *tapas* (austerity). They lived like hermits taking vows of poverty and silence, and enduring the weather of the high mountains. I spent mornings doing translation sēvā for Amma on the computer and the afternoons doing my duties in the monastery. We did four hours of Catholic sādhanā in Latin every day. At first, my relationship with Amma seemed not to be an issue, and it never was for the nuns. But it ended up being an issue for the main priest who was expecting me to stay and fully embrace Catholic dogma.

Those months away from Amma's physical presence were full of sadness and longing. After the pandemic hit, Amma started recording bhajans in foreign languages. One day I got a message asking if I could write one in my native language. I had never done such a thing, but I knew that with Amma's grace anything is possible. I wrote a bhajan in Spanish, and I also started writing bhajans in Malayāḷam like a Malayāḷi[79] kid would do. So besides the Catholic immersion, during the pandemic I also learned to compose bhajans.

This bhajan reflects my bhāva (attitude) during those evenings alone, wondering how long I would have to wait to be in Amma's physical presence again:

> *ēkāntata enne kṣhaṇikkunnu*
> *ennuṭe aṭuttāṇu kṛiṣhṇan*
> *nī eviṭe bhagavān?*
> *nī eṅgōṭṭāṇu pōkunnatu?*
> 'Solitude is calling me
> Kṛiṣhṇa is near me
> Where are you, Bhagavān?
> Where are you going?'
>
> *divasaṅgaḷ kaṭannu pōkunnu*
> *ippōzhuṁ nī enne kaṇunnilla*
> *ennōṭoppaṁ kṛiṣhṇan maṭaṅgi varika*
> *nī eviṭe kṛiṣhṇan?*
> *nī eṅgōṭṭāṇu pōkunnatu?*
> 'The days are passing by
> Even now you do not see me
> Come back with me, Kṛiṣhṇa

[79] A person from Kerala.

Where are you, Kṛiṣhṇa?
Where are you going?'

ēkāntata enne kṣhaṇikkunnu
ennuṭe aṭuttāṇu kṛiṣhṇan
'Solitude is calling me
Kṛiṣhṇa is near me'

The long months away from Amma and the āśhram were some of the most spiritually challenging months of my life, but also absolutely rewarding and worthy. Those months of isolation have allowed me to go deep within. I have learnt that we can always pray to Amma for the help and strength to discover her grace hiding beneath all of our pain and suffering. In April 2021 I was able to finally return to Amma's physical presence and be reunited with my ashram family. I made it back home.

22

Hot Chai and Cold Lassi

Benjamin - Germany

Amma is the beacon of my life. I am so blessed and beyond happy that she cares for me. How can we describe in words what can't be written down? The indefinable — Our Amma. The *Śhrī Lalitā Sahasranāma* glorifies Dēvī in a thousand beautiful mantras. I suppose their composer stopped at one thousand not for lack of inspiration, but simply for lack of breath.

It is an honor to present this satsang since I have no pre-qualifications or scriptural knowledge. I am not even an āśhram resident, but only a 'tourist' in India. I had the privilege of being just the fifth international tourist to arrive in Kochi airport on November 15th, 2021 since the Covid lockdowns started in 2020.

To help us deal with the pain of separation from Amma during the pandemic, Amma blessed us with daily broadcasts of the Amritapuri meditation, satsang, and bhajan programs that continue to this day. It is challenging to fit it into our daily schedule, I admit. Kudos to those on Pacific Standard Time that get up at 3:30 a.m. for meditation. Or those on Central European Time that can only see Amma in the middle of a busy workday. Each time zone has its challenges, but it's good to try to tune in at least once or twice a week. Amma has certainly not forgotten us, so should we forget her? Amma is like the sun that sustains and gives life on earth. She is the sun that shines within each one of us. We just need to open our hearts to her.

It was not easy to stay sane during Covid. Not going on Amma's tours dealt a major blow to my wife and me. And when my sports rowing club closed for a couple of months due to the lockdowns, I thought I would 'lose it.' For the sanity of all around me, especially my wife, I have to keep busy, including having strenuous physical activity as part of my daily routine. Venturing out into nature and staying active helps me a lot. Nature calms and grounds us. It is full of beauty and splendor and is a reflection of Amma near us. It doesn't have to be the 'wild outdoors.' A garden or beautiful tree will do. At least there you don't get eaten by bears.

As much as I love the outdoors and am fascinated by new cities and countries, when on tour with Amma we rarely go outside the program hall. The most magnificent nature and architecture pales against the splendor of Amma giving darśhan.

Often people say, "Amma came into my life on such and such a day." But hasn't Amma always been with us? We are like babies slowly opening our eyes and seeing our mother for the first time. What do we really know? After my parents first met Amma in 1989 on Amma's Europe Tour in Germany, they took us kids the next year. I was thirteen. Not the fresh green grass that can easily be molded that Amma talks about, but not concrete either. We all fell in love with her. At that time, darśhan was very informal and there weren't too many rules and regulations. Or if there were, I ignored them and went for darśhan as often as I could...multiple times a day. Forgive me Amma. I thought of myself as a little kid. Even now I still do, just my body got much older.

I learned early on that Amma could read my mind. Once, I really wanted one of Amma's prasād candies. They looked so good. But could I go for darśhan just to get a candy? No! A typical kid's dilemma. Before long, darśhan was over. Amma stood up and we all prostrated. Suddenly I felt someone yanking on my hair. It was Amma laughing wholeheartedly as she gave me a candy.

Only now can I appreciate the enormous faith my parents had in Amma. At the tender age of fifteen they let me go on the Europe Tour with Amma. There were no tour buses with hundreds of staff and several trucks and cargo vans. There were just a couple of vans with Amma and the swāmīs. I was not part of the in-crowd, so I had to organize everything by myself. I got an interrail train ticket that gave me access to all trains all over Europe, and a thick timetable book that had the schedule for every train in every country. Remember, back then there were no cell phones, no internet, and I barely spoke any English. Either it was my parent's faith...or...were they trying to get rid of me?

Other than the train ticket I had nothing organized. I only had a naive and blind faith that Amma would take care of me. And Amma's devotees did take care of me. Not once did I go hungry or sleep on a park bench. Amma watched out for me and asked me how I was doing. When I didn't turn up for a morning program she'd ask where I'd been. Most memorable was when I got invited to ride with Amma's group in the TGV train from Bordeaux to Paris. Finally they were using my mode of transportation!

We arrived at the station in separate cars, and then I found myself with Amma. She invited me to sit next to her on a bench by the platform. If you ever have to wait for a train, there is nothing that could possibly be better than having Amma sitting next to you. I promise, you won't mind the train being late. I remember that Amma teased me saying, "You will soon go off to college and see pretty girls, and then you will forget all about Amma." Fortunately, that didn't come true. She also said that being in the world is like putting sugar in your mouth and trying not to salivate.

I managed to get through France and Italy. My English was bad, but I quickly realized that other people's English was even worse. And yet I caught each train that I needed to catch, and changed trains at the right stations. Again — no smart phones. Just a timetable book and lots of Amma's grace.

My mom had a moment of fear when I didn't show up on the first day of the Belgium program. She was going to join me there. Worried, she started inquiring. Some other devotees said that they had seen me in London, but they were traveling by car and had lost contact with me since I was traveling by train. Concerned, my mom went to Amma and asked about me: "Amma, where is my son? He didn't show up." Amma simply closed her eyes for a moment, then opened them and said that I was fine and that my mom needn't worry.

It seems like I am nothing but trouble for my two moms. I was stuck at the port city of Dover in the U.K. because my train was late and I had missed the last ferry. Back then there was no tunnel. It didn't even occur to me to call someone. Either that, or I was simply too stingy to spend my last precious pound-sterling on a costly international phone booth call.

***

In my first years with Amma I would just sit near her, watch, and meditate. I wondered, "Why isn't everyone doing this? Just sitting here, it's so beautiful. People must be so restless that they have to do other stuff around Amma. Sēvā must be just for people who can't sit still." I am a slow learner and I'm still trying to make up for it. Now I enjoy sēvā and have a hard time sitting still on the floor. I shift around and wish I had taken my dad's offer to teach me the lotus position at a young age. Now I am as stiff as a broomstick.

Amma has taught me the beauty of sēvā. Although I often fail, I try to practice her advice to always help others when asked. Each opportunity is a blessing. As long as we can move our body and mind, we can find a way to contribute. Slowly we understand that giving is more beneficial than taking.

When I was younger, every year Amma asked me about my studies. Study? Why did Amma keep asking about my studies? I was too arrogant to see that Amma wanted me to do well, or to realize how important it is to find a job and earn a living. Luckily, I somehow got through school reasonably well. By Amma's grace I have managed to make a living as an architect, but still have so much more to learn.

Amma keeps emphasizing scriptural studies. I always thought just listening to Amma was sufficient, and if I couldn't put even half of what Amma says into daily practice, why burden myself with even more? I now see two aspects to scriptural studies: first, it positions Amma's teachings in a much wider and historic context. Secondly, it always helps to find inspiration and directions when viewing a topic from other angles. Amma's scholarly young children have inspired me to learn more about the *Bhagavad Gītā* and the *Rāmāyaṇa.*

While Amma's love is boundless, our ego seems endlessly resistant. By clinging to 'I' and 'mine' we shut ourselves out from our true Self. We are having an identity crisis. Amma keeps telling us that we are the self-effulgent sun and not a mere candle. A lot of rewiring needs to happen, and Amma is the expert mechanic to see it through. Little by little she brings us face to face with our misconceptions and opens us up. Why do we love Amma so much? It is her innocent beauty that connects us to our innermost being. We see our true Self in her. Amma captivates us with her love.

Surrender to the Guru is essential, but it is a concept almost impossible for people in the West to grasp. A typical thought process is like this:

> "Yes, it is fine to accept a teacher for math or music, but a teacher for the science of life, living and the Self? No way. I know myself. I don't need a teacher for that. Or do I? I admit I'm a mess. I don't know what is going on in me, but it is my mess. Somehow, I feel I am in control of things. At least I think so. Religion is fine, but God is somewhere, and I am here. God in a person? No way. And that person and I are one? I don't understand it. It's too much. Give me a break."

It is very difficult to overcome this way of thinking. It is heavily ingrained in our society and examples of successful Guru-disciple relationships in Western culture are rare. Individualistic thinking and ego predominate. Why would the ego willingly give the Guru, its archenemy any place in its life?

Amma is patient, and so loving and sweet. She knows we get scared easily. Too much challenge and we run away. One stern look and we think Amma doesn't love us, and we turn our back on her. Why do we think we know better than she does and want everything on our terms? Let's not be fools. We need to have our own experiences to learn, but the quicker we realize that we have little control over what happens in our life, the better. Let's concentrate only on what we can control. There's a story about a fisherman who was asked how he could remain so calm in the face of bad weather at sea. He replied, "I have no control over the wind and the water. All I know is how to steer the ship. That's all I concentrate on." What an inspiration! Mindset is key. I'll give you an amazing example for this later.

***

When preparing this satsang, a friend suggested I talk about something I know. When I said I don't know anything, he said, "Talk about Indian snacks and the Europe tour." If you have ever been on a Europe tour, you will remember 'samosas' and 'onion bhajis' and 'hot masala chai' — all a distant memory since Covid.

In every city we'd set up our big kitchen tent, fully equipped with floors, lighting, electricity, water lines, gas lines, fryers, fridges, ovens, and sound system...everything. Setup is a major undertaking and Amma's tight schedule leaves no time for twiddling our thumbs. Typically we'd arrive at a venue around midnight, sleep for a few hours and then start setting up at 5:00 a.m. Three hours later the cooks would start cooking. It's amazing how Amma's children willingly pull together to make something like that happen. Our love for Amma and for one another can shift mountains.

Amma protects us, and she ensures her children don't cause too much trouble. Her teachings and example can also greatly influence her children to have the right mindset to help diffuse difficult situations. Here's an example:

During Dēvī Bhāva, one of the 'Indian Snacks' jobs is to keep the people happy who are waiting in line for hours for darśhan, by providing them snacks and chai. We'd walk alongside the darśhan line with trays of chai and shout, "Chai, chai, chai" (like /they do on Indian trains). One time in Toulon, I was carrying a tray full of hot chai and cold lassi. Huge numbers of people were sitting on the floor, and we had to carefully balance the hot drinks. At one point I needed to catch my breath, so I set my tray on a plastic pillar next to the queue of seated devotees.

I didn't realize that what I thought was a sturdy support for my tray of steaming hot chai and delicious cold mango lassi was nothing but an illusion of stability. The plastic bent under the weight of the tray then snapped back. Five servings of hot chai catapulted into the air and landed on an unsuspecting lady seated next to the pillar. What a shock! I was scared stiff. Getting burned by one spilled chai is bad enough, let alone five! The lady had a rude awakening from whatever state she was in.

To my surprise, except for a little gasp she wasn't screaming in pain. In disbelief I kept asking her, "Are you ok? Are you ok? Are you hurt?" I assumed she was just in shock as she kept insisting she was fine. Picture this: her immaculate white dress dripping with chai and mango lassi. Then I realized the chai and lassi had mixed and made a perfect lukewarm mixture in midair; here was another miracle! I apologized profusely but the lady insisted she was fine. I offered to get her a new dress from the Amma shop since hers was ruined, but she said she had a second dress in her car. She was so calm, composed and kind. It was as if I had handed her a bouquet of flowers instead of sudden chai-lassi abhiṣhēkam.[80] Salutations to such equanimity. She had every reason to be upset and scream at me. She chose to remain totally unaffected.

***

When I was eighteen or nineteen, I traveled to see Amma in Amritapuri. There was no internet at that time, so I just assumed that Amma would be there at that time of year. So naive. Thankfully I have been blessed to generally keep my cool in the midst of chaos.

I had an Air India connecting flight from Frankfurt to Mumbai and Mumbai to Kochi. When we landed in Mumbai, a

---

[80] Ceremonial bath, usually given to deities in a temple.

frantic Air India representative told us that the airline was on strike, and I couldn't proceed to Kochi. They would put us up in a hotel. He couldn't say how long the strike would be. One day, two...nobody knew. I wasn't going to stick around and shared a rickshaw with some Americans going to the domestic terminal. Gosh! Those Americans talk a lot! Unfortunately, they failed to mention that they were on their way to an Amma program...

At the airport I went to every single airline counter to see if they could fly me to Kerala, and if they would accept the Air India ticket I was waving at them. I finally found one airline who accepted the ticket and told me that they flew to Calicut. I didn't even have to pay anything extra.

My plan was that once I got to Kerala, I would just hop on a train. I reached Calicut in an airplane that seemed mostly held together by duct tape. Calicut has a tiny airport and the terminal seemed like an oversized living room. When I went to the money exchange counter, to my shock they didn't accept traveler cheques. I was exhausted by that time and stranded with no money even for a taxi into town. A businessman took pity on me and exchanged one hundred dollars worth of rupees for one of my cheques. Usually, the cheque needs to be countersigned in the presence of the teller. When I signed, I was shaking with exhaustion and my second signature didn't match the first one. God bless him. He saved me.

When I reached the Calicut railway station that morning, I learned that the next train for Karunagappally wasn't until late afternoon. Finally, boarding the train without a reservation and with a yelling train conductor who almost threw me out, we went rolling on into the night. I didn't see any station names, and it was only by the kindness of my fellow passengers that I knew where to get off. They advised me to take a hotel in Kollam and go to the āśhram during the day, however, I just wanted to reach the āśhram.

The Karunagappally train station was absolutely deserted and pitch black. I found a single rickshaw with a driver sleeping in it. I woke him with, "Amma, āśhram." These keywords set him in motion. I reached the ferry jetty right at sunrise, and saw the āśhram buildings from across the backwater. I felt like crying.

As I climbed the stairs to the Kāḷi temple in the āśhram, a fellow German greeted me saying, "Welcome Benjamin. Did you know that Amma is leaving in an hour? We are going to a program in Calicut. I'll find you a seat on the bus." Later I saw Amma at a chai stop on the road. She gave me a hug but didn't seem at all surprised to see me. No wonder. She had been with me the whole time.

23

Faith in Guru and God

Guramrit - USA

The journey of a sādhak (spiritual seeker) continues for many lifetimes. Śhrī Śhaṅkarāchārya said, "There is no title in all the three worlds suitable for a Satguru." Swāmījī says, "For the true disciple or devotee, there is no other God than his Guru. He remembers his Guru with every breath." A Hindi couplet by Sant Kabīrjī says,

> *guru gōvind doū khaḍe, kāke lagūṅ pāōṅ*
> *baliharī guru apne gōvind diyō batāyē*

> 'Both God and the Guru are before me, whose feet do I bow down to?
> O my dearest Guru, it is you...for by your blessings I could attain the Divine.'

Once Amma was asked, "Who is greater, God or the Guru?" Amma said:

> "In principle, God and the Guru are the same. The Guru's grace is something unique. If the Guru wants, he can remove [...] the effect of God's displeasure. But even God cannot remove the sin that comes from dishonoring the Guru."

Guru Nānak Dēvjī, the founder of Sikhism, says in the *Śhrī Guru Granth Sāhib*[81]:

---

[81] The central sacred text or scripture of Sikhism.

> "One who enters the holy śharaṇāgati (refuge) of the Satguru, so chooses the lotus feet of the Satguru, so surrenders himself at his feet, has actually been accepted and saved by the Guru. A Sikh (or any disciple) who does not leave the Guru, the Guru never leaves him. He who truly loves the Satguru, the Satguru loves him much more. He who chooses the divine, has already been chosen by the divine."

Sant Kirpāl Singhjī says:

> "In the garb of man, God comes into the world and dwells amongst us for the sake of suffering humanity and we cannot know of God in spite of his presence everywhere. Through the Guru's saving grace, he takes upon himself the many responsibilities for our shortcomings. And highly charged with higher consciousness, He injects the jīvas (individual souls) with his life impulse. There is no friend greater than Satguru; He is the protector here and everywhere. Search for such a one right and left, high and low, and never rest until he is found."

During a question-and-answer session, Amma was asked, "How can we tell if we are in the presence of a true Guru?" Amma said, "A true Guru will be a role model for others, and is like a policeman disguised as a thief in order to catch a thief — to help us realize our mistakes and guide us along the right path."

In the absence of a living master like Amma, we cannot develop the devotional attitude necessary on the spiritual path. In one of Amma's Guru Pūrṇimā messages, she says:

> "The Guru-śhiṣhya (Guru-disciple) relationship becomes complete only if the disciple has faith and

> self-surrender. It is rightly said that spirituality can neither be bought nor taught, but it may be caught like an infection, from one highly infected himself."

Amma's life purpose is to inspire the divinity within each of us. She doesn't want us to abandon our faith, but instead understand that the very essence of all religious teachings is to deepen our connection with God.

A recent video showed Amma in the swimming pool rowing a boat made of recycled plastic bottles. Afterwards, Amma told us that if we were to row a boat with just the oar of faith but without the oar of self-effort, then our boat would only go in circles. And if we rowed the boat with only the oar of effort without the oar of faith, then our boat would still go in circles. Amma said that we need to blend together faith, self-effort, and being intent on the goal for our boat to row smoothly.

Amma says as spiritual seekers we should have the intensity of a fish out of water. It flutters, striving for water as it suffocates, gasping for life. I used to struggle to chant the *Śhrī Lalitā Sahasranāma* archana along with my Sikh prayers. I asked Swāmī Rāmakṛishnānanda if it was really necessary to chant the thousand names. Swāmījī said that Amma doesn't force anyone, and that I need not do it if it was too much. But he added that chanting the thousand names was most beneficial. Not only does it purify the atmosphere, but all the basic needs of the spiritual aspirant who regularly chants it are met.

By Amma's grace, chanting the Śhrī Lalitā Sahasranāma became an integral part of my spiritual practices. When Amma told me to pray during a difficult period in my life, I took Amma's words to heart. By putting maximum effort into our spiritual practices we invoke God's grace. Maintaining spiritual discipline has given me faith and strength to accept whatever comes, and I feel Amma's hand always guiding me.

Amma once said, "Each and every drop of Amma's blood, each and every particle of her energy, is for her children. The purpose of this body and of Amma's whole life is to serve her children." Nowhere in history has such sacrifice ever been seen. Amma's every breath works like an infinite factory of compassion. She takes every jīva's heavy karma, dilutes its potency, fills it with her grace and restores it with her unconditional love. Just one divine hug heals lifetimes, and the karmic restoration work begins. Before Amma's First World Tour in 1987, Amma said, "My children are everywhere. They are crying for Amma but cannot find me. Amma must go to them."

***

Since then, Amma has traveled the world for more than thirty years, lighting the lamp of divinity and returning each year to rekindle the flame with her loving embrace. My sister Nihsimajī and I have been blessed to accompany Amma on most of her western tours. There is no greater miracle than watching Amma's compassionate embrace transform millions of lives. Amma sits for hours pulling humanity into her arms. Amma cultivates the spirit of self-sacrifice, unity, and service in her children all over the world.

Amma's programs are the most magnificent festivals. The program halls are transformed into glorious sanctuaries, brimming with love and joyful selfless service. Thousands of meals and drinks are served, pots get scrubbed, bathrooms get cleaned, and endless hours of troubleshooting happen with only one goal in mind — to follow Amma's example.

Sanātana Dharma[82] rightly demonstrates that the whole world is one kuṭuṁbam (family).[83] Amma's teachings take us beyond our cultural differences and personal desires. A few years back in the early morning during an extremely large Dēvī Bhāva in Milan, Italy while everyone's eyes were on Amma, I saw an elderly man hunched over a broom, meticulously sweeping the far end of the balcony. He must have been eighty-plus years old. Hours later, he was still sweeping. This joy of giving knows no bounds. It's as if the great gates of heaven open for every thirsty soul to drink the rejuvenating amṛit, the nectar of Amma's selfless love, and awaken to their higher purpose.

This earnest yearning and collective outpouring of hearts brings Amma back each year to hold and comfort all her darling children. For the first time in more than thirty years, Amma has not been able to visit her children due to Covid. Amma deeply feels their sadness. Out of deep love and compassion, Amma has showered her grace on us by giving the daily webcast of her meditations, spiritual discourses, satsangs and bhajans.

After a year spent away from Amma because of Covid, as well as having had many opportunities to travel with Amma and be with her in Amritapuri, I've had time to reflect, "What does it mean to be 'with' Amma? To see Amma? To listen to Amma? To follow Amma? To bow down to Amma? To embrace Amma? And what does it really mean to have faith in Amma?"

In one Guru Pūrṇimā satsang Swāmī Amṛitaswarūpānandajī said, "Listen to Amma – not with ears. Touch Amma – not with hands, but with your soul." Swāmī Shāntāmritānandajī said, "If we want to see the real Amma, we must remain open

---

[82] 'The Eternal Way of Life,' the original and traditional name of Hinduism.

[83] Reference to the popular phrase from *Mahā Upaniṣhad*: 'vasudhaiva kuṭumbakam' – 'the world is one family' (6.72). Kuṭumbakam is synonymous with kuṭumbam.

and receptive, and simply be in her holy presence, with the surrender and openness of a small child." But how can we have complete surrender? Amma says:

> "Surrender means accepting everything in life. It is like remaining still on God's operation table, and we can only put forth our best effort and surrender the rest to the divine will. In that state of surrender, the Lord accepts all our burdens."

I always struggled with surrendering my workload to Amma. I thought Amma had enough to take care of, and I often found myself burdened by the sense of doership created by my lack of awareness. Once, after my darśhan, Amma called me back and exclaimed, "Sēvā sēvā sēvā!" Amma's attendant translated that Amma said, "I was doing a lot of sēvā." Actually, I felt that Amma was saying I should do more sēvā.

For many years, one of my sēvās was to help coordinate Amma's visit to San Ramon. The San Ramon temple is the smallest program hall in North America. To accommodate large crowds, I had to make sure that there was enough seating for everyone before and during every program, remove all the extra chairs that had been added at program's end, then reset the hall seating for the next day. However much I tried, I could not find any easy solution for this exhausting routine year after year. One evening, as I glanced at Amma hopelessly, I realized how small my role was in Amma's divine play. All I needed to do was to offer my sēvā to Amma and focus on being a well-tuned instrument in her hands. After all, was it not really Amma seating all her darling children?

Amma orchestrates the perfect master plan for each of us with sēvās that will help us transcend our personal limitations of body and mind, and become fully aware of our ego. Amma once said that we should never miss an opportunity to serve. It is like winning the lottery. Now, when a new sēvā opportunity comes my way, I simply smile and think of all the new doors and windows opening to help me release my hidden vāsanās. By surrendering my responsibilities to Amma, instead of feeling burdened, I pray to Amma to make me worthy of serving her and her children.

***

I grew up in Delhi in a traditional Sikh family from Punjab, where Gurus play a central role, and grew up with the teachings of Guru Nānak, the founder of Sikhism. He was born into a Hindu brāhmin family, and like Amma he taught the oneness of God and humanity. He also insisted that women be allowed to serve as spiritual leaders in the Sikh faith.

My father followed a strict religious discipline and liked to meet different saints. He also blessed me with my name – Guramrit. We often had religious gatherings at our home, and my mother taught us spiritual values and to honor the lives of the Sikh Gurus who fought for dharma. Both my parents have had a strong influence in my life. Growing up, I would often feel the pain of the poor and the less fortunate. I wondered why so many people had to suffer while we lived so comfortably.

When I was sixteen, I went to study in a boarding convent college in Himāchal Pradesh for three years. I was away from my family nine months of the year. The strict monastic discipline gave me the strength to overcome many difficulties later in life. When I was eighteen, both my mother and grandmother passed away suddenly in a car accident. This was my first lesson in the spiritual truth that death is the most inevitable reality of our existence.

Amma says, "We cannot change situations in life, but we can change our attitude towards them." A few years later our prārabdha karma took my family to the U.S. where we settled near San Francisco. There, my son was diagnosed with a severe bleeding disorder that required constant intravenous infusions to treat spontaneous internal bleeding. With Amma's infinite grace, he has always exemplified great courage, true surrender, and acceptance.

In Amma's words, "Only when one gets a few blows in life does one learn to look within. It is when we experience tragedy that we wish to learn how to transcend sorrow." My life struggles served as my first Guru, and each experience paved my way to Amma. In Śhrī Paramahaṁsa Yōgānandajī's words, "If the devotee is persistent in his prayer and in faith, God will surely respond by sending that soul a true Guru to guide him." I started praying to Guru Nānak Dēvjī to meet my Guru.

A few months later, I saw Amma's photo on the front page of a local newspaper featuring the 'hugging saint from India.' Just then a beautiful image of Lord Kṛiṣhṇa flashed in my mind. Amma's Northern California program in November 2000 was held near our home. My sister and I hadn't heard of Amma before, so we went to receive her darśhan. The atmosphere in the hall was serene and familiar. After darśhan, the emptiness I had experienced before was now filled with the deep love that a mother has for her long-lost child. Lifetimes of tears gushed out as we soaked in the holy river of Amma's loving, compassionate embrace.

I returned that evening for Dēvī Bhāva and received my mantra from Amma. I never imagined that my prayers would be answered so quickly and that my Guru would come in the form of a loving mother, speaking a language that I'd never heard before. My family has also been blessed to receive Amma's darśhan.

My brother, who has courageously faced many adversities in life, had resisted coming to Amma, holding onto his strong Sikh faith and beliefs. I felt such joy when Amma answered my prayers and he finally came for Amma's darśhan as well.

As he waited by the entrance of the San Ramon temple with palms folded and eyes closed, Amma arrived, stepping out of a white car. Just then to his amazement, he saw his beloved Guru Gōbind Singhjī dismounting his white horse and entering the hall. My brother stood there in complete reverence. Later he also received a mantra from Amma and started chanting the thousand names.

By 2010, my father started showing signs of decline. I anxiously asked Swāmī Dayāmṛitānandajī about which rites to perform when my father passed away. Swāmījī assured me not to worry, as Amma would take care of everything.

A few months before Amma's Summer U.S. Tour in 2014, I felt a strong desire to help take care of my father. Not long after, he fell and suffered a brain hemorrhage. We felt Amma was taking care of everything. Our satsang family sang bhajans in the ICU room, and a Punjabi Sikh doctor appeared from nowhere and arranged the best room in the hospital for us. We took turns staying up at night doing archana, and Sikh hymns played nonstop. A beautiful altar graced the room, and our father was surrounded by family at all times.

On the fifth morning, as I was telling my brother that the biggest blessing a father can give his children is to bring them to God, my brother felt Amma's divine presence enter the room, and just then we watched our father take his last breath. The Sikh chant, "*Wāhe Guru, Wāhe Guru, Wāhe Guru*" (O Wondrous Guru, O Wondrous God), resounded nonstop through me. One doctor had tears in her eyes, saying the energy in the room was filled with light. In keeping with tradition, we really wanted my father's cremation to happen the very next day, but it was impossible due to the medical certificates needed. However, Amma worked out all the details. Early next morning a priest from the Sikh temple accompanied us for the last rites. Later, Swāmī Dayāmṛitānandajī and our satsang fulfilled my heartfelt desire by attending a memorial service that we hosted near our father's home. Later, when my sister and I went to Amma, and before we could say very much, Amma said that she was very happy that we were all there together with my father. What else could a daughter ask for?

I bow down to Amma in humility for compassionately showering her grace upon us all. In this life with Amma, she has shown me that her infinite power makes the unmovable move, the unchangeable change, and the weak become strong. This power is present in all of us, but we need her grace to be a dāsa (true servant). By having faith in Amma, I am able to let go of my attachments. Only by surrendering at my beloved Guru's feet can I be free. Amma says:

> "Children, God doesn't have any hands or feet of his own. He works through us, through our eyes, ears, and hands. So we have to bring him into our hands, into our feet, into our tongue, our eyes, and our hearts. We ourselves have to become God."

Amma's super GPS tracking system goes beyond the realm of each of our births and deaths. Once, Amma asked me if I just had my birthday. I said yes and wondered, "Amma you see so many children, how can you know that it's my birthday?" Today, twenty-one years later, I am deeply grateful to Amma to offer this satsang on the eve of my sixtieth birth year tomorrow.

The sixtieth year signifies the 'ṣhaṣhtipūrti' milestone — the completion of half of one's lifetime. It emphasizes the vānaprastha and sannyāsa[84] stages of life. This is also an occasion to offer gratitude for this rare and precious life given by God and Guru. In this birth we are all truly victorious, in spite of our inner and outer struggles as we have been given the highest blessing to have Amma as our Guru — the one who has taken birth to bring us back to our true abode. I pray that we don't waste this rare gift of human life.

> *tū kāhē i dōlah prānīā tudh rakhaigā sirjanhār*
> *jin paidāis tū kīā sōī dēi ādhār*
> 'Why do you waver, O mortal being? God shall protect you.
> The one who has created you will also take care of you.'
>
> A popular verse from *Guru Granth Sahib*

[84] Vānaprastha: 'forest life;' a reference to the retired life dedicated to spiritual practices; the third of the four stages of life. Sannyāsa: the formal vow of complete renunciation; the fourth and final stage of life.

24

Gratitude

Govinda Rohkitte - Germany

The topic of my satsang is gratitude. In Sanskrit it's called kṛitajña. 'Kṛita' means cultivated, and the root 'jña' refers to a state of consciousness. 'Cultivated consciousness' could also mean 'enlightened awareness.' This shows us that to be grateful, a higher consciousness or awareness is needed. Due to lack of awareness, many people are unaware of their good luck, and therefore cannot appreciate it. Very often in my life I have counted myself in this category.

When I consider the great fortune I've had to be blessed by meeting Amma, and that she has accepted me as her devotee, I feel a deep gratitude in that moment. I am even more thankful because I never had a religious education, nor did I have a wish for spiritual things. It was through suffering that I finally made my way to God.

Amma knows me as the little kitten that is often 'meowing' when I come to her for darśhan. Mostly I meow about suffering from a depressed mind, or that I'm deeply disappointed because of a relationship. The last time I told Amma that I don't want to live like this anymore, she explained to me how precious life is, and that I have to carry on! "I have to carry on?" I thought. That was not what I wanted to hear, but it helped me enormously to better accept myself and my life, and to become stronger and more self-confident. Today I want to present myself from a different angle, and I want to express my gratitude.

When I was born, my mother was a child herself, only fifteen years old. She was brought to the hospital by her mother who left her there all alone for the delivery. She was very anxious and had no idea what was going to happen next. Later she told me that I was the one who had fought with all my strength to come into this life. My father left us when I was only a few months old. My mother then married another man, and I grew up not knowing that he was my stepfather.

I had a nice childhood amongst a lot of beautiful nature. We had a dog, a Saint Bernhard who always went out for walks with me. I had friends to play with and I had my own room with a lot of play toys. Everything appeared to be fine, except for the fact that my mother beat me regularly. I often missed her because she worked ten hours every day and wasn't home during the daytime.

I grew up mostly with my step-grandmother. At first she was displeased when her son came home with a young girl and her so-called 'bastard' son. Later on however, I think due to my innocence, she grew to like me. She had her own small supermarket business to run, so I was often left alone spending time by myself. The feeling that no one really cared for me or that I wasn't worthy of being loved arose in me.

Amma says the truth should be spoken kindly, without harming the other person. When I was fourteen years old, my mother told me that I was 'old enough,' and that she had something to tell me. "Your father is not your real father," she said. Then she showed me a piece of an old newspaper.

The headline was: 'Tragedy in Store, Man Shoots Woman then Shoots Himself'

I didn't understand!

"That was your father," my mother replied.

You can imagine my shock. But when I ran to my friends to tell them what I had just learned — my father is not my father! — they were astonished that I was just finding this out now. They told me that everybody in the village had known this for a long time; so how was it that I hadn't found out? I was shocked and lost all confidence in myself because I was the son of a murderer. I lost all my trust in others as well, at the same time. Two years later, my mother moved out and soon she and my step-dad divorced. I stayed a few months more with my step-dad, until he threw me out one day. Six months later, I made my first suicide attempt.

***

It took six more years with some time spent in mental hospitals before my stepfather suggested seeking out a non-medical practitioner. This specialist was able to help me in a better way. He had a picture of his Guru on the wall. I was curious and asked who the man in the photo was, because his eyes were so fascinating. He told me the man's name was Swāmī Nārāyaṇānanda. I thought, "Oh dear..."

But then I read some of his books and discovered that God is 'sat-chid-ānanda' — 'the all-pervading truth, consciousness, and bliss' — and I felt that for the first time in my life, I heard the truth in my heart. Not a God presiding over heaven while sitting on a throne and judging and punishing everyone for their transgressions, but a God who is ever blissful, compassionate, and in the form of true knowledge itself, residing in our own hearts.

I started to meditate, do yōga and mantra japa, and to read spiritual books. Because Swāmī Nārāyaṇānanda had already left his body, I prayed to meet a living master. In the summer of 1993, my prayers were answered when I met Amma for the first time in Cologne. The hall was dark yet full of light. Around fifty people gathered in front of the small stage where Amma sat.

When Amma gave darśhan, she spent so much time with each person. Perhaps you know the feeling of time and space seeming to disappear while being held in Amma's embrace. Everything was filled with the sense of unreserved security, love and being unconditionally accepted. That was how I felt when I got my first darśhan.

A year later in December 1994, I came to Amritapuri for the first time, and I'm so very grateful for that! It was still early times around Amma, without many of the comforts we can find in the āśhram today. We did a lot of sand sēvā, tile sēvā, and concrete sēvā during those days; moving sand and other construction materials, mixing and pouring concrete etc. Even though there wasn't any cappuccino, coke, burger, or french fries to enjoy afterwards, as there would be today, it was a wonderful experience to be a part of this community. It gave me so much self-confidence and made me stronger.

Over the next few years, I came to Amritapuri almost every year, spending five or six weeks at a time. I remember one visit when the building for the brahmachāriṇīs was being built, I was staying in the men's dorm above the Kālī temple. One day, I fell sick. I felt weak and had a cold and a little fever, so I stayed in bed.

After lunch, someone rushed into my room saying, "Ōm Namaḥ Śhivāya,[85] we need more men to help with concrete sēvā." "I'm sorry, I feel sick today," I replied. But this guy wouldn't take 'no' for an answer and told me I should try and see how it goes. I said, "No man. I mean, I really feel sick. I have a fever!"

Again he came forward, saying things like, "Amma will give you the strength," and so on. What can you reply to that

[85] A famous mantra meaning 'Salutations to Śhiva, the auspicious one, the inner Self' that is used as a greeting in Amma's āśhrams.

when you like to call yourself an Amma devotee? Finally he got to me. I slowly got out of bed, put on my work boots and dhōti,[86] and went to the fifth floor of the new building. Standing there with a fever in the heat of the day, I started working. We formed a human chain, passing these small bowls filled with concrete from one person to another. As time went by, I felt better and better. Of course, I was sweating, but who wasn't at that moment and who wouldn't while doing that kind of sēvā? For me it was kind of a miracle. Earlier, I never would have imagined I'd be able to work that day. I am so very grateful for this experience! It helped me to see how we can overcome our own weaknesses and our doubts by putting in the effort to help others, or for a higher purpose.

***

In 2000 I came to Amritapuri to see if I could stay for a longer period of time, to see if this was the place I could call home. Ultimately I ended up spending four months in the āśhram. During that time, I joined the North India Tour for the first time. Before that, I had only attended the five-day programs in Trivandrum and Calicut, so this was a big challenge for me. I loved the experience of traveling with Amma and especially enjoyed bathing in rivers with Amma, where she washed our faces with soap to wash away our vāsanās. We also savored the chai and meditation stops in open fields. Then, of course, there were the huge crowds at the programs, which were quite challenging.

One unforgettable experience was the inauguration of the Brahmasthānam temple. There was so much energy during that program. Eagles circled auspiciously above the temple. I'm so grateful that I was there.

---

[86] Sarong-like cloth wrapped around the waist, worn by men in India.

When we returned to Amritapuri it took only a few weeks for my old habits and depression to return. One day, when I went for darśhan and told Amma about my negative tendencies, Amma looked at me and said, "Too much tension. Go and come back." The next day I left the āśhram and felt so relieved. Time passed; two years later my daughter was born. I was so happy and very grateful that she was born healthy!

***

According to the teachings of Sanātana Dharma there are five categories of beings to which we should pay homage on a daily basis. These are known as the *Pañcha Mahāyajñas* or the five great sacrifices. They form the basic framework for expressing gratitude, especially by householders:

1. *Pitṛu yajña* to our parents and ancestors — we can express our gratitude through honoring, serving, and caring for them. Another way is the performance of pūjās (ritualistic worship) like Vāvu Bali, which is an ancestral offering performed in Kerala on a new moon day in July, intended to bring peace to the departed souls and ensure their unobstructed onward journey.
2. *Dēva yajña* to the demi-gods or celestial beings who manage the universe and manifest in the natural world as forces of nature — we can express our gratitude through offering a portion of the bounty that we have received from them, like flowers, incense, water, fire, or fruits. Hōmas or fire rituals also belong to this type of sacrifice.
3. *Brahma yajña* to the ancient sages as well as to our teachers who impart scriptural and other forms of knowledge to us — we can express our gratitude by respecting them, studying well and passing on the knowledge we have received by teaching others.

4. *Manuṣhya yajña* to all members of society — we can express our gratitude by contributing to social service works, feeding and clothing the poor, and just by being a good and caring citizen observing our duties.
5. *Bhūta yajña* to the environment, which is our life support system — we can express our gratitude by caring for the forests, rivers, oceans, feeding birds and animals, separating and reducing waste, and applying ecologically sustainable principles.

In Chapter 3, verse 11 of the *Bhagavad Gītā,* Lord Kṛiṣhṇa says:

> *dēvān bhāvayatānēna tē dēvā bhāvayantu vaḥ*
> *parasparaṁ bhāvayantaḥ śhrēyaḥ param avāpsyatha*
> 'By your sacrifices the celestial gods will be nourished and they will nourish you; thus by pleasing one another you shall attain the highest good.'

Gratitude with awareness leads to love, and love leads to happiness. Amma always tells us that happiness is a decision. Mostly I really didn't understand this because I have suffered from depression since my youth. But now I actively work on gratitude and I feel better. Amma says a real master teaches you to accept everything in life. Such a master helps you to be thankful for good and bad, for friend and enemy, to feel gratitude for those who hurt you, for those who help you, for those who coop you up, as well as for those who free you from your cage.

It was a long journey through many difficult experiences that made me understand this. When I was in a relationship with a woman from 2006 to 2009, I would do almost anything for her. I looked to her for love, hoping she would finally see that 'I am her man.' But in vain! It resulted in my having a mental breakdown and four-month stay in a mental hospital! At that time, I was full of hatred and anger, completely disappointed, insanely jealous, and suicidal. It took me a few months to come back to Amma again. I was so angry and upset with her. Why did she let me suffer like this?!?

It has all been purged — the jealousy, the anger, the hatred, and the desperation. Today I'm able to see the situation from a different perspective. I'm thankful for this experience and that this girl and I have not become enemies. Through Amma, we were able to forgive each other after some time. Amma saved me from a love that brings only involvement, dependency, and discontentment, and I guess she also cleaned my mind a bit. She helped me so much with these lessons. I gained more self-confidence and independence. But it took a long time for me to get the right understanding. Today, I'm thankful for these lessons!

Amma says, "Gratitude is an inner connection between us, God, and the entire universe." I know that I can never repay what I have received, and I cannot express enough gratitude towards my Guru, but at least I want to try to express my gratitude to Amma: I thank you, Amma, for your guidance; your endless patience with me; for every precious moment in your presence; for every lesson you have given me; for your unconditional love; and for accepting me when I couldn't accept myself.

Thank you for saving my life several times; for all the good and the bad in my life; for every opportunity to do sēvā; and the chance to become a bit more selfless. Thank you for all my sisters and brothers in faith. Thank you for all the talents you have given me. Thank you Amma for protecting me and for the gift of my daughter.

Thank you, Amma, for all the support I received in Amritapuri and at home when I most needed it. Thank you for giving me shelter and food every day.

Finally, Amma, thank you for taking me as your devotee and for all those things you have done for me (and are still doing) that I'm unaware of — *Vaḷareyadhikam nandi Ammē* (Thank you so much Amma).

25

Compassion is the Answer

Amritasri - Spain

I met Amma when I was eight years old. In that way, I don't really know any life without her. I don't have formal education in scriptures, so I will share some of my life experiences through which Amma has taught me significant values. I hope some of you can relate or feel inspired by these experiences.

I was lucky to be born in a family that was spiritually inclined. My parents were very involved in the Transcendental Meditation organization from before I was born. Growing up, meditation and worshiping God were the norm in our household.

My grandmother used to tell me that when I was around four years old, at bedtime I would sometimes curl up on one side of my bed and stare at the other empty side. She would ask me what I was looking at? I would tell her a woman full of light with long, dark, wavy hair, dressed in a beautiful white dress was sitting at the edge of my bed, smiling at me. I have no doubt this was Amma, already looking after me even before we physically met.

I met Amma physically in 1995. It is said that if you take one step towards God, God will take one-hundred steps towards you. In Amma's case, she gets on a plane and travels thousands of kilometers to reach her children longing to be with her. In my family's case, she came all the way to a tiny town in the north of Spain.

My parents heard of an Indian saint coming to the north of Spain, and decided to leave us kids home to take a day trip to visit her. They drove five hours and reached a little church in a tiny town where Amma was giving darśhan. When they entered the church and saw that they had to sit on the floor and wait in line to get darśhan they said, "Us? Sit on the floor and wait in line? Who do these people think they are?!? No way! We're leaving." Believe it or not, they left!...or at least they tried to leave. They started the car, intending to leave that tiny town. However, they kept getting lost and wound up back in front of that church!

After the third time this happened, they understood the message, went back inside, sat in line, and waited until they reached Amma. They loved her. They loved her so much that they stayed the whole three days. Then they drove all the way back home, packed our bags and drove us all (Grandma, two brothers, one sister, and me, with us kids ranging in ages between four and eight years old) to Amma's next stop in France.

Being a shy kid I didn't like interacting with strangers, never mind physical contact. However Amma's darśhan felt totally natural, like she was no stranger at all. It felt like it was just meant to be.

After that first day I prayed every day for my parents to take us to the next stop. Amma must have heard me because we did go to the next stop...and the next one, and the next one. We ended up doing the whole Europe Tour in our van. After that tour, many more followed. I bow down to my parents in eternal gratitude for bringing me to Amma in this life, and giving me the chance to grow up with her. By the end of that first tour two things happened:

Number one: Everyone thought I was a boy. I was a little bit of a rebellious kid (that hasn't changed much). I didn't accept anyone telling me how a girl should be, look or behave — that was my way of rebelling. This story has given Amma a good laugh quite a few times. Seeing her face bright with laughter when she looks at me and remembers the little boy-looking kid that I was, is worth everything.

Number two: My entire family fell in love with Amma. So much so that on the last tour stop in Helsinki, my parents asked her if we could all move to India. Amma told us that we had to study first, and then if we still wanted to, we could go later on. This truly made an impression in my mind. If Amma wouldn't let us do something as important as going to live with her at her āśhram because we had to study, then studying must be extremely important to her. This thought that she planted in me has stayed with me my entire career, and really helped me move forward during some challenging times.

When we finally got back home after our first tour, I remember having a deep feeling of incompleteness and emptiness. I wanted to know more about this feeling, so I read some Amma books and finally found an explanation that a kid like me could understand: the analogy of chocolate and carob (a plant-based chocolate substitute). If you've only had carob, you may be content with it. But once you taste real chocolate, carob will never satisfy you again. Likewise, once you experience a small taste of true happiness — your own true Self — nothing else will ever compare to it. My focus became: when will I see Amma next?

I was soon introduced to the āśhram motto taken from the *Vēdas* [87]:

> *tyāgēnaikē amṛitatvamānaśhuḥ*
> 'By renunciation alone is immortality attained.'
>
> *Kaivalya Upaniṣhad*, verse 3

---

[87] Most ancient of all scriptures, originating from God, the Vēdas were not composed by any human author but were 'revealed' in deep meditation to the ancient seers.

The aim of renunciation is to break the sense of 'I' and 'mine.' If we put a fence around a piece of land and say, "This land is mine," isn't it actually still part of the entire earth? By calling it 'mine' I label it and treat it as separate. If I say, "I like this" or "I did this," then I limit myself to this body, this 'me,' and forget that I am one with creation. The aim of renunciation is to break the fence we create around ourselves.

It is difficult to cultivate detachment and often we are scared to renounce things we may like or feel we need. However, through our love for her, Amma helps us and gives us detachment almost without us knowing it. Love gives life purpose and meaning. The greatest human achievements have happened out of love. For love we live and for love we die. Love is the energy of life.

Where there is true love, detachment and renunciation happen naturally. You don't have to strive or make sacrifices for it. We are so lucky to have Amma both as our mother and our Guru. What stronger love is there than the love of a mother for a child? Amma is universal motherhood in a human body. At the same time, what to say of the love of a child for a mother? When we think of Amma, we can't help but feel deep love. Most of Amma's devotees are ready to do anything for her without thinking twice, and that is only out of love. Love for Amma has given me strength and self-confidence throughout life. At the end of the day, nothing really matters. Only Amma matters.

***

Starting when I was around fourteen years old, my father went bankrupt twice. The first time, he ended up going to jail for a couple of years. He was the only income earner in the family, and we were left with absolutely nothing within just a few days. Some Amma devotee friends welcomed us into their house. We all slept in their living room for months until we could recover financially. In the beginning we didn't have money for food, so we had to get it from a charity organization. In that situation, not even knowing what we would eat the next day, the only thing I was upset about was that we wouldn't be able to travel with Amma that year. I cried about that for many nights. I didn't care about where we were sleeping, eating, or how we were going to school. The truth is that if Amma hadn't been in our lives, I would have cried anyway for material things. At least in this way, my tears were all for Amma.

On the back of the archana book is a quote by Amma that says:

'Dēvī (the Divine Mother) will always protect those who chant the *Lalitā Sahasranāma* with devotion every day. They will never face a shortage of food and basic necessities and will also gain spiritual growth.'

I used to read this quote regularly knowing that Amma doesn't only speak the truth, but truth follows her words. Love for Amma protects me from crying for worldly possessions; and faith in her gives me the confidence to move forward without fear, knowing that she only gives us what is best for us. If we truly love Amma then, even when we have nothing, Amma will be all that we want. And when life becomes prosperous, Amma will still be all we want. Our minds will remain untouched by outer or inner circumstances. I pray to Amma that our love for her stays forever strong and unshakeable.

Life is teaching me that without experience we can never truly understand those who endure similar hardships. Without personal hardships we should at least educate ourselves on social issues. How can we help others if we are ignorant of the problems they face?

One of the times I expressed how hard it was for me to be away from Amma physically, her answer was beautiful and full of meaning. She said:

"There are stars in the sky even when it's daytime, but we can't see them. Likewise, Amma is always with you. A camel can cross the desert because it stores water in its hump. Your water is your good memories of when you're with Amma. Hold on to those while you are physically away."

Later I realized this message had an even deeper meaning. These memories have helped any time I had thoughts such as, "I have to work so much extra if I want to go on this tour;" or "I'll have to study so many more hours if I skip these classes;" or "Taking time off will be so hard to arrange with work." Whenever I think like this, my Amma memories snap me right back into reality. My precious Amma memories always help me to get out of my comfort zone. Then the magic happens. As Amma says:

"The Guru's ways are incomprehensible. Once the sapling grows it doesn't only need good conditions, but also storms etc. to make the roots strong and give the sapling the strength to withstand them. But the sapling doesn't know that. Likewise Amma gives her children everything necessary to become true disciples and realize the truth."

***

Having to come and go from Amma's physical presence made me realize that Amma is not confined to her five-foot body, and also how finite being in her physical presence can be. Change is the nature of the world. If we manage to find Amma in our heart, we will never feel apart from her. Eventually my focus shifted from "When will I see Amma next?" to "How can I see Amma in myself and others?"

As I mentioned earlier, Amma always gave a lot of importance to education. Amma's selflessness and self-sacrifice inspired me to want to help her in her mission. I wanted to study something that would serve as a tool to serve others as well. So with her blessings, I decided to become a doctor. Getting an MD degree is a long and time-consuming process. Despite that, and some financial hardships during my university years, Amma blessed me with many opportunities to travel with her. Our pact was unspoken, but in my heart it was as real as if she had written and signed it herself. The deal was Amma would help me skip school to see her as much as possible, as long as I kept my grades at the top of the class. Amma made everything work out with exquisite perfection.

I wrote exams walking straight in from Dēvī Bhāva. I did whatever I could to go to India. Sometimes I would take a break from work so I could run back to Amma's program on the other side of the city. Once, instead of attending a three-day European cardiology convention, I went to Amma's Paris program to do sēvā. The examples are endless. Amma still keeps her side of the deal, as long as I keep mine. Amma taught me how her grace will move mountains for us, but only through our own effort.

I'm reminded of a story. Two little birds had built a nest by the ocean and laid eggs. Unfortunately, an ocean wave took the eggs. The mother bird was heartbroken. To console her, her husband said, "Don't worry, dear. We'll search for them in the ocean." They started trying to empty the ocean by filling their beaks with ocean water, then unloading the few drops of water onto the shore. Repeating this over and over, they forgot sleep and food for days.

The dēvas (demi-gods) were impressed by their unwavering determination. News of this got to Garuḍa, the celestial king of birds. Observing their despair and intense effort, he felt compelled to help and started flapping his powerful wings to dry up the ocean. Now, the ocean got scared and immediately returned the lost eggs to the birds. Our self-effort is like the birds trying to dry up the ocean with every beak-full of water they carry to the shore. Even our biggest efforts may not get us very far. But they will invoke God's grace by which even the seemingly impossible becomes attained.

Amma's life is all about selfless service. Amma says: "Meditation and studying the scriptures are like two sides of a coin, the coin of spiritual life. But the engraving on that coin is selfless service, and that is what gives it its real value."

Compassion and selfless actions take us to the depths of spirituality. Through selfless action we eradicate the ego that hides our true Self. Detached, selfless action leads to liberation. Such action is not just work — it is karma yōga.[88] It's beautiful to see everyone doing sēvā together, no matter their education or social status, happily doing whatever needs doing, even scrubbing toilets.

One time, during a busy season in the Western Café in Amritapuri, an accountant on my right was flipping pancakes on one grill. I, a cardiologist, was making omelets on the other grill, and a mechanical engineer to my left was breaking eggs for the omelets. We don't need a degree or formal education to help others. As Amma says, a simple smile or kind words are ways of helping others. In that way I've had many jobs before and after becoming a doctor: from serving samosas and coffee... to handing out darśhan tokens. Very long hours and always being on call was a little bit like being on a hospital shift, except that it was coupled with periodic bus travel days. Our beloved Amma makes everything worth it. At the same time, Amma is

[88] The path of selfless action.

an expert in finding and pushing our most hidden buttons to help us get over our latent tendencies.

I also learned a lot from distributing darśhan tokens. One of the most important things it taught me is that what happens at Amma's program is what Amma wishes to happen. The more in-tune we are with Amma the more we can 'help' run her program. When we allow our ego to overpower us and the more notion of doership we have, the more it becomes an obstacle for doing Amma's work. This exact thing is applicable in life. Amma, our Guru, will take us to the goal; we just have to let her. As Amma says, "When you have a Guru, it is like traveling in an express bus. You can reach your destination much faster."

In the hospital, I have met colleagues and also patients who truly try to help others, despite not being 'spiritual.' This inspires me and gives me hope for humankind. A hospital is an environment where basically anything you do is for helping others when they most need help and compassion. I am so grateful for my medical degree. For this I am so grateful to Amma. I couldn't possibly have done it without her.

Amma says: "It is compassion towards the world, which allows the shoot of the mind to open up and blossom into the all-encompassing Mind." Even though selfless service gives meaning and purpose to my life, intellectually I never truly understood why a sādhak (spiritual seeker) had to cultivate compassion. After all, on the spiritual path, isn't there just oneself and God? What is the need of feeling compassion towards others?

I got a tiny glimpse of what Amma is talking about when the first wave of Covid-19 struck. When faced with uncertainty, the mind expects the worst. The world was gripped by fear. I was working in a cardiovascular ICU in the south of France. I left Amritapuri in January 2020 to work until the U.S. Tour in

May. I couldn't know that those few months would become a few years. Within days, the U.S. Tour was canceled, and for the first time ever, I had no idea when I'd see Amma again. Life as I knew it crumbled. I felt lost, sad, and isolated. But eventually, like when I was a teenager and throughout my whole life, love and faith in Amma made me move forward without fear.

Amma says, "Never lose your mental strength. That is the real failure. Never fall prey to your mind. Be strong. Be courageous. Failing in external situations is ok, but losing mental strength is true failure."

***

Just as happiness is a decision, fearlessness is also a decision. I just refused to live in fear despite the media pressure, the hospital pressure, and the uncertainty. That gave me the courage to go to work every day and serve in whatever way I could. The support underlying this decision — 'I will not live in fear' — was Amma, since I truly knew that whatever happened to me came from her.

In my feeling of sadness and isolation, I wanted to help Amma, do something for her, but I didn't know how. Finally, Amma made clear in my mind what we all know: the best gift I can give her is to treat others like she would, to treat others like I would treat her, because selfless service and compassion is her mission. By helping others, we contribute to her mission wherever we are in the world. So when the first wave of Covid raged through the world, I tried to help others and treat them with compassion...for Amma. That intention was the only thing that got me up in the morning in those very dark and hard times.

In the past, whenever I have been physically away from Amma, I could feel her presence most in nature, God permeating every element of his untainted creation. But I never felt this with human beings. My own mind and ego could never go beyond other people's minds and egos to see the underlying creator in all. This time though, I realized that by trying to help and treat others with compassion, I felt closer and closer to them — a sense of unity, and somehow I could catch a glimpse of the light pulsating through us all. This experience was temporary and short-lived, but I pray to Amma to give me this experience more and more often and for longer periods of time. The *Chhāndōgya Upaniṣhad*[89] says: "There is a light that shines beyond the world, beyond everything. Beyond all, beyond the highest heaven. This is the light that shines within your heart."

This experience helped me understand that Amma asks us to be compassionate and loving not so much for others to feel good, but for us to realize this unity of all beings and God. Expressing compassion is more for our own upliftment than it is for those who receive it. Actually, on the spiritual path there is not just you and God. There's only God.

Compassion is the answer to the question, "How can I see Amma in others and myself." It's like putting on a pair of glasses that enables you to skip people's mind and ego, and see right through to their true self. Compassion will help us reach the ultimate renunciation, which is dissolving the sense of 'I,' the sense of being boxed up in a human body and lets us realize that we are one with creation.

Amma summed up this experience in a beautiful and simple way. She said:

> *kāruṇyattil āṇu prapanchaṁ nilanilkkunnatu*
> "In compassion lies the whole universe."

---

[89] One of the oldest principal 'Upaniṣhads,' which are the philosophical part of the *Vēdas* dealing with the subject of Brahman, the supreme truth, and the path to realize that Truth.

I am so grateful for all the grace that Amma so generously showers upon us again and again and again.

Glossary

abhiṣhēka: ceremonial bath, usually given to deities in a temple.

abhyāsa: unrelenting spiritual practice, constant effort.

adharma: unrighteousness; deviation from natural harmony.

Ādi Śhaṅkarāchārya: saint revered as a *Guru* and chief proponent of the *advaita* (non-dual) philosophy.

advaita: 'not two;' non-dual philosophy that holds that the *jīva* (individual soul) and *jagat* (universe) are essentially one with *Brahman*, the supreme reality.

AIMS Hospital: Amrita Institute of Medical Sciences, a super-specialty hospital in Kochi, Kerala.

AMMACHI Labs: an academic and research center at Amrita Vishwa Vidyapeetham that brings an interdisciplinary approach to addressing societal challenges. AMMACHI Labs creates innovative educational tools and skill development solutions to help uplift entire communities, especially women and girls in rural villages in India.

amṛit: nectar of immortality, a divine substance symbolizing eternal life and spiritual liberation.

Amrita Vishwa Vidyapeetham: a private, deemed, multi-campus, multidisciplinary university, currently ranked among the best in India.

Amṛitakuṭuṁbam: lit. 'family of nectar or immortality;' Amma's initiative wherein devotees meet regularly in their locality for *bhajan*, chanting and *satsang*.

Amṛitānandamayī: 'full of immortal bliss,' the name by which Amma is universally known.

Amritapuri: the international headquarters of Mata Amritanandamayi Math, located at Amma's birthplace in Kerala, India.

AmritaSREE: Amrita Self-Reliance, Employment & Empowerment, a network of self-help groups managed by the Mata Amritanandamayi Math and aimed at empowering unemployed and economically vulnerable women by providing them with skill and vocational training and by encouraging those who are interested to become entrepreneurs.

ārati: a traditional ritual involving the waving of a lighted lamp to the *Guru* or deity usually done towards the end of *pūjā* or worship. At some of Amma's programs, multiple devotees take turns waving the lighted lamp to Amma as she showers them with flower petals and the ārati song is sung.

archana: chanting of the 108 or 1,000 names of a particular deity (e.g. '*Lalitā Sahasranāma*').

āsana: physical posture, usually referring to *yōga* postures or sitting postures during meditation. Also, the seat on which one sits for spiritual practice.

āśhram: 'place of striving.' A place where spiritual seekers and aspirants live or visit, in order to lead a spiritual life. It is usually the home of a spiritual master, saint or ascetic, who guides the aspirants.

aṣhṭōttaram: litany of 108 attributes of a deity, divine incarnation or saint; short form of *aṣhṭōttara-śhatam* (108) or *aṣhṭōttara-śhata-nāmāvalī* (108 names).

ātmā (ātman): the true Self. The essential nature of our real existence. One of the fundamental tenets of *Sanātana Dharma* is that we are not the physical body, feelings, mind, intellect, or personality. We are the eternal, pure, unblemished Self.

Awaken Children: one of the first compilations of Amma's teachings written by Swāmī Amṛitaswarūpānanda.

bhaga: the six blessed qualities, viz. *jñāna* (knowledge), *aiśh-varya* (sovereignty), śhakti (energy), *bala* (might), *vīrya* (valor) and *tējas* (spiritual splendor). One who has all these qualities is known as *Bhagavān* (God) or *Bhagavatī* (Goddess).

Bhagavad Gītā: 'Song of the Lord,' it consists of 18 chapters of verses in which Lord Kṛiṣhṇa advises Arjuna. The advice is given on the battlefield of Kurukṣhētra, just before the righteous Pāṇḍavas fight the unrighteous Kauravas. It is a practical guide to overcoming crises in one's personal or social life and is the essence of *Vēdic* wisdom.

Bhagavān : God, one who has all the six divine qualities pertaining to *bhaga* (see *bhaga*).

Bhāgavata Purāṇa: also known as *Bhāgavatam*, one of the eigh-teen *Purāṇas,* a devotional Sanskrit composition narrating the life, pastimes and teachings of various incarnations of Viṣhṇu, chiefly that of Lord Kṛiṣhṇa.

Bhaja Gōvindam: a devotional work in Sanskrit composed by Ādi Śhaṅkarāchārya.

bhajan: devotional song or hymn in praise of God.

bhakta: devotee.

bhakti: devotion for God.

bhakti yōga: the path of devotion.

bhāṣhya: commentary or exposition of a text.

bhāva: divine mood or attitude.

bhōgī: one who indulges in sense-pleasures.

Brahmā: Lord of Creation in the trinity of Brahmā, Viṣhṇu (Lord of preservation), and Śhiva (Lord of destruction).

Brahma Sūtras: a central philosophic text synthesizing the teachings of the *Upaniṣhads*, also known as the *Vēdānta Sūtras.*

brahmachārī: celibate male disciple who practices spiritual disciplines under a *Guru's* guidance; '*brahmachāriṇī*' is the female equivalent.

brahmacharya: celibacy; see āśhrama. *Brahma* also means *Vēda.* So, *brahmacharya* is the stage of life in which one pursues the study of the *Vēdas* with self-discipline under the guidance of an āchārya (teacher).

Brahman: the absolute reality, supreme being; the Whole; that which encompasses and pervades everything, and is One and indivisible.

Brahmasthānam: 'abode of *Brahman.*' The name of the temples Amma consecrated in various parts of India and one in Mauritius. The temple shrine features a unique four-faced idol that symbolizes the unity behind the diversity of divine forms.

Brāhmin: also known as *brāhmaṇa*, a member of the priestly caste, whose duty it is to study and teach the *Vēdas.*

Chhāndōgya Upaniṣhad: one of the oldest principal *Upaniṣhads.*

chēchi: 'older sister' in Malayāḷam.

daivī sampad: divine qualities or virtues.

darśhan: audience with a holy person or a vision of the Divine. Amma's signature darśhan is a hug.

dāsa: devoted servant or follower.

dēva: deity or god; divine being; celestial being. *Dēva* is the masculine form. The feminine equivalent is *dēvī.*

Dēvī Bhāva: 'the divine mood of Dēvī;' occasion when Amma reveals her oneness with the Divine Mother.

dhōti: traditional Indian outer garment worn by men around the waist and legs.

dīkṣhā: initiation. Transfer of spiritual power from the *Guru* to the disciple.

Draupadī: wife of the Pāṇḍavas, also known as Pāñchālī.

Dvāpara Yuga: see *yuga.*

Gaṇēśha: deity with an elephant head and human body, son of Lord Śhiva and Goddess Pārvatī.

Gaṅgā: most sacred river in India. Known as the Ganges river in English.

Gāyatrī Mantra: a revered *mantra* from the *Vēdas.*

gōpī: milk maiden from Vṛindāvan. The *gōpīs* were known for their ardent devotion to Lord Kṛiṣhṇa. Their devotion exemplifies the most intense love for God.

Guru: spiritual teacher.

Guru Granth Sāhib: the central scripture of Sikhism.

Guru Pūrṇimā: the full moon ('*pūrṇimā*') day in the Hindu month of Āṣhāḍha (June – July) in which disciples honor the *Guru*; also, the birthday of Sage Vyāsa, compiler of the *Vēdas*, and author of the *Purāṇas, Brahma Sūtras, Mahābhārata* and the Śhrīmad *Bhāgavatam.*

Halāhala: poison produced during the churning of the Ocean of Milk in *Purāṇic* lore.

hōma: ancient *Vēdic* fire ritual in which oblations are offered to the gods by offering ghee into a consecrated fire.

IAM: Integrated Amrita Meditation Technique® is a meditation practice formulated by Amma that integrates gentle relaxation stretches with an effective and easy-to-practice breathing and concentration technique. It is based on traditional methods and designed for the time constraints of modern life.

Īshavāsya: also known as Īśha *Upaniṣhad*, one of the principal *Upaniṣhads*.

iṣhṭa dēvatā: preferred form of divinity.

Jagadambā: 'Mother of the Universe,' a name of the Divine Mother.

japa: repeated chanting of a *mantra*.

-jī: an honorific suffixed to names or titles to show respect.

jīvātmā: individual soul or self. Sometimes referred to as just '*jīva*.'

Kaivalya Upaniṣhad: one of the minor *Upaniṣhads*.

Kaḷari: original small temple where Amma used to hold *Kṛiṣhṇa Bhāva* and *Dēvī Bhāva darśhans*.

Kālī: Goddess of fearsome aspect; depicted as dark, wearing a garland of skulls, and a girdle of human hands; feminine of *kāla* (time).

Kālī Temple: main temple in Amritapuri dedicated to Kālī.

Kali Yuga: the present dark age of materialism and ignorance (see *yuga*).

karma: action; mental, verbal and physical activity; chain of effects produced by our actions.

karma kāṇḍa: ritualistic portion of the *Vēdas*.

Kṛiṣhṇa: from '*kṛiṣh*,' meaning 'to draw to oneself' or 'to remove sin;' principal incarnation of Lord Viṣhṇu. He was born into a royal family but raised by foster parents, and lived as a cowherd boy in Vṛindāvan, where he was loved and worshiped by his devoted companions, the *gōpīs* (milkmaids) and *gōpas* (cowherd boys). Kṛiṣhṇa later established the city of Dwāraka. He was a friend and advisor to his cousins, the

Pāṇḍavas, especially Arjuna, whom he served as charioteer during the *Mahābhārata War*, and to whom he revealed his teachings as the *Bhagavad Gītā*.

kṛitajña: grateful.

Kumbha Mēla: a major Hindu festival occurring every three years in one of four sacred riverbank pilgrimage places in North India.

kuṭumbam: household, family.

lakṣhya bōdham: focus on the goal (of liberation).

Lalitā Sahasranāma: thousand names of Śhrī Lalitā Dēvī, a form of the Goddess.

līlā: divine play.

lōka: world.

lōkāḥ samastāḥ sukhinō bhavantu: 'May all beings in all the worlds be happy.' A prayer for universal peace and wellbeing.

Mahābhārata: ancient Indian epic that Sage Vyāsa composed, depicting the war between the righteous Pāṇḍavas and the unrighteous Kauravas.

mahātmā: 'great soul;' term used to describe one who has attained spiritual realization.

mālā: garland; rosary, usually made of *rudrākṣha* seeds, *tulasī* wood or sandalwood beads.

Malayāḷam: language spoken in the Indian state of Kerala.

Malayāli: one whose mother-tongue is Malayalam.

manasthiti: attitude (lit. 'state of mind'). Often contrasted with *paristhiti* (circumstance).

mantra: a sound, syllable, word or words of spiritual content. According to *Vēdic* commentators, *mantras* are revelations of *ṛiṣhis* arising from deep contemplation.

Matruvani: 'Voice of the Mother.' The āśhram's flagship publication dedicated to disseminating Amma's teachings and chronicling her divine mission. It is currently published in seventeen languages (including nine Indian languages).

māyā: cosmic delusion, personified as a temptress; illusion; appearance, as contrasted with reality; the creative power of the Lord.

Mīrābaī: great female devotee of Kṛiṣhṇa who lived in the 16th century.

mōkṣha: spiritual liberation, i.e. release from the cycle of births and deaths.

mumukṣhutva: intense desire for liberation.

Nāchikēta: also called Nāchikētas, a young boy mentioned in *Kathōpaniṣhad* who asked Lord Yama to reveal the secret of death.

(Ōm) Namaḥ Śhivāya: 'Salutations to Śhiva, the auspicious one, the inner Self,' a famous *mantra*; greeting used in Amma's āśhrams.

Nārada: wandering sage ever engaged in singing the praises of Viṣhṇu. He composed the *Nārada Bhakti Sūtras*, aphorisms on devotion.

Nārāyaṇa: name of Viṣhṇu.

Navarātri: nine nights of worship of the three aspects of the Divine Mother, as Durgā, Lakṣhmī, and Saraswatī.

nimittamātram: lit. instrument, usually used with reference to *Bhagavad Gīta* Verse 11.33 to indicate being 'a mere instrument in the hands of the divine.'

Ōm: primordial sound in the universe; the seed of creation. The cosmic sound, which can be heard in deep meditation; the

Holy Word, taught in the *Upanişhads*, which signifies *Brahman*, the divine ground of existence.

Ottoor Unni Namboodiripad: composer of *Amma's Aşhţōttaram (108 Names of Amma).*

pāda pūjā: ceremonial washing of the feet as a form of worship.

pādukā: traditional Indian footwear like sandals that may be used in worship symbolically representing the *Guru's* auspicious feet.

pañcha mahāyajñas: five great sacrifices to be performed daily by householders, viz. *brahma-yajña* (studying / teaching the *Vēdas*); the *tarpaṇa* (offering libations of water to deceased ancestors) is *pitṛu-yajña*; the *hōma* is *dēva-yajña* (offerings to the gods); the *bali* (offering a portion of the daily meal of rice, grain, ghee, etc. to all creatures) is *bhūta-yajña*; and the honoring of guests is *nṛu-yajña.*

Pāṇḍavas: the five sons of King Pāṇḍu, and cousins of Kṛiṣhṇa, who are the main protagonists in the great *Mahābhārata* epic.

parā vidyā: 'highest knowledge,' knowledge of the Self or *Brahman.*

Paramahansa Yōgānanda: spiritual master (1893-1952), author of '*Autobiography of a Yogi;*' one of the prominent figures who promoted Indian spirituality in the West.

paramātman: supreme Self, *Brahman.*

Parāśhaktī: supreme power, personified as the Goddess or Empress of the Universe.

Pārvatī: consort of Lord Śhiva.

Prahlāda: son of the powerful demon-king Hiraṇyakaśhipu known for his staunch devotion to Viṣhṇu.

praṇām: salutation; greeting.

prārabdha: also known as *prārabdha karma*, the results of past actions that are the cause of one's birth and whose effects one is destined to experience in this lifetime.

prasād: blessed offering or gift from a holy person or temple, often in the form of food.

prasāda-buddhi: the attitude of seeing everything one receives as a gift from God.

prēma: deep love.

prēmabhakti: highest form of love of God, comparable to *parābhakti*.

pūjā: ritualistic or ceremonial worship.

Purāṇas: compendium of stories, including the biographies and stories of gods, saints, kings and great people; allegories and chronicles of great historical events that aim to make the teachings of the *Vēdas* simple and available to all.

pūrṇimā: full moon.

Rādhā: eternal companion of Lord Kṛiṣhṇa, *gōpī* who exemplifies the highest form of devotion.

rājasūya: Rajasuya is a *mahāyajña* (great sacrifice consisting of hundreds of smaller *yajñas*). It lasts for nearly eighteen months. It is done only for the coronation of an emperor (*chakravartī*) in the presence of kings who are his vassals.

Rāma: divine hero of the *Rāmāyaṇa*. An incarnation of Lord Viṣhṇu, he is considered the ideal man of *dharma* and virtue. 'Ram' means 'to revel;' one who revels in himself; the principle of joy within; one who gladdens the hearts of others.

Rāmakṛiṣhṇa Paramahaṁsa: spiritual master (1836 – 1886) from West Bengal, hailed as the apostle of religious harmony. He generated a spiritual renaissance that continues to touch the lives of millions.

Ramaṇa Maharṣhi: spiritual master (1879 – 1950) who lived in Tiruvannamalai, Tamil Nadu. He recommended Self-inquiry as the path to Liberation, though he approved of a variety of paths and spiritual practices.

Rāmāyaṇa: 24,000-verse epic poem on the life and times of Lord Rāma.

Rāmcharitmānas: a devotional retelling of *Rāmāyaṇa* composed in Awadhī language by Gōswāmī Tulsīdās. *Rāmcharitmānas* is said to be mainly based on *Adhyātma Rāmāyaṇa* (which is a part of *Brahmāṇda Purāṇa*) and not on *Vālmīki Rāmāyaṇa*. Its devotional character is borrowed from *Adhyātma Rāmāyaṇa.*

ṛiṣhi: seer to whom *mantras* are revealed in deep meditation.

sādhak (sādhaka): spiritual aspirant or seeker, one dedicated to attaining the spiritual goal, one who practices *sādhanā.*

sādhanā: regimen of disciplined and dedicated spiritual practice that leads to the supreme goal of Self-realization.

samādhi: oneness with God; a state of deep, one-pointed concentration, in which all thoughts subside. The mind enters into a state of complete stillness in which only pure consciousness remains as one abides in the ātman or Self.

saṁsāra: cycle of births and deaths; the world of flux; the wheel of birth, decay, death and rebirth.

saṁskāra: imprints or impressions left on the mind as a result of past experiences, actions, and thoughts. These imprints shape an individual's character, tendencies, and reactions in future situations. For this reason, traditional rites in *Sanātana Dharma* are also called saṁskāras.

Sanātana Dharma: 'Eternal Way of Life,' the original and traditional name of Hinduism.

saṅkalpa: divine resolve, usually used in association with *mahātmās.*

sannyāsa: a formal vow of renunciation.

sannyāsin: monk (or nun) who has taken vows of renunciation. Also called *sannyāsī.*

sāri: traditional outer garment of Indian women consisting of a long, unstitched piece of cloth wrapped around the body.

sat-chit-ānanda: lit. 'existence-consciousness-bliss,' a description of the subjective experience of the Supreme.

Satguru: 'true master.' All *Satgurus* are *mahātmās*, but not all mahātmās are Satgurus. The Satguru is one who, while still experiencing the bliss of the Self, chooses to come down to the level of ordinary people in order to help them grow spiritually.

satsang: 'communion with the supreme truth.' Also, being in the company of *mahātmās*, studying the scriptures, and listening to the enlightening talks of a mahātmā; a meeting of people to listen to and/or discuss spiritual matters; a spiritual discourse.

Satya Sai Baba: spiritual master (1926-2011) from Andhra Pradesh, India.

Saundarya Laharī: devotional hymn by Śhrī Śhaṅkarāchārya addressed to the Divine Mother.

sēvā: selfless service, the results of which are dedicated to God.

Śhabarī: a woman belonging to a hunter tribe who was an ardent devotee of Rāma.

śhakti: personification of cosmic will and energy; strength; see *māyā.*

śhāstra: science; authoritative scriptural texts.

śhiṣhya: disciple.

Śhiva: the static aspect of *Brahman* as the male principle. Worshiped as the first in the lineage of *Gurus*, and as the formless substratum of the universe in relationship to the creatrix Śhakti. He is the Lord of destruction in the trinity of Brahmā (Lord of creation), Viṣhṇu (Lord of preservation), and Śhiva. Usually depicted as a monk, with ash all over his body, snakes in his hair, wearing only a loincloth and with a begging bowl and a trident in his hands.

Śhivarātri: annual festival also known as *Mahā* Śhivarātri, 'the great night of Lord Shiva.'

śhlōka: verse.

śhraddhā: attentiveness; faith.

Śhuka: son of sage Vyāsa and spiritually-illumined soul; main narrator of the Śhrīmad *Bhāgavatam.*

sūtra: aphorism.

swāmī: title of one who has taken the vow of *sannyāsa* (see *sannyāsin*); *swāminī* is the female equivalent.

tapas (tapasya): austerities, penance.

Tripurasundarī: name for Durgā.

tyāga: giving up, renunciation.

Upaniṣhad: portions of the *Vēdas* dealing with Self-knowledge.

upāsanā : worship as a spiritual practice.

vairāgya: dispassion.

vānaprastha: 'forest life;' a reference to the retired life dedicated to spiritual practices; the third of the four stages of life (see *aśhrama*).

vāsanā: latent tendency or subtle desire that manifests as thought, motive and action; subconscious impression gained from experience.

vāvu bali: ancestral offering done on a new moon day in July in Kerala.

Vēdānta: 'end of *Vēda*.' The philosophy of the *Upanishads*, the concluding part of the Vēdas, which holds the Ultimate Truth to be 'One without a second.' A *Vēdāntin* is a follower of Vēdānta.

Vēdas: most ancient of all scriptures, originating from God, the Vēdas were not composed by any human author but were 'revealed' in deep meditation to the ancient seers. These sagely revelations came to be known as the Vēdas, of which there are four: *Ṛig, Yajur, Sāma* and *Atharva*.

vidyārambham: first writing ceremony of a child. One of the rites regularly performed by Amma.

Viṣhṇu: 'all-pervader,' Lord of sustenance in the trinity of Brahmā (Lord of creation), Viṣhṇu, and Śhiva (Lord of destruction).

Vivēkachūḍāmaṇi: a *Vēdantic* work by Ādi Śhaṇkarāchārya.

Vṛindāvan: sacred site in Mathura district in Uttar Pradesh, celebrated as the place where Kṛiṣhṇa passed his early days as a cowherd.

Vyāsa: lit. 'compiler.' The name given to Sage Kṛiṣhṇa *Dvaipāyana*, who compiled the *Vēdas*. He is also the chronicler of the *Mahābhārata* and a character in it, and author of the eighteen *Purāṇas* and the *Brahma Sūtras*.

yajña: form of ritual worship in which oblations are offered into a fire according to scriptural injunctions, while sacred *mantras* are chanted.

yama: restraints for proper conduct (the 'don'ts'); the first 'limb' of the *aṣhṭāṇga yōga* (eight limb path) formulated by Sage Patañjali. They include *ahiṁsā* (non-violence), *satya* (truthfulness), *astēya* (non-stealing), *brahmacharya* (chastity) and *aparigraha* (non-covetousness); often mentioned in association with *niyama* (the 'dos').

yōga: 'to unite.' Union with the Supreme Being. A broad term, it also refers to the various methods of practices through which one can attain oneness with the Divine. A path that leads to Self-realization.

Yōga Sūtras: '*Patañjali Yōga Sūtras*,' aphorisms composed by Sage *Patañjali* on the path to purification and transcendence of the mind.

yōgī: a practitioner or an adept of *yōga*; *yoginī* is the female equivalent.

Yudhiṣhṭhira: the eldest of the righteous Pāṇḍava brothers who waged war against the Kauravas, their unrighteous cousins, in the *Mahābhārata*.

yuga: according to the Hindu worldview, the universe (from origin to dissolution) passes through a cycle made up of four *yugas* or ages. The first is *Kṛita* or *Satya Yuga*, during which *dharma* reigns in society. Each succeeding age sees the progressive decline of dharma. The second age is known as *Trēta Yuga*, the third is *Dvāpara Yuga*, and the fourth and present epoch is known as *Kali Yuga*.

Pronunciation Guide

Vowels can be short or long:

a – as 'u' in but; ā – as 'a' in far
e – as 'a' in may; ē – as 'a' in name
i – as 'i' in pin; ī – as 'ee' in meet
o – as in oh; ō – as 'o' in mole
u – as 'u' in push; ū – as 'oo' in hoot

ṛi – as 'ri' in crisp; ṛu – as 'ru' in Spanish 'Peru'
ḥ – pronounce 'aḥ' like 'aha,' 'iḥ' like 'ihi,' and 'uḥ' like 'uhu.'

Some consonants are aspirated (e.g. kh); others are not (e.g. k). The examples given below are only approximate:
k – as 'k' in 'kite;' kh – as 'ckh' in 'Eckhart'
g – as 'g' in 'give;' gh – as 'g-h' in 'dig-hard'
ch – as 'ch' in 'chat;' chh – as 'ch-h' in 'staunch-heart'
j – as 'j' in 'joy;' jh – as 'dgeh' in 'hedgehog'
p – as 'p' in 'pine;' ph – as 'ph' in 'up-hill'
b – as 'b' in 'bird;' bh – as 'bh' in 'rub-hard'

r – as 'r' in ride
ñ – as 'ny' in 'canyon;' ṅ – as 'ng' in 'sing'

The letters ḍ, ṭ, ṇ are pronounced with the tip of the tongue against the hard palate, the others with the tip against the teeth.
ṭ – as 't' in 'tub;' ṭh – as 'th' in 'lighthouse'
ḍ – as 'd' in 'dove;' ḍh – as 'dh' in 'red-hot'
ṇ – as 'n' in 'naught'
ḷ – as 'l' in 'revelry'
ṣh – as 'sh' in 'shine;' śh – as 's' in German 'sprechen'

With double consonants the sound is pronounced twice:
chch – as 'tc' in 'hot chip'
jj – as 'dj' in 'red jet'

Acknowledgements

This book is the fruit of the collaboration of Amma's children done in the spirit of offering. I especially want to thank Karnaki Nolan for tirelessly completing an initial edit, as well as Anita Raghavan, Rajani Menon, Veena Erickson, Murali Sreenivasan, and James Conquest for their invaluable behind-the-scenes support. My deepest gratitude goes to Jagannath Maas for his meticulous layout work and to Arun Raj for yet another mesmerizing cover design. Swāmī Vidyāmṛitānanda was instrumental in crafting the comprehensive glossary. Swāmī Jñānāmṛitānanda's unwavering guidance has been our pillar of strength. To all of you I express my heartfelt gratitude.

Julius Heyne